William Symington

PENMAN OF THE SCOTTISH COVENANTERS

by Roy Blackwood

with Michael LeFebvre

REFORMATION HERITAGE BOOKS
Grand Rapids, Michigan

William Symington: Penman of the Scottish Covenanters
Copyright © 2009 Roy Blackwood and Michael LeFebvre

REFORMATION HERITAGE BOOKS
2965 Leonard St., NE
Grand Rapids, MI 49525
616-977-0599 / Fax 616-285-3246
e-mail: orders@heritagebooks.org
website: www.heritagebooks.org

Library of Congress Cataloging-in-Publication Data

Blackwood, Roy, 1925-
  William Symington : penman of the Scottish covenanters / by Roy
Blackwood ; with Michael LeFebvre.
      p. cm.
  ISBN 978-1-60178-066-9 (pbk. : alk. paper)
  1. Symington, William, 1795-1862. 2.
Covenanters--Scotland--Clergy--Biography. 3.
Presbyterians--Scotland--Clergy--Biography. 4. Scotland--Church
history--17th century. I. LeFebvre, Michael. II. Title.
  BX9225.S96B43 2009
  285'.2092--dc22
  [B]
                        2009028252

*For additional Reformed literature, both new and used,
request a free book list from the above address.*

TABLE OF CONTENTS

PREFACE

This book is about a man and his ministry—a man named William Symington. Symington was a pastor and theologian in Scotland during the early ninteenth century. The pages which follow recount Symington's life, his ministry, and offer a study of his most important writings. Sadly unknown to many interested in church history and Reformation theology, it is hoped the present volume will help introduce Symington to a wider audience.

Yet this book is really about much more than William Symington. There is a more important "recovery operation" at the heart of this book—a concern to recover a forgotten trophy of Reformation theology. William Symington was a "Covenanter." That is, he was an ecclesiastical heir of the Scottish Reformers who, in the seventeenth century, came to be known as "Covenanters." Important contributions to Reformation theology emerged from the afflictions and expositions of the Covenanters. By the time of William Symington, however, the Scottish church was in danger of losing (or, worse yet, misunderstanding and denigrating) many of the Covenanter attainments.

William Symington pastored, preached, and wrote with an earnest prayer that this would not happen. In his own vibrant and colorful ministry, Symington served to keep Covenanter theology alive within his own community and time. In his books and published sermons, Symington labored for the propagation of these Scottish Reformation fruits even more widely. To study the works of William Symington, then, is really just a focal point for recovering the testimony of the Scottish (Covenanted) Reformation.

My own "discovery" of the Scottish Covenanters, and of William Symington, began in 1996 when I moved to Indianapolis, Indiana. Dr. Roy Blackwood, senior pastor at the Second Reformed Presbyterian Church of Indianapolis, was teaching seminary-level courses on church history at that time. I moved to Indianapolis as a theological student, and enrolled in Dr. Blackwood's courses. I also had the privilege of getting close to Roy Blackwood and watching him (and his wife Margie) in the ministry.

Dr. Blackwood had done his Ph.D. research on William Symington, with the University of Edinburgh (Scotland), in the late 1950s and early 1960s. By the time I arrived in Indianapolis, the church which had been planted through the Blackwoods' labors there was thirty years old and thriving. Roughly half a dozen more churches, daughtered across central Indiana over the years, were also growing. (Since the RP Church is an *a cappella* Psalm-singing denomination, this growth was obviously not part of modern church growth techniques!) One of the reasons I chose to pursue my theological education by moving to Indianapolis was to learn in a context where solid, Reformed preaching and discipleship were bearing such fruit. Getting close to Roy and Margie Blackwood, and the other ministers working with them, was an education in itself.

I heard the name "Symington" frequently in my conversations with the Blackwoods. It was evident Dr. Blackwood's research into this man's ministry had been a profound influence on his own ministry. When I finally got around to reading Dr. Blackwood's dissertation on Symington, and some of Symington's works directly, I felt like I was making acquaintance with an uncle or grandfather I never knew I had. So much of the ministry I had been privileged to witness from the inside out in Indiana bore the unmistakable stamp of what I found in Symington—which, of course, Symington had himself learned at the feet of the old Scottish Reformation Covenanters. It was therefore with great delight that I welcomed the opportunity to work with Dr. Blackwood on the preparation of this book that you now hold in your hand.

I offer this window into the personal history behind this book for the following reason. It seems to me that these ties—from the Scottish Reformation to William Symington, and from Symington to a present-day Covenanter (Roy Blackwood)—illustrate the vitality of the doctrines touched on in the present volume. These doctrinal expositions (in Symington's books) and applications (in his ministry) are not mere artifacts for historical fascination. They are vibrant truths that were mined from the pages of Scripture by faithful ministers, huddled on the moors and in the caves of Reformation Scotland, as they sought to understand the reign of Christ in a land of persecution and bloodshed. They are, furthermore, truths which have continued to nurture the faith and life of the church in Symington's day, and on the opposite side of the world in our own day.

This volume has been prepared, therefore, with an awareness that the Covenanter testimony has much to offer the church in all times and conditions. In fact, in light of recent world events—many of which raise the importance of rethinking church and state relationships—the Covenanter testimony on that important subject might be deemed of particular urgency in the twenty-first century.

For Christ's Crown and Covenant
Michael LeFebvre

INTRODUCTION

CHAPTER 1

Introduction to the Life and Work of Dr. Roy Blackwood

The life of William Symington is both fascinating and instructive. The reader will be richly rewarded for making Symington's acquaintance through this book—the first volume to be published on Symington's life and ministry. Before taking up the story of Symington, however, it is worthwhile to meet Roy Blackwood, the man whose study produced this book.

Birth and Early Life in New Concord, Ohio

Roy was born into a family with deep roots in the Reformed Presbyterian Church. The Blackwood family descends from Scottish stock, including such men as James Blackwood (1793–1851), a minister of the gospel who came to America in 1824 to serve in the Reformed Presbyterian Church of North America,[1] laboring as a home missionary in western Pennsylvania and southeast Ohio.[2] Though not a direct descendant of James, Roy was born into that branch of the Blackwood family which continued in the Reformed Presbyterian Church in Ohio.

---

1. The Reformed Presbyterian Church of North America dates from the erection of the Reformed Presbytery of America in Philadelphia, PA, in May 1798, to serve congregations of "Covenanter" immigrants coming from Scotland and Ireland to settle in various parts of North America in those days. The Reformed Presbytery was divided into three presbyteries under the authority of the Reformed Presbyterian Synod, constituted on May 24, 1809. Today the Synod of the RPCNA comprises 76 churches, 4 missions, and 7 presbyteries, in the USA, Canada, and Japan.

2. See the ministerial sketch of James Blackwood in William Melancthon Glasgow's *History of the Reformed Presbyterian Church in America* (first published 1888; reprinted by Reformation Heritage Books, Grand Rapids, 2007), 443–445.

Roy was born on February 7, 1925. He was the fifth child of Roy Samuel and Lena Shipe Blackwood. Mr. Blackwood was a farmer with 120 acres on the western outskirts of New Concord, Muskingum County, Ohio. Lena was a godly wife and mother who "looked well to the ways of her household." Tragically, however, Lena's maternal care for her family was not to continue long after Roy's birth. In early 1928, Lena contracted a disease called erysipelas.[3] The family doctor did what he could, but with none of the antibiotics known to modern medicine available at that time, five children were soon left motherless. Roy had just turned three when his mother died. His father made a valiant attempt to care for the children himself, while continuing to run the farm; but he eventually found it necessary to send Roy into New Concord to live with his grandmother, Martha Blackwood, and two maiden aunts, Emma and May.

So Roy grew up under the watchful care of his grandmother and aunts. Apart from his changed family circumstances, Roy's childhood was similar to that of other Ohio boys in those days, romping through the woods, playing marbles, hunting groundhogs, and sliding down the banisters when no one was looking. His grandmother and aunts devoted themselves faithfully to his spiritual nurture. Roy's grandmother faithfully read the Bible to him, and "Auntie May," a retired school teacher, insisted that the lad memorize passages from it. Psalm 19 was one of the passages in which she diligently drilled the youngster, beginning with the words, "The heavens declare the glory of God; and the firmament sheweth his handywork."

A neighbor also took a spiritual interest in Roy and his family. John Herschel Glenn, Sr., was a ruling elder in Westminster Presbyterian Church (PCUSA) on Liberty Street, and came over to pray with the Blackwoods. Many years later, in 1962, Roy would have opportunity to return the same ministry to the Glenn family, praying for them as they anxiously watched their son, John Herschel Glenn, Jr., preparing to launch into space aboard the *Friendship 7* to become the first American to orbit the earth.

---

3. Erysipelas is a streptococcus infection of the skin, which if not checked, can spread to the internal organs of the body and cause death.

Another spiritual influence in Roy's upbringing was his distant cousin, Dr. Andrew Blackwood. Andrew Watterson Blackwood (1882–1966) was ordained to the ministry in the United Presbyterian Church of North America in 1908, went on to become professor of homiletics at Princeton Theological Seminary from 1930 to 1950, and was the author of many books on preaching, worship, and pastoral work.

Professor Blackwood took a keen interest in the heritage and spiritual nurture of his extended family. In the summer of 1939, at a Blackwood family reunion in Ohio, Andrew preached from Isaiah 51:1, "Look unto the rock whence ye are hewn." Andrew urged his fellow Blackwoods in America not to forget their Scottish Covenanter forebears, and not just their cultural and ethnic heritage, but their deep love for Christ.

All these influences—a mother's love, an aunt's Bible memory drills, a neighbor's prayers, a cousin's preaching, as well as the ministry of the pastors at the New Concord Reformed Presbyterian Church[4] where his family faithfully attended Sabbath day services—were planting seeds in Roy's heart which would not come to full fruition for many years. But Christ was preparing Roy, even from a young age, for His own purposes.

Off to War, but without Christ

In the spiritual culture in which Roy was reared, it was assumed that knowledge of the Bible and the Shorter Catechism, faithful attendance on Sabbath worship, and diligent use of the means of grace were sufficient to make one a Christian.[5] The idea of personal faith in Christ was not well articulated, and certainly not a topic of daily conversation. Roy showed all the right outward signs of a boy raised in the church, so his family and church assumed he was

---

4. For an account of the early history of the New Concord RP Church, see William M. Glasgow, *History of the Reformed Presbyterian Church in America*, 316–318.

5. Helen Hooven Santmyer (1895–1986), for many years Dean of Women and head of the English Department at Cedarville College, described her upbringing as a Presbyterian in Xenia, another Ohio community much like New Concord, in "Church," Chapter VI in her book, *Ohio Town: A Portrait of Xenia* (New York: Harper & Row Publishers, 1962), 125–156; much of this material was later incorporated into her historical novel, *"...And Ladies of the Club"* (New York: G. P. Putnam's Sons, 1882).

a Christian; but it would be many years before Roy would come to saving faith. But even if Roy did not yet know Jesus in a saving way, Jesus was fully mindful of Roy—and He would use a world war to begin making Himself known to Roy.

On December 7, 1941, Roy had just finished reciting an oration on peace for a speech contest in nearby Zanesville, Ohio, when his family heard the news of the surprise Japanese attack on the fleet of US warships anchored at Pearl Harbor, Hawaii. As America entered World War II, Roy was in his junior year at high school. He promptly began service for his country. Roy became New Concord's air raid warden, and began his first position in service for his country patrolling the streets to enforce the town's nighttime blackout requirements.

At the end of his junior year, Roy left high school and was allowed to enroll in Muskingum College.[6] After a year at Muskingum, Roy enrolled as a Naval Reserve cadet, and was sent to Ohio Wesleyan University in Delaware, Ohio, to finish his college education. After completing college and going on to finish midshipman's school in New York, Roy was commissioned to serve in the United States Navy on March 6, 1945. Once in the Navy, Roy was trained as a pilot and then transferred to navigators' school. He was eventually posted as ship's navigator on an aircraft carrier, the *USS Petrof Bay*.[7]

As a navigator, Roy spent his nights taking sightings on the stars. With his sextant frequently in hand, it was Roy's responsibility to insure that the ship was always where she was supposed to be, and he relied on the regularity of the stars to do so. Then one day Roy was given the opportunity to study the instruments in the cockpits of captured Japanese fighter planes that the *Petrof Bay* was bringing back to the States. Clambering into the cockpit of one such aircraft, Roy recalls seeing Japanese characters on the controls that he could not read; but he also found he could immediately understand the Japanese navigational charts.

---

6. Muskingum College, New Concord, OH, is a four-year liberal arts school, founded in 1837, and until 1958, under the control of the Synod of Ohio, United Presbyterian Church of North America, and the *alma mater* of numerous United Presbyterian ministers and missionaries.

7. For an online history of the *Petrof Bay*, go to: http://home.comcast.net/ ~ivorjeffreys/history.html

"At that moment," Roy later recalled, "my mind flashed back to those days when Auntie May made me memorize Psalm 19:1–4a:

> The heavens declare the glory of God; and the firmament sheweth his handywork. Day unto day uttereth speech, and night unto night sheweth knowledge.
>
> There is no speech nor language, where their voice is not heard.
>
> Their line is gone out through all the earth, and their words to the end of the world."

That night, as Roy found himself back on the deck, once again taking measurements of the stars with his sextant, his thoughts reached beyond the stars to contemplate the truth and trustworthiness of their heavenly Creator. Christ was beginning to draw Roy to Himself.

Studies at Geneva College, the RP Seminary, and New College, Edinburgh

After the war, the *Petrof Bay* was decommissioned and Roy returned to school. He enrolled at Geneva College[8] in Beaver Falls, Pennsylvania, to study chemistry. During his years at Geneva, attending College Hill Reformed Presbyterian Church, Roy became convinced that there is a God and that he, Roy Blackwood, needed to be right with Him. The seeds planted in Roy's heart over many years were watered by the Spirit, and Christ brought Roy to Himself. Roy came to trust and love Jesus Christ as his personal Savior. Suddenly Roy found his interests in his chemistry studies eclipsed by his hunger for God's Word; but he learned to honor God in his schoolwork even as he sought to know the Scriptures more.

In addition to the study of chemistry and his blossoming faith, Roy also became interested in another "subject" at Geneva College: a young woman by the name of Margaret Graham. Margie was the daughter of Dr. Thomas E. Graham, Geneva College alumnus and pastor of the United Presbyterian Church (UPCNA) of Ambridge,

---

8. Geneva College was founded by Reformed Presbyterians in Northwood, OH, in 1848, and relocated to Beaver Falls, PA, in 1880; it is operated today as an institution of higher education belonging to the Synod of the Reformed Presbyterian Church of North America.

Pennsylvania.[9] Margie was persuaded that God was calling her to remain single and to teach as an unmarried woman, but the Lord faithfully guided Margie's heart and Roy's patience, and gave them both confidence that Christ would be honored to use them as a married couple. Roy received his Bachelor of Science degree from Geneva on June 1, 1948, and promptly enrolled at Reformed Presbyterian Theological Seminary[10] in Pittsburgh. He married Margie Graham on November 20, 1948.

Roy completed his course of study at RPTS in 1951 and decided to use his G.I. Bill benefits to pursue post-graduate studies overseas. While considering where to go and what to study, Roy was encouraged by Andrew Blackwood to study church history in Scotland. Following this counsel, Roy and Margie crossed the Atlantic and moved into a third-floor flat not far from the University of Edinburgh. Roy enrolled in New College, the university's school of theology.[11]

As Roy began his studies, looking for a subject for his thesis work, New College church historian Hugh Watt (1879–1968) recommended that Roy research the life and ministry of the Scottish Reformed Presbyterian minister, William Symington (1795–1862).[12] It was a course of study which was to have a deep influence on Roy's own life and ministry, and became the focus of his postgraduate work. Only later did Roy learn that Professor Watt had arrived at this choice of research topic through consultation with Watt's close personal friend in the United States, none other than Professor Andrew W. Blackwood of Princeton Seminary.

---

9. For a brief history of Reformed Presbyterianism in Ohio, see Thomas Graham's article, "The Reformed Presbyterian Church—Those Sturdy Ohio Covenanters," in *Buckeye Presbyterianism,* E. Burgett Welsh, ed. (published by Collier for the United Presbyterian Synod of Ohio, 1968), 37–47.

10. Reformed Presbyterian Theological Seminary was found by the RP Synod in 1810, in Philadelphia, PA; since 1923 the Seminary has operated at 7418 Penn Avenue, Pittsburgh, PA 15208.

11. New College was founded to train ministerial students for the Free Church of Scotland after the Disruption of 1843; the name was retained when the college was united with the University of Edinburgh's Divinity Faculty in 1929.

12. For a brief account of Symington's life and work, see Roy Blackwood's article, "William Symington," in the *Dictionary of Scottish Theology* (Downers Grove, IL: InterVarsity Press, 1993), 808–809.

Initially Roy's research was primarily historical, getting to know the events of Symington's life, ministry, and times. But the more Roy became acquainted with Symington, the more he began to recognize the passion for Christ's mediatorial kingship that filled Symington's heart and life. And the more Roy studied the doctrinal truths that shaped Symington's ministry, the more Roy found his own heart captivated by them.

Ordination and Ministry in Bloomington, Indiana

In 1953 Roy returned to the United States, intending to complete his dissertation after entering the pastorate. He was ordained to the ministry and served the Reformed Presbyterian Church of Bloomington, Indiana,[13] until 1960. During those years Roy's close friend and fellow RP pastor, Kenneth G. Smith, introduced Roy to Leroy Eims of the Navigators.[14]

Founded in California by Dawson Trottman in the 1930s, the "Navs" began reaching out to military personnel and students on college campuses, presenting the gospel and discipling new Christians, with special emphasis on personal Bible study, Scripture memorization, and prayer. The goal was for each Christian to learn how to communicate his faith to others by engaging in personal evangelism and discipleship.

It was through Ken Smith and Leroy Eims that Roy began to learn the importance of men discipling men after the manner taught by the apostle Paul: "and the things that thou hast heard of me among many witnesses, the same commit thou to faithful men, who shall be able to teach others also" (2 Tim. 2:2). Ken and Leroy helped Roy learn to train young men as "reproducing" disciple-makers.

This new "classroom" was providing an important complement to Roy's study of Symington's work in the doctrine of Christ's mediatorial kingship. In particular, if Jesus Himself had proclaimed the kingdom of God through a disciple-making ministry, then Roy

---

13. Bloomington RPC was organized in 1821 by Reformed Presbyterians who chose to uproot their families and make a new start in Indiana rather than remain among slaveholders in South Carolina. Today it is a vibrant and growing church housed in a historic building not far from the campus of Indiana University.

14. Leroy Eims later paid tribute to Dr. Blackwood and "The Indianapolis Model" in Chapter I of his book, *The Lost Art of Disciple Making* (Grand Rapids: Zondervan Publishing House, 1978), 25, 26.

realized that he, as a pastor with a passion for that kingdom (as he was learning it from Symington) ought to "do Jesus' work Jesus' way" (as he was learning disciple-making from Ken and Leroy). Roy was not making much progress on writing his dissertation, but the Lord was teaching Roy important lessons directly connected to his passion for Christ's kingship. Roy began reaching out to university students on the Bloomington campus of Indiana University, witnessing to and discipling men.

Further Study in Edinburgh

While the years of ministry in Bloomington were rewarding and important, it gradually became apparent that Roy would not be able to complete his dissertation so long as he remained so actively involved in campus ministry. Roy decided to return to Scotland in order to complete his study on William Symington, though now with a deeper appreciation for Symington's work and the pastoral importance of the doctrine of Christ's mediatorial kingship and kingdom. In the spring of 1960, Roy and Margie embarked with their three children[15] on a ship bound for Scotland, and Roy returned to his work at the University of Edinburgh.

Influenced by his own experiences in the pastorate, Roy continued his studies with keener insight into Symington's ministry as a pastor-theologian. His dissertation was finished in 1963, and Roy received his Ph.D. in church history, but the most exciting years of his ministry were only beginning.

Church Planting in Indianapolis, Indiana

In June of 1963 Roy arrived back in Indiana, now taking up residence in Indianapolis. There was no Reformed Presbyterian Church in Indianapolis, and on October 22 of that year, the Illinois Presbytery of the Reformed Presbyterian Church appointed Roy to undertake church-planting work there. Roy embraced this ministry, convinced that, as the state capital, Indianapolis would be a prime location to proclaim the gospel of the kingdom of Jesus, with concern for its application to the state as well as the church.

The Lord had blessed Roy's ministry with students in the past, and Roy took this as the Lord's direction to begin the new work with

---

15. William, Beth, and Robert Blackwood.

ministry to students on the many college and university campuses in Indianapolis and throughout Indiana. The Lord also opened doors for Roy to develop a significant ministry to businessmen and government leaders. Christ had been preparing Roy for this ministry now opening before him in Indianapolis, and it was evident that Christ was blessing the work as young people and businessmen came to faith, and a congregation began to form.

In 1964, with Christ's evident blessing on these labors, a new church was organized and given the name Second Reformed Presbyterian Church.[16] Roy served as pastor of this congregation for the next forty-four years.[17] During those years, Christ continued to build the congregation where Roy ministered.[18] The Lord was also pleased to use Second RPC in the planting of ten more churches throughout central Indiana in the succeeding decades. Christ was at work, doing something extraordinary in Indiana from those small beginnings in Indianapolis.[19]

As Roy himself is quick to point out, there was nothing about him that could account for the remarkable fruitfulness of those years. Nor can such growth be attributed to the introduction of "church growth" methods[20] in the Reformed Presbyterian Church of North

---

16. There was a Reformed Presbyterian Church in Indianapolis in the tumultuous years after the Civil War, from 1867 to 1870. The new congregation organized in 1964 took the name "*Second* Reformed Presbyterian Church" to honor that previous work in the city. Second RPC is housed in facilities located at 4800 N. Michigan Road, Indianapolis, IN 46228.

17. At his request, Dr. Blackwood was released from the pastorate of Second RPC by action of Great Lakes/Gulf Presbytery (RPCNA) at its meeting in Orlando, FL, on Friday, Feb. 29, 2008.

18. Everyone who knows Dr. Blackwood has heard him disavow the notion that ministers build churches, holding that if the minister builds the church, then it isn't Christ's church, for Christ said, "I will build my church" (Matt. 16:18); ministers are only instruments that Christ uses to that end.

19. An account of the development of the ministry in Indianapolis, and the church planting ministries in other cities around central Indiana, can be found in an unpublished paper by Keith R. Magill, "A Brief History of the Reformed Presbyterian Church of North America in Central Indiana" (March, 1980).

20. "Church Growth" has more than one meaning today. Originally it meant the use of the methods and findings of the social sciences to understand what promotes, and what impedes church growth. Later, it came to mean using the methods of marketing to "sell" Christianity as a product, allowing these methods to dictate

America. Rather, Jesus was showing Himself faithful to His promise, "I will build my church" (Matt. 16:18). Furthermore, as Roy has often emphasized, the additions and growth in the Reformed Presbyterian Church in those years were a fulfillment of Jesus' promise, "Seek ye first the kingdom of God, and his righteousness; and all these things shall be added unto you" (Matt. 6:33). Roy and the men he was discipling were learning to focus on "seeking first the kingdom," and Jesus was faithfully building His church.

Symington's Example and Influence

Rarely does the church experience a ministry as prolific and wide-reaching as the years of Roy Blackwood's service in Indianapolis. There is, however, a parallel to Roy's ministry in the life and work of William Symington, the subject of this work. The parallel is worth noting as we embark on the book that follows, for two reasons.

First, it is a familiar writer's axiom that to write the story of a great life requires a great life. The providential influences and divine grace that shaped the life of Roy Blackwood have aptly suited him to the task of recovering the testimony of William Symington from the annals of 19th century Scottish church history.

Second and more importantly, the extensive ministries that characterized both Roy Blackwood and William Symington illustrate the kind of vision which flows from the "kingdom doctrine" these men had been taught more or less from their youth (and which is one of the primary themes that emerges in the pages that follow):

> God has given the exercise of all authority to the Lord Jesus Christ.
>
> Christ is the Divine Law-Giver, Governor, and Judge. His will concerning the purpose of civil government and the principles regarding its functions and operation are revealed in the written Word of God.... Every nation ought to recognize the Divine institution of civil government [and] the sovereignty of God exercised by Jesus Christ... [and] should enter into covenant with Christ and serve to advance His Kingdom on earth....

---

the content of preaching, the form and content of worship, etc., regardless of biblical requirements.

The Christian must profess publicly and the church must witness, that Christ is the ruler of every nation ... Both the Christian and the church have a responsibility for witnessing against national sins and for promoting justice.[21]

Ultimately, it is Christ who came "preaching the gospel of the kingdom" (Matt. 4:23), and who calls us to "let this mind be in you, which was also in Christ Jesus" (Phil. 2:5). It is not the insight of Roy Blackwood or of William Symington which is at the heart of the doctrine in this present volume, but the royal claims of Jesus Himself which Symington and Blackwood, like other churchmen through the ages, have delighted to discover and apply.

Careful attention to Jesus' royal claims has profoundly shaped the service of churchmen throughout the ages—early Church Fathers like Augustine,[22] Reformation churchmen like John Wycliff,[23] Martin Bucer,[24] and the Scottish Covenanters (whose doctrine was aptly compiled by Symington). Standing in this heritage, at the dawn of the Industrial Revolution, William Symington brought this historic commitment to Christ's priestly and kingly claims into the modern era.

In other words, the wide-reaching ministries that characterized Symington and Blackwood are two historically recent examples in a long history of "kingdom minded" churchmen. Furthermore, they

---

21. Excerpted from "The Testimony of the Reformed Presbyterian Church, adopted August 1980," Articles 23:2, 4, 17, and 22, published in *The Constitution of the Reformed Presbyterian Church of North America* (Pittsburgh: Crown & Covenant Publications, 2004), A-70 to A-75.

22. Augustine wrote *The City of God* around 430 A.D., just after Rome had fallen, in which he articulates his understanding of the kingdom of Christ which transcends the kingdoms of men.

23. At the dawn of the Reformation, John of Wycliff wrote *De Dominio Divino* (1366) and *De Civili Dominio* (1371) to distinguish the kingdom of Christ from the kingdoms of men, and to show their vital relationship in the proper service of Christ's authority over both church and state.

24. Widely recognized as a friend of Martin Luther and a mentor of John Calvin, Bucer wrote *De Regno Christi* in 1550, summarizing the lessons he had learned about the kingdom and kingship of Christ during his years laboring for reformation in the city-state of Strasbourg. Bucer dedicated his book to Prince Edward VI of England, and presented it to the prince on New Year's Day, 1550. It was designed to serve as a guide for Edward in his role as a civil ruler under Christ in "Christianizing" the nation.

are examples that remind us that the study which follows is not a mere work of academic curiosity. It is a vision of Jesus Christ's crown rights, prerogatives, and purposes as King of kings and Lord of all. It is a profoundly practical study, and one with profound implications for all those who love and serve this great King. It is a study which enriches and energizes the ministry of all those who with grace in their hearts anticipate and sing of the coming time, "when all things shall be subdued unto him" (1 Cor. 15:28):

> All ends of earth, remembr'ing Him,
> Shall turn themselves unto the LORD;
> The kindreds of the nations then
> To Him their homage shall accord,
> Because the LORD the kingdom owns
> And rules above all earthly thrones.[25]

Mono to Theo doxa.[26]

Compiled by Michael LeFebvre and Ray Lanning, in interviews with Roy Blackwood and consulting notes prepared by Brad Johnston.

---

25. Metrical version of Psalm 22:27, 28 in *The Book of Psalms for Singing* (Pittsburgh: Board of Education and Publication, Reformed Presbyterian Church of North America, 1973), No. 22-I.

26. Greek, "To God alone be glory," William Symington's chosen motto.

CHAPTER 2

Introduction to William Symington and the Reformed Presbyterian Church

William Symington (1795–1862) was ordained to the gospel ministry in 1820. Until his death four decades later, he faithfully served
his Savior in the Reformed Presbyterian (RP) Church of Scotland.
This title—*Reformed Presbyterian*—summarizes the reason for this
denomination's distinct place within the wider church. It is a title
which gives ongoing witness to the attainments of the Scottish
Reformation.

It was around the year 1560 that the Reformation took root in
Scotland. Periods of reformation progress were often punctuated by
periods of persecution and digress. One of the most violent periods
of persecution took place between the years 1660 and 1688. During those years, virtually everything which had been gained in the
previous century of Reformation was systematically dismantled. In
1688, peace was restored to Scotland with the placement of William
and Mary on the throne. However, the *National* Church (that is, the
state-recognized or, established "Church of Scotland") was reorganized at that time along lines of political expedience. Much of the
Reformation progress of previous generations was ignored in the
re-constitution of the mainline presbyterian Church of Scotland.

A body of Scottish believers refused to join this, as they saw
it, compromised church. Instead, these believers contended for the
continuation of all that had been previously won by reformation. It
is this other body of Scottish presbyterians which eventually came
to be known as the *Reformed* or *Reformation* Presbyterian Church of
Scotland. The title is meant to represent this church's witness to the
full embrace of Scotland's Reformation attainments.

Numerous other presbyterian bodies have since appeared in
Scotland and have planted more presbyterian churches around

the globe. These other Scottish presbyterian bodies have emerged out of divisions within the National Church of Scotland or, on at least one occasion, from a split within the Reformed Presbyterian Church. These two bodies, however—the Church of Scotland and the Reformed Presbyterian Church—uniquely trace their roots directly to the Scottish Reformation period. Of these two, it is the claim of the *Reformed Presbyterian* Church that theirs is the heritage which embraces not only a continuity of existence, but a faithful *continuity of doctrine,* with the Reformation.

As will shortly be seen, this claim was not intended as a boast or to be divisive. For many years, these dissenters from the National Church actually refused to organize as a distinct church themselves. For over six decades, in fact, these outside the National Church met in worship assemblies they called the "United Societies." Their name and their operation were explicitly non-ecclesiastical, because these dissenters did not view themselves as "another church." Originally, at least, this organization called themselves "societies" rather than "churches" because they expected the National Church to be restored to her Reformation heritage. When that happened, they could reintegrate with her. Even when the Societies did organize as a distinct ecclesiastical body called the Reformed Presbyterian Church (in 1743), they continued to witness to the compromised National Church in hopes of her restoration and eventual reunion.

William Symington, one of the ablest preachers of the 19th-century RP Church, became the penman *par excellence* of the Reformation Presbyterian testimony. His book entitled *Messiah the Prince,* in particular, is probably the most comprehensive articulation of that doctrine which was the centerpiece of Scotland's Reformation—the doctrine of Christ's Mediatorial Dominion—and this doctrine's implications for the church, the state, and church–state relations.

Symington not only composed the standard text on this doctrinal trophy of the Scottish Reformation, but he actively labored to see it applied. As an RP churchman in nineteenth-century Scotland, Symington labored for a greater observance of Christ's dominion in his own church. He also continued the RP labors for the National Church's recovery of this fundamental Reformation doctrine (with a surprising measure of success, it might be added). Symington also pressed the implications of Christ's kingly reign upon the matters of civil government in his day, and on the affairs of the wider church and community as well. In short, Symington provided both an eminent exposition of Christ's mediatorial dominion in his writings and a vigorous example of its practical implications for the church and society in his own labors.

It is these facts which make the life and writings of William Symington of particular importance. For the theological student, Symington offers a window into the doctrinal centerpiece of the Scottish Reformation. For the church historian, Symington's life and writings play a pivotal role in one of the most eventful periods in post-Reformation Scotland. For the minister and elder, Symington bears witness to the throne of Christ as it instructs the faith, life, hope, and labors of the Christian congregation in a godless world. For the civil servant, Symington produces a rare explanation of civil government's place within heaven's royal agenda. For the Christian, Symington points the way to a clearer vision of Christ's reign and the believer's comfort and obedience to that reign. For the unbeliever still inquiring after the teachings of the Christian faith, Symington gives access to one of those teachings which lurks beneath the surface of the whole system of Christian faith and yet receives remarkably little attention: the universal, sovereign rule of Jesus Christ.

The present volume represents an attempt to make the life and writings of Symington more accessible to the general public. This book is organized in two parts. The first section introduces the life and work of William Symington. Only a sketch of his ministry has here been ventured. It might be hoped that a full, proper biography on Symington will yet be written. What is here offered is not such a biography, but rather a selective sketch of one minister's *practice* of the reign of Christ. It is hoped that, by reading this life section, the *principles* later discussed from his books will be easier to appreciate.

It is the second section of this book which is probably the most important. It is there that the doctrines championed by Symington will be taken up. Two productions of Symington's pen, in particular, are important: his 1834 work on the *priesthood* of Christ, and his 1839 work on the *kingship* of Christ. It is the latter for which Symington is best known, but the latter really cannot be properly understood without the former. After all, it is the work of Jesus on the cross (as our High Priest) that gives reason to his work on the throne (as our

King). Therefore, both of these principal works of Symington are here dealt with.

The ideal, of course, is for the reader of Symington to acquire and read his books directly. Two factors make this difficult, however. First of all, neither title has been readily accessible until recently. His work on the priesthood of Christ—*On the Atonement and Intercession of Jesus Christ* (1834)—has only recently been reprinted after remaining out of print for over a century.[1] His work on the kingship of Christ—*Messiah the Prince or, On the Mediatorial Dominion of Jesus Christ* (1839)—has fortunately been reprinted several times in recent years.[2] None of these reprints are by major publishing houses, however, and only with the advent of internet book sales (e.g., through Amazon.com) have these titles become readily available. Until recently, this lack of availability has been one hurdle to general study of Symington's works.

A second difficulty is posed by the difference in writing style between Symington's day and our own. Modern readers may find sections of Symington's works laborious, although in his own day these books were hailed as lucid and markedly devotional. The difficulty is not one of Symington's writing style so much as the changed expectations of our own times. Nonetheless, readability is a second hurdle to be surmounted in the study of Symington's works.

On account of these two obstacles, it is hoped that the "retelling" or "summarizing" of Symington's two main works here will help a wide circle of interested readers get at the biblical truths expounded in them. This is the purpose for the second part of the present volume.

It has commonly been said that a Christian has two avenues of witness. It is said that a Christian's "walk talks" and that his "talk talks." What follows is an introduction to the Christian witness of William Symington through an observation of his "walk" (that is, his life in Part One) and a hearing of his "talk" (that is, his words in Part Two).

---

1. Recently republished by Reformation Heritage Books (Grand Rapids, 2006), Kessinger Publishing (Whitefish, MT, 2008), and Bibliolife (Charleston, SC, 2008).

2. Most recently by Christian Stateman Press (Pittsburgh, PA, 1999) and Kessinger Publishing (Whitefish, MT, 2008).

A Brief History of the Scottish Reformation

For readers unfamiliar with the events of the Scottish Reformation, the emergence of the United Societies, and the Reformed Presbyterian Church of Symington's time, the following overview will help to set some important historical context.

Even as long ago as Old Testament times, reformation has always been a gradual and complicated process. Reformation frequently extends over several generations and faces numerous setbacks along the way. Such was certainly the case in Scotland, where John Knox famously observed, "The face of the Kirk must be always reforming."

The sixteenth and seventeenth centuries were taken up with the long, painful process of reform in that land. And although there were numerous setbacks along the way, the potency of one particular period of setback has led historians to speak of there having been *two* reformations in Scotland. The First Reformation extended from 1560–1637. The deformation toward the end of that period called for a *Second* Reformation extending roughly from 1638–1651.

The First Reformation (1560–1637)

In relation to other lands like Germany, France, and Switzerland, reformation came late to Scotland. In Germany, Martin Luther had rediscovered the biblical teaching on justification (that salvation is by faith alone), and nailed his famous "95 Theses" to the door of the Castle Church in Wittenberg in 1517. Working in Geneva, John Calvin published his *Institutes of the Christian Religion* in 1536. This, Calvin's *magnum opus,* compiled together many of the fruits of those early Reformation years, including his own particular contributions on such doctrines as biblical worship and scriptural teachings on the Holy Spirit.

These and other biblical truths had for too long been distorted and misunderstood. For too many long years, unbiblical superstitions about salvation, worship, and the Christian faith had been permitted to modify, and even contradict, the Bible's own teachings on those subjects. The Reformation was, in essence, a Europe-wide Bible study recovering the "raw" biblical teachings on such important truths. Scotland's Reformers followed in the wake of these early theologians from the European Continent.

The leader of the Reformation in Scotland, John Knox, had been discipled by Calvin in Geneva. Knox was later to reflect on his experience in Geneva, calling Calvin's school there, "the most perfect school of Christ since the days of the apostles." Knox brought the Reformation doctrines he learned at Geneva to his native Scotland. Scotland had had her "morning stars" of the Reformation in earlier times (most notably the pre-Reformation martyrs, Patrick Hamilton and George Wishart). Knox also had begun preaching Protestant doctrine prior to his time with Calvin in Geneva. Nonetheless, the major momentum for national reform culminated after Knox's 1559 return from Geneva.

As latecomers to Reformation, Scotland inherited the doctrinal clarity already worked out by her predecessors. This First Scottish Reformation was squarely grounded in the doctrines worked out on the Continent. Nonetheless, the Scottish Reformers also made important, further contributions to the doctrinal recoveries of that period. In particular, the exposition of biblical teachings on *church government* found its fullest development in the Scottish wing of the Reformation with the implementation of presbyterianism.

The First Reformation in Scotland was characterized by the replacement of Roman Catholic doctrine and church hierarchy with Reformation doctrine and presbyterian church government.

As was often the case in Reformation lands, however, opposition came not only from Rome but from civil government as well. Sometimes kings were known to resist reformation in concert with the Roman pope. Sometimes kings and governments introduced obstacles to church reform independent of the papacy. In Scotland, Roman Catholic dogma and hierarchy were eventually purged. Nonetheless, the avowedly Protestant kings, James VI and his son Charles I, endeavored to reshape the Protestant Church of Scotland in subjection to civil authority. That is, the Church of Scotland, though a professedly Protestant church free from Roman control, was now being brought under state control.

Between 1567 and 1637, a long series of struggles ensued between the Reformation movement in the church, and the royal agenda for the church. By the end of that period, the attainments of the First Reformation lay in shambles. In his history of the period, Johannes G. Vos aptly summarized the situation in 1637, thus:

The destiny of the Church of Scotland hung in the balances.

Presbyterian government was gone; Presbyterian worship was about to be destroyed. If the constitution and worship of the Church of Scotland [achieved in the First Reformation] ... was to be saved from total destruction, it was necessary that decisive action be taken....[3]

It was in this period of desperation—and in the face of the church–state problem specifically—that a "Second" Reformation emerged. In this Second Reformation period, the biblical doctrine of *church* government (presbyterianism) would continue to be championed. But in addition to this, biblical teaching on *state* government, and on the proper relationship between church and state, was to emerge as a further important contribution of the Scottish Reformation.

The Second Reformation (1638–1651), and its Ongoing Adherents

Seeds of the Scottish Reformation doctrine of the state, and its relationship with the church, can be found as early as John Knox's reasonings with Mary Queen of Scots. Reformers in other lands had also written on church-and-state issues in earlier times.[4] Nevertheless, the events of 1638 and thereafter were to bring this subject squarely to the forefront of reformation efforts in Scotland. In the Scottish Second Reformation, the subject of civil government was to receive what was probably its most rigorous examination from Scripture. It was to be a study worked out, not in the context of a palace court or a university hall, but in the refining forge of fire, sword, persecution, and desperate prayer.

Whereas the First Reformation was a reformation *of the church* in Scotland, the Second Reformation was to seek reformation *of church and state* in Scotland. Whereas a doctrine of *church government* (presbyterianism) was to be a notable fruit of the First Reformation, a biblical doctrine of *civil government* was to be the fruit of the Second Reformation.

The whole of that Second Reformation period is too complex to review in detail here. Nevertheless, the highlights of the Second Reformation, and of the years immediately following the Reforma-

---

3. Johannes G. Vos, *The Scottish Covenanters* (1998), 44.

4. E.g., John Wycliffe's *De Dominio Devino* (1336) and his *De Civili Dominio* (1371). Also, Martin Bücer's *De Regno Christi* (1550).

tion up to Symington's time, can be indicated through the following seven events.[5]

1. The National Covenant of 1638 — The pivotal event, opening the Second Reformation period, was the signing of the National Covenant of 1638. King Charles I had been systematically undoing the First Reformation in Scotland. The Reformation doctrines of worship were replaced by a forcibly imposed Service Book. The Reformation church government was altered by royal decrees, putting a hierarchy of politically appointed bishops in place, and these answerable to the king. This last point was particularly devastating, for it placed the church under the headship of a man—King Charles I —rather than leaving the church in direct subservience to Christ (and His Word) as her sole Head and King.

When Charles resisted all appeals for the restoration of the church's Reformation order, the defenders of Reformation orthodoxy resorted to public *covenanting*. In previous generations, covenanting had been an important means for securing Reformation aims in the face of seemingly insurmountable crises. John Knox had drawn up a "band" (or, covenant) with the "gentlemen of Mearns" in 1556. During the early years of James VI, the first covenant of *national* proportions was drawn up. Commoners, lords, nobles, and the king himself signed their allegiance to the aims of national Reformation outlined in that National Covenant of 1580.

Covenanting had been a practice throughout the Scottish Reformation for unifying—and propelling—biblical reforms forward in the face of serious apostasy. Covenanting was another of those particularly Scottish contributions to the doctrines of Reformation, as this practice is one which was learned from the pattern of Scripture (e.g. 2 Chr. 15; Neh. 9–10) and worked out most clearly in Scotland. Two elements were particularly important in such covenants: national repentance for the sins which had brought the present distresses; and national vows to turn from those sins in specific ways.

In 1638, rather than simply complaining at King Charles's belligerency, a series of public sermons was called for. Preachers were

---

5. J.G. Vos, *The Scottish Covenanters* (Edinburgh: Blue Banner Productions, 1998) has been particularly useful for many details in this summary of the Second Reformation.

asked to identify and biblically confront the sins of the nation. If *God* had permitted a mere man—Charles I—to undo the Reformation so long and laboriously constructed, the people must be called to self-examination to consider whether God's wrath was upon them. Out of this period of public examination, a National Covenant of corporate repentance and reform was drawn up. At its heart was the old covenant from 1580. The same promises made by the nation in 1580 were renewed. A new list of present offenses needing to be corrected was also appended. The result was the National Covenant of 1638 which was circulated around the nation in multiple copies. Literally tens of thousands of the Scottish population, from commoners and ministers to lords and officials, signed their names to that Covenant. Its salient features can be noted through a few citations from it.

The first part of the National Covenant was a restatement of the 1580 Covenant. As such, it detailed the reforms necessary to restore *the church* to her Reformation moorings. It begins with:

> We all and every one of us under-written, protest, That, after long and due examination of our own consciences…we are now thoroughly resolved in the truth by the word and Spirit of God…. And therefore we abhor and detest all contrary religion and doctrine….

Following this opening profession is a long description of errors of faith and practice requiring nationwide repentance in particular relation to the church (or, the "kirk," in the Scotch vernacular).

Further along, then, the Covenant turns its attention to matters of *the state,* with this profession of loyalty to the king: "We protest and promise with our hearts, under the same oath,… that we shall defend his person and authority with our goods, bodies, and lives…." This was not a document of sedition against Charles, only a document affirming the biblical grounds (and boundaries) of his place. At that point, the restatement of the 1580 Covenant ends, and a new legal section further expanding the state reforms necessary follows.

In several long paragraphs, specific Acts of Parliament from previous years are listed. These Acts of Parliament are those which had been enacted in previous years in cooperation with the First Reformation. This list demonstrated the legal grounds—and pattern—for restoring Reformation orthodoxy with state support. After detailing these laws, the coronation law of Scotland's kings is quoted verbatim:

> That all Kings and Princes at their coronation, and reception of their princely authority, shall make their faithful promise... [to] serve the same eternal God, to the uttermost of their power, according as he hath required in his most holy word ...[and] shall maintain the true religion of Christ Jesus [according to the Reformation Confessions]....

In other words, Charles I (who took that coronation oath in 1633) is due full honor as Scotland's head of state. However, Charles is himself, *as head of state,* bound to rule the nation *according to the laws of God* (i.e., "in his most holy word"). It was the claim of this Covenant that Scripture requires kings to rule in submission to Christ, and that the coronation oath taken by Charles I had already bound him as Christ's subject. Charles I was therefore legally obliged to uphold, not dismantle, the church of Christ as biblically reformed.

Quite explicitly, the Covenant summarizes its aims as twofold: (1) the defense of "the true religion" *(the church)* as taught from Scripture alone, and (2) the upholding of "the King's Majesty" *(the state)* according to his biblical prerogatives. The Covenant concludes that these two realms—church and state—must be "so straitly joined [that is, united in concert], as that they had the same friends and common enemies, and did stand and fall together."

This National Covenant was nothing less than a call for the Reformation of church *and* state. Both must be made harmonious subjects to the Crown of King Jesus. Each must govern its distinct jurisdiction, without meddling with one another, yet in mutual and cooperative service to the same heavenly laws. The National Covenant of 1638 laid down the gauntlet for the Second Reformation—a reformation of church and state under the crown of King Jesus.

Charles did not take kindly to the National Covenant of 1638. Nevertheless, after its initial signing at Greyfriars Kirkyard in Edinburgh, copies were circulated throughout Scotland. Tens of thousands of commoners, ministers, officials, and men and women of rank subscribed together to that national bond. These signatories were professing their obligation to continue the work of reformation under a higher crown than that of Charles.

2. The Solemn League and Covenant (1643)—A significant development in the Second Reformation period took place in 1643, when the rest of the British Isles also embraced the above Covenant. During a period of severe unrest (i.e., the English Civil War), England and Ireland joined with Scotland in what came to be known as the Solemn League and Covenant.

This Solemn League and Covenant was a word-for-word copy of the Scottish National Covenant of 1638, only expanded and updated to address the reformation needs of all three nations:

> We, noblemen, barons, knights, gentlemen, citizens, burgesses, ministers of the Gospel, and commons of all sorts, in the kingdoms of Scotland, England, and Ireland...having before our eyes the glory of God, and the advancement of the kingdom of our Lord and Saviour Jesus Christ,... after mature deliberation, resolved and determined to enter into a Mutual and Solemn League and Covenant, wherein we all subscribe, and each one of us for himself, with our hands lifted up to the Most High God....

Unfortunately, England was later to ignore that Covenant. In later years, England turned away from the kind of Christian government defined by the Solemn League and Covenant. Nevertheless, its subscription was an important step in pressing the reformation of church and state throughout the British Isles.

One important and lasting fruit did, however, come from that expanded Covenant: the Westminster Standards. The Westminster Assembly, which was just beginning its labors for doctrinal reformation in *England* that same year (1643), was expanded under the terms of the Solemn League and Covenant. Scottish Commissioners were added into the Assembly, and the Confession produced at Westminster was composed as the unified doctrinal standards for the Reformation Church throughout England, Scotland, and Ireland.

3. The Coronation of Charles II (1651)—The years of the mid-seventeenth century were rife with unrest in England and Scotland. The Civil War between the English Parliament and King Charles had ended with the king's execution by beheading. The Scottish had generally opposed this execution, still desiring a *reformation* of the crown rather than its overthrow.

One of the results of this Scottish/English tension was that *Scotland* crowned Charles I's heir (Charles II), while England refused to acknowledge him. On January 1, 1651, Charles II was crowned king of Scotland at the traditional coronation site in Scone.

Prior to that coronation, however, the Scots had required that Charles II sign the Solemn League and Covenant. Furthermore, in his coronation oath and as the conditions for his authority, Charles II swore his allegiance to govern according to the Solemn League and Covenant:

> I, Charles, King of Great Britain, France and Ireland, do assert and declare, by my solemn Oath, in the Presence of Almighty God, the Searcher of Hearts, my Allowance and Approbation of the National Covenant, and of the Solemn League and Covenant, above written, and faithfully oblige myself to prosecute the Ends thereof in my Station and Calling....[6]

In that year—1651—Scotland at last achieved, at least in broad strokes, the Covenanted Reformation of church and state. This achievement ought not be overlooked for its significance, even though it was sadly not long lasting.

Oliver Cromwell and the Parliament in England were not keen to see Charles II on Scotland's throne. Furthermore, Charles II was eager to march a Scottish army into England to re-secure his reign there, as well. Within a few months, Cromwell's army soundly defeated Charles II and drove him back into exile. English troops then forcibly subjected Scotland to the English Protectorate of Oliver Cromwell. After Cromwell's death in 1658 (and the inability of Cromwell's son, Richard, to fill his shoes), England too was to welcome Charles II back to the throne. In 1660, Charles II became king of the whole of Great Britain—England, Scotland, and Ireland. But the terms of Charles's coronation in Scotland nine years before were quickly abandoned.

Even in 1651, some of the Scottish Covenanters had suspected Charles of insincerity in his oaths. Once he had full power back in

---

6. Transcribed from the original Covenant signed by Charles II (which is in the Bodleian Library, Oxford) by James King Hewison, *The Covenanters: A History of the Church in Scotland from the Reformation to the Revolution* (Glasgow: John Smith and Son, 1908).

his hands, however, his duplicity became obvious. From 1660 to 1688, Charles II (and his heir, James VII) prosecuted a period of terrible persecution against the Covenanters in Scotland. Charles II was determined to keep the church firmly under his thumb.

4. *The Sanquhar Declaration (1680)*—When Charles II came back to the throne in 1660, among his measures to resubjugate the church to his crown, was a 1662 edict ejecting large numbers of ministers from their pulpits. This was followed by a series of "Indulgence" acts, whereby ministers could return to their pulpits *if* they accepted Charles's order for the church. Many ministers submitted to Charles's demands. These came to be known as the "indulged curates" of the National Church. Those who refused these terms and remained outside the State Church came to be known as the "Covenanters."

These Covenanter ministers took their preaching to the hills and fields of Scotland. Thousands of believers faithful to the Covenants gathered for worship outside the State Church. Charles tried to outlaw such "conventicles" (as they were called), even instituting military force against them. Blood was shed. The Covenanter leaders began to be hunted down and killed. Sometimes the Covenanters rallied in self defense, but they were little match for the king's forces.

In the summer of 1680, one of the Covenanter leaders—a minister named Richard Cameron—rode into the town of Sanquhar with a small band of fellow Covenanters. There, they read and posted a formal declaration of the Covenanters' allegiance to the *Reformation* Church and State. The church and state of Charles II, however, were not that Reformation church and state. In that document, the Covenanters expressed their position that Charles II had abandoned his coronation oath by his rejecting the Covenants he swore to uphold. Consequently, while the Covenanters continued to express loyalty to the Scottish throne in principle, they could no longer recognize *Charles* (and his dynasty) as legitimate. He had abdicated.

The declaration read, in part:

> Therefore, although we be for government and governors, such as the Word of God and our covenant allows; yet we, for ourselves, and all that will adhere to us as the representative of the true Presbyterian Kirk and covenanted nation of Scotland,... disown Charles Stuart, that has been reigning,

or rather tyrannising, as we may say, on the throne of Britain
these years bygone, as having any right, title to, or interest in,
the said Crown of Scotland..., as forfeited..., by his perjury
and breach of covenant both to God and His Kirk..., and
many other breaches in matters ecclesiastic, and...in matters
civil....

All this serves to highlight the seriousness with which the
Covenanters embraced the need for a reformed church *and* state.
The Second Reformation was about the establishment of a biblical
church *and* a biblical state. Without *both* jurisdictions operating in
common submission to the crown of Christ, *neither* was safe from
the intrusions of the other.

Cameron and others paid with their lives for publishing that
declaration. Nonetheless, the Covenanters continued in their witness to the crown rights of Jesus, as claimed by Him in Scripture
over every human kingdom (e.g., Ps. 2). The Sanquhar Declaration
affirmed the Covenanter call for reformation ecclesiastical and civil,
with the bold implication of proclaiming Charles II a usurper.

5. Formation of the United Societies (1681)—Persecution of the Covenanters continued throughout Charles II's reign. Covenanter
ministers were tracked down and killed. Meeting in conventicles
for worship, in wide open fields, became increasingly dangerous
and difficult. Such mass Covenanter gatherings, in obscure places,
continued for communion and such important services. Otherwise,
Covenanters began to meet for worship in smaller groups which
came to be known as "Praying Societies." Careful rules were drawn
up and circulated to maintain the orderliness of these Praying Societies (often simply called, "Society Meetings").

As these Societies increasingly became the focal point of
Covenanter worship and doctrinal instruction, a "general correspondence" was set up among them. The *United* Societies were
organized into this system of shared study and mutual account-
ability in 1681. It was explicitly stated that these Societies were *not*
ecclesiastical nor civil societies. In their organizing declaration, the
United Societies professed:

> These meetings...[being] neither Civil nor ecclesiastick Judi-
> catories..., in this time of extreme persecution, [are] gathered
> together in their generall Correspondence...for our preser-

vation, & the propagation of our Testimony, according to the word of God...& laudable practices of our antient Covenanted Church & Nation, acting...by way of consultation, deliberation, & admonitary determination.[7]

That is, the Covenanters were not organizing another church (nor, for that matter, a shadow state). They remained, expressly, "anti-sectarian."[8] The expectation was still for reform of the National Church (and the state).

Societies met in local areas for prayer, worship, and study of the Scriptures. Four times a year, delegates from each of the local Societies gathered together. This quarterly assembly was the "general correspondence" which "United" the Societies. Although originally organized as a temporary measure, it was these United Societies which, six decades later, would become the *Reformed* Presbyterian Church of Scotland.

6. *The Revolution Settlement of 1688*—Charles II died in 1685. He was succeeded that year by his younger brother, James VII (known as James II in England). The new king was not only opposed to the Covenanters, but he was opposed to Protestantism as a whole. James had publicly converted to Roman Catholicism a decade earlier, and once on the throne he set about to restore Roman Catholicism in the British Isles.

The years 1685–1688 were the bloodiest yet for the Covenanters. They came to be known as the "Killing Times," and they marked the climax of nearly three decades of persecution. According to John Howie's classic, *The Scots Worthies*, "above 18,000 people ...suffered death, or the utmost hardships and extremities" under the oppressions of Charles II and James VII.[9] (Of particular interest

---

7. James Renwick and Alexander Shiells, *An Informatory Vindication of a Poor, Wasted, Misrepresented Remnant, of the Suffering, Anti-Popish, Anti-Prelatic, Anti-Erastian, Anti-Sectarian, True Presbyterian Church of Christ in Scotland, United Together in a General Correspondence, By Way of Reply to Various Accusations, in Letters, Informations and Conferences Given forth Against Them* (Edinburgh: R. Drummond, 1744 [reprinted from original edition, 1687]), head 1, subdivision 3, page 47.

8. Note the "anti-sectarian" claim in the title of their vindication, in note 7, above.

9. John Howie, *The Scots Worthies* (Edinburgh: Oliphant, Anderson, and Ferrier, 1781), 626.

to American readers: included in Howie's number are 1,700 exiled to penal colonies in America). Much of this violence against the Covenanters took place under James.

Nonetheless, James's tyranny was soon overthrown. The Covenanters had eight years before denounced Charles II as having abdicated his right to rule. They had also, in that same Sanquhar Declaration, already denounced James' eligibility to the throne as well, seeing he was even at that time a professing Roman Catholic. Although the Covenanters had stood alone in these civil protests from 1680, their claim was vindicated by the general masses of Scotland and England in 1688.

In that year, James VII's queen bore him a son, and it became evident to all that Britain was on the verge of a long line of Roman Catholic rulers. Because the king, by law, was obliged to swear loyalty to the Protestant church in his coronation oath, James VII was summarily proclaimed to have abdicated. In other words, the Sanquhar Declaration and its claim that a king could be pronounced illegitimate for having violated his coronation oath, was now the common stance of the United Kingdom. James VII fled to France, never to resume the throne.

The next in line to reign were William and Mary of Holland. Mary was James VII's daughter, and William also was related to the British royal line. Parliament ministers in London invited the Protestant rulers, William and Mary, to assume the crown in Great Britain. In November 1688, William and Mary landed in England. A new dynasty was inaugurated through a bloodless revolution.

William and Mary went about consolidating their new dominion. In England, they restored the Protestant Anglican church. In Scotland, they restored the Protestant presbyterian church. However, the restorations instituted in Scotland specifically ignored the Covenants and all the achievements of the Second Reformation period. Instead of affirming the legally ratified *Covenants* of 1638 and 1643 as the basis for reform, William and Mary reinstituted a Presbyterian Charter *from way back in 1592!* That document—the so-called "Great Charter of Presbytery" of 1592—had been an important step forward during the First Reformation. It was now a strange step backward, sidestepping all that had been gained under the Covenants and Acts of Parliament recorded in them.

Many Christians in Scotland, content just to have peace again, accepted William and Mary's Revolution Settlement. The National Church became presbyterian again, *but it remained a church subject to the king's authority.* It was a Protestant and presbyterian church, but it was not the Reformation Church of Scotland. Many believers, though grateful for peace, remained conscientious of the oaths they had sworn in the National Covenants. Conscience bound them to continue their adherence to Jesus *alone* as King and Head of the church. There were many who could not lightly accept the "partially restored" order of the new Revolution Settlement.

On March 3, 1689, an assembly of Covenanter Societies gathered at a site called Borland Hill. There, they prayerfully renewed their commitment to the promises they had made to Christ in the National Covenant. Appeals to the State Church to remember her Covenanted principles would continue; but in the meantime, the United Societies continued outside the State Church.[10]

7. Organization of the Reformation Presbytery (1743) — The United Societies persisted in their hope for the reformation of church and state in Scotland. However, as a non-ecclesiastical society — that is, a Christian body not itself claiming to be a church — the Covenanters had no means for training and ordaining ministers. There had only been a handful of ministers remaining after the Killing Times. By the early eighteenth century, it was evident that, to maintain their witness for the gospel church and the Christian state both allied under Christ's crown, the Societies would have to organize as a church.

Lacking ordained ministers, however, the Societies continued to abstain from the sacraments and from church organization until the Lord would provide legitimately ordained ministers. John Macmillan was the first thus raised up for the Societies. Macmillan had been ordained in the National Church. After long wrestling with his conscience, however, he left the National Church and joined the Societies in 1706. For many years, he was the only minister to administer sacraments and preach for some twenty Societies includ-

---

10. For a fuller account of reasons for abstaining from the Established Church, see, John Graham, "The Revolution Settlement and the Church of Scotland," which is Lecture IV in Andrew Symington, ed., *Lectures on the Principles of the Second Reformation* (Glasgow, 1841).

ing 7,000 members. In 1743 however, Thomas Nairne also joined the United Societies. Nairne had been ordained in the National Church before embracing the principles of the Covenanters. In the year of Nairne's coming, a plurality of ordained ministers made it possible to organize a presbytery. This was done on August 1, 1743.

The original minutes from that meeting are lost; however, a document written ten years later by John Macmillan's son (John Macmillan II), reports the event and its reason, thus:

> The Reverend Mr. John MacMillan and the Reverend Mr. Thomas Nairn...with their respective elders did, by solemn Prayer, constitute themselves into a Presbytery, immediately under Christ their Head, under the name of The Reformed Presbytery. By which Title they understood...a Presbytery professing to adhere and bear Testimony to our covenanted Reformation, as it was carried on in the Nations betwixt the years 1638 and 1649.[11]

William Symington was born into a Covenanter family fifty years later. By Symington's time, the Societies were continuing to meet as Societies while a small (but growing) number of ministers were shared amongst them. There were also regular congregations in places where ministers resided. The Reformed Presbyterian Church was still making its transition from non-ecclesiastical Societies into a fully operating Reformation and presbyterian church. Symington was to prove an important participant in that process, helping to work out the applications of Covenanter principles to the practices and ministry of the Covenanter congregations.

It also was to fall to Symington to become the penman of those Covenanter principles. As a Reformed Presbyterian theologian, living in those years when peace afforded the leisure to document, Symington took up his pen for the Covenanter testimony. Symington was a diligent student of the scattered confessions and sermons of his Covenanter forefathers. He was also, himself, an active participant in the ongoing witness of Covenanter doctrine in his own day.

Symington was the first to assemble the various doctrinal contributions of these Covenanter testimonies, and to write out, in a

---

11. *A Serious Examination and Impartial Survey of a Print Designed the True State, etc., by a Pretended Presbytery at Edinburgh...Published in the Name and by the Authority of the Reformed Presbytery* (1754), 42–43.

systematic and comprehensive whole, the biblical teaching on Christ's mediatorial dominion and its application to church and state.

One of the anonymous publications of the Covenanters during the persecution years had self-consciously described their Reformation labors in this way:

> Whereas other Churches have asserted and contended for his [Christ's] *Priestly* and *Prophetical* offices, the lot seemeth to have fallen upon *Scotland,* to assert and wrestle more eminently than many others for the *Crown* and *Kingdom* of Jesus Christ.[12]

A century later, William Symington took up his ministerial mantle and his pen to perpetuate and explain that Covenanter testimony—"For Christ's Crown and Covenant."

---

12. *Naphtali, or The Wrestlings of the Church of Scotland for the Kingdom of Christ* (1667), 16.

BIOGRAPHY:

The Life and Ministry
of William Symington

CHAPTER 3

Youth and Early Influences:
Mono To Theo Doxa

William Symington was born on the outskirts of Glasgow, Scotland, in 1795. His birth was at a time when Scotland was undergoing significant changes, and in a place where those changes were most keenly felt.

Glasgow was still a relatively young city. Its counterparts—the ancient cities like Aberdeen, Edinburgh, and St. Andrews—had grown up along the east coast through trade with the European continent. Glasgow (on the west coast) only began to expand in the seventeenth and eighteenth centuries, largely through trade with the American colonies, even though trade with America suffered somewhat in the wake of the American Revolution, late in the eighteenth century. Nevertheless, the prodigious income of those early years enabled Glasgow to invest in the latest technologies of the Industrial Revolution also then underway. By the 1790s, Glasgow was established at the heart of Scottish manufacturing and was positioning itself as "The Second City of the British Empire" (i.e., after London). At the time of Symington's birth, agricultural Scotland was in the throes of industrialization—with all its cultural benefits and banes.

The Symington family was directly affected by the foment of the age. For centuries, the Symingtons had occupied a farming tract in central Scotland. The property had been assigned to a fourteenth-century ancestor by Robert the Bruce, and continued as the family home over the four subsequent centuries. Its location in the medieval barony of Symundstoun is the origin of the family name.

William Symington's father, also named William, had been born on that family farm in 1761. His was the last generation born on the ancestral land. He was raised on the farm, and grew spiritually under the instruction of the Covenanter ministers and in the Society Meetings in Southwest Scotland. Nevertheless, when he came of age, William Sr. was among the thousands swept from farm to city by the irresistible and often ruthless currents of the Industrial Revolution. He settled in Paisley on the southwest edge of Glasgow.

In Paisley, William Sr. engaged himself in the growing textile industry. Paisley shawls were becoming a particularly profitable commodity of the time. William Sr. began his career as one of the so-called "philosophical weavers"—an influential class of respectable and well-read craftsmen who helped build the industry and earned good wages doing so. Eventually, however, possibly due to health concerns, he left the loom and became a linen and woolen merchant. Symington's mercantile venture proved successful, allowing him to maintain a respectable, middle-class home in Paisley.

William Sr.'s continuing Christian devotion through his business years can be seen in his choice of a bride. In 1784, he married Marion Brown, a woman described as having "strong natural good sense and [of] sterling Christian worth, and the member of a family distinguished for godliness."[1] Mr. Symington is also frequently mentioned in church records at Paisley, having been active in the work of the Societies in that community. His labors earned him recognition as one of the "principal pillars" in the eventual organization of a Reformed Presbyterian church in Paisley. As an elder, he was also active at the presbytery level and was among the constituting members of the first Reformed Presbyterian *synod*, organized in 1811.

A memorial to William Symington Sr., published after his death in the *Reformed Presbyterian Magazine* (March, 1862), remembered him as a "pious merchant in Paisley,... shrewd, genial, and yet deeply religious." He was one who "evinced in his religion much of the 'joy unspeakable.'"

It was into the home of this devout businessman, in the summer of 1795, that William Symington (Jr.) was born. Although it was this son who bore his father's name, William was the sixth in a family of eight. The oldest boy was named Andrew and was ten years William's senior. Andrew was to prove an important influence in his

---

1. "Memoir of the Author" by Symington's sons (pp. xvii–ciii of the 1881 edition of *Messiah the Prince*), xix. (Hereafter cited simply as "Memoir.")

Glasgow University's "Old Main Gateway." Presently the entrance to the university's Pearce Lodge, during the time Symington was a student at the school this gate was its main entrance.

younger brother's life, not only in childhood but on into adulthood as well. In many ways, Andrew was a "second father" for William, and a positive influence in every way.

Not all of those reared in the predominantly religious homes of agrarian Scotland successfully passed on their faith to the new generation raised in the new pressures of industrial cities. Nevertheless, family descriptions speak of the Symington parents as those who faithfully taught their family "as they had themselves been trained, in intelligent attachment to the principles of the Scottish Covenanted Reformation, and in the love and practice of holiness."[2] The Lord honored the faithfulness of the parents in the face of new social pressures, bringing fruit in the lives of their children.

Andrew (the oldest) flourished under this parental nurture. Upon completing studies at the University of Glasgow, he entered the Reformed Presbyterian Theological Hall and from thence

---

2. "Memoir," xix.

accepted a call to the pastorate of the Paisley congregation. Andrew was also to become the professor at the Theological Hall from 1820 to 1853. Undoubtedly, Andrew's example was one of the important influences in William's own study for the ministry. It is also said that William's parents had especially dedicated him to the ministry.

The generally pious upbringing enjoyed by William does not mean that his youth was unmarked by the temptations of the world, however. William later wrote of his childhood with an acknowledgement of youthful temptations and his all too oft surrender to them. "I plunged into all the frivolities of thoughtless childhood," he was later to reflect on his early schooling years,

> The wicked practices of my associates, in which I too readily joined, shall always be remembered with pungent grief. Here (the Grammar School) the bad example all around was too powerful to be counteracted by the pious instruction and sober walk of the domestic circle in which I lived.[3]

As important as his parents' instruction and example would prove to be in William's life, their devotion could not restrain his own heart's leanings. His youth was marked by all the same struggles of any child facing the competing claims of his father's faith and the world's allure. The latter would have been especially strong in the utopian zeal of the new industrial age.

The temptations of the city were especially real for the boy when he moved to university at age fifteen. He described himself in that period as "a thoughtless youth of fifteen in the heart of a great and licentious city...[without] a parent's eye to watch over my youthful steps, or to awe into the external observance of moral and religious duty."[4] College was to be a decisive period in young William's life.

He was by no means slothful in his studies, however. The diligence with which he applied himself to his courses is evidenced by his various distinctions. William's mastery of Latin in previous schooling enabled him to enroll directly into Greek class his first year. His fourth-year essay in Greek won top honors. William also took courses in logic, natural philosophy, mathematics, astronomy,

---

3. "Memoir," xxi–xxii.
4. "Memoir," xxiv.

geography, and other fields, records of which are incomplete, but which indicate a student with high marks.

It was during his college years that William resolved his commitment to the faith in which he was reared. The temptations which college life proffered would likely have contributed towards his contemplation about divine justice. A severe attack of scarlet fever in the early summer of 1811—just after completing his first year— added to his thoughts about his soul. The primary influences on his spiritual development, however, were the summer communion seasons in 1811 and especially 1812.

In those days, communion was preceded by an extended "season" of preparation through daily preaching services. Only those with a public profession of faith (and church membership) were admitted to participate in the sacrament, though others could attend the sermons. Although a child of Christian parents and of the Paisley congregation, Symington had not made his own profession of faith. During the communion services of 1811, sixteen-year-old William began to speak seriously with his mother about the sacrament and to ask of her about "the pre-requisites of those to whom it was dispensed."[5]

It was the communion season of the following summer (1812) that Symington was to regard as "the commencement of my serious impressions about divine things."[6] Sitting daily under the preaching of God's Word, Symington began to examine his relationship with Christ. "I retired in the evening," he recalled of one particular day,

> to an adjoining forest for the purpose of secret devotion.... My meditations and reflections were overpowering. I fell upon my knees and poured forth to God a fervent prayer that he would open my eyes to see the spiritual import of the sacred ordinance I was soon to witness, give me a personal interest in the glories which it represents, and prepare me in due time for sitting down at his table.[7]

Soon after, William moved home to Paisley for the summer, where one of the elders came to call on him. The elder spoke to William of his need to make a public profession and join the church

5. "Memoir," xxvii.

6. "Memoir," xxvii.

7. "Memoir," xxviii.

at the upcoming communion. William informed the elder of his "motives to postpone" this decision, but the elder warmly answered the lad's concerns with a series of subsequent meetings together. Although William does not reveal what his particular hesitancies were, he later recalled those private conferences as having been an important help to him in overcoming his apprehensions.

As a result of that elder's private conferences with him, and the contemplations which followed from them, Symington writes, "I gave myself away to the Lord in a solemn personal covenant."[8] He had grown up in a Covenanter household, and a personal covenant responding to Christ's covenant was the sensible way for him to express his surrender. This "solemn personal covenant" was followed by application for church membership and public participation in the Lord's Supper. "This step of my life," Symington later wrote, "shall never be forgotten, and as I have had reason to reflect upon it with feelings of satisfaction and delight, I earnestly hope they may continue through eternity."[9]

Symington's testimony reminds us of the value of a godly businessman (his father) who is not so concerned about his success as a merchant to overlook his need to be a successful teacher to his children as well. It is also a witness to the value of a church elder's pastoral interest in the young. If it had not been for the "frivolous" draw of his classmates in school years, Symington thought he might have come to his own public profession earlier in life. Nevertheless, the foundations laid through godly parents and his church equipped Symington to think intelligently about the claims of Christ when he did turn his serious attention to religion. In a sense, young William's head had already been well instructed in the faith, so that when his heart "caught up" that summer of 1812, his was already a well-grounded faith. And that was to prove important.

That next autumn, as William began his third year of study at university, he was enrolled in one of the most challenging tests of his newly covenanted faith: Professor Mylne's infamous Moral Philosophy class.

Professor Mylne was well known as a skeptic who took great relish in stirring doubt in the minds of his students. One period

---

8. "Memoir," xxviii.

9. "Memoir," xxviii.

writer, and former student of Mylne's, described the professor and his course in the following manner:

> He was…a sceptic; and, indeed, he set himself, in a quiet but effectual way, to shake the belief of his students. He openly denied and argued against eternal punishment, and sneered at some of the cardinal doctrines of Christianity besides. Few came away from his class without sharing, more or less, in the infection, if not of his actual doubts, at least of his cold, sceptical, materialistic spirit. The Moral Philosophy Class was a kind of ice-bath, in which we shivering novices were plunged; some of the weaker perishing, and even the stronger more chilled than strengthened by the operation.[10]

In later years, Symington was to recall Mylne's course as having pushed him to think in more thorough and careful ways than he had before. He must have done well, both in maintaining his own faith and in defending his views in class debate. He is listed among the prizes for having produced the best composition in the class, and he also was awarded for his "eminence" in class discussion. Mylne's "ice bath" must have been a proving ground for Symington's faith, but it also served to strengthen his ability to articulate himself in a philosophically rigorous manner.

The years at the University of Glasgow were intellectually and spiritually stimulating for William. When he completed his courses there, he proceeded to enroll at the Reformed Presbyterian Theological Hall, at that time located north of Glasgow in Stirling. The Theological Hall provided courses in four, eight-week sessions, held only during the autumn-time. William attended theological courses each autumn from 1814 to 1817. In between sessions, William worked as a tutor for the Tennant family and took advantage of his brother Andrew's counsel and library for study. William also traveled by horse throughout Scotland during those years, as a "probationer" preacher. Records from the period show that William was frequently requested for sermon supply by various congregations. He was already becoming widely known for his ability as a biblical expositor.

A letter from Mrs. Tennant to William, dated August 26, 1815, reveals that William was also contemplating a move to America

---

10. George Gilfillian, *The History of a Man* (1856), 89–90.

during this time. "I find you are still thinking of the Atlantic," Mrs. Tennant wrote to William, "You have a great deal to do before you cross it, and tho you should, it would neither separate you from the [affections] of your friends, or prevent the manifestations of it by letters."[11] William never was to cross the Atlantic, although through his writings he would later have an important ministry in America. Nonetheless, whatever William's contemplations may have involved during that time, his extensive travel among the Scottish congregations and Societies must have served to bind his heart to his native land and ground his concern for the needs of his countrymen.

On the completion of his studies at the Theological Hall, William sustained licensing examinations before the presbytery. Two congregations issued calls for him to be their pastor: the congregation in Airdrie just outside Glasgow, and the congregation of Stranraer along the southwest coast. At the Synod meeting of May, 1819, William announced his acceptance of the call to minister at Stranraer. At an assembly in Stranraer on August 18, with between four and five thousand attending, William was ordained to the ministry.

It was not insignificant that two of the men who had had the greatest influence in his preparation for that moment took part in the ordination service. It was Rev. Andrew Symington, the older brother and mentor, who was appointed by the Presbytery to lay hands on William in the prayer of consecration, and to preach the charge to William and the congregation. Furthermore, William's father (an elder in another presbytery) was asked to take an "honorary" position in that assembly for William's ordination. The elder William was gratified to accept.

The results of all these early influences in William's life can best be summarized by the life motto which he chose for himself during this period. It is first noted in a journal entry for September 19, 1816, although he was to refer to it many times more over the years. Above all else, it had become the whole desire of this young man to live, *"mono to theo doxa"*—Greek for, "to the glory of God alone."

---

11. MS Letter, dated 26 August 1815, to "Mr. Wm. Symington Junior" and signed "Mrs. C. Tennant." (See also, "Memoir," xxxiv.)

CHAPTER 4

The Stranraer Years I:
Disciplines of a Covenanter Pastor

The Royal Burgh of Stranraer is the only natural port on Scotland's southwest coast. Its population in 1819, when Symington took up ministry there, was around 2,500. Although not the major transatlantic port that Glasgow was to the north, Stranraer was the closest port for reaching English and Irish markets. As such, it served the commercial interests for the entire Scottish southwest. Roads ran from Stranraer throughout the region. These factors were to make Stranraer an excellent location for ministry.

Stranraer was a sort of "gateway" for the whole Southwest, and this region had been historically significant for the Covenanters. During the seventeenth-century persecutions, many of the Covenanter martyrs had been from the southwest. Likewise, during the years when the Covenanters were barred from the Established Church and lacked their own ministers, it was in this area that the Societies were most numerous and best organized.

As the Lord began to raise up ministers for the Covenanters in the late eighteenth century, a minister named John Reid was ordained to serve the "Galloway Congregation." Galloway referred loosely to the whole coastal region where Stranraer is located. At the first Galloway communion service, held not long before Reid's 1783 ordination, there were some ten to fifteen thousand in attendance. (It is no wonder Reid was to complain, in later years, of being overworked!)

In 1796, the Societies in Stranraer and nearby Stoneykirk were formed into a separate congregation and called their own minister. This divided the care for Galloway between two ministers. Robert Douglas served as the first minister of the Stranraer congregation (and outlying Societies), pastoring there from 1796 to his death in

1800. The second minister in Stranraer was John Cowan, whose death in 1817 left the vacancy Symington was called to fill.

As the foregoing facts will make evident, although Symington was appointed to the pulpit in Stranraer, there was a very real sense in which Symington was actually the pastor for a much wider area. There were something like twenty Societies affiliated with the Stranraer church at that time. That Symington's ordination in Stranraer was attended by four to five thousand—double the population of the city itself—is some indication of the strength of the Covenanter Societies in the area.

It was to prove a strenuous pastorate for Symington, requiring him to travel to homes and preaching stations the length and breadth of the county. It nevertheless proved a fertile location for his early labors. It was in Stranraer that Symington established himself as a Covenanter churchman, theologian, and family man.

Symington the Family Man

On moving to Stranraer, Symington initially took up residence in the home of Mrs. Cowan, the widow of the previous minister. His journal, letters, and frequent trips back to Paisley, however, reveal the young minister's already-forming intentions to establish his own home. His journal speaks of his regular prayers for his "intended partner in life," at places identifying her as, "My D[ear] Agnes."

The summer after his ordination, on June 27, 1820, Symington was united in marriage to Miss Agnes Speirs of Paisley. Agnes and William set up house in Stranraer where they were to enjoy the next twenty years, and where the Lord was to bless them with seven children.

Symington took his responsibilities as a father seriously. Recalling his own, early distractions from Christ through the pressure of school peers, Symington purposed to educate his children at home. He did find himself comfortable enrolling some of his children in a school in Glasgow after moving there in later years, and in home education he hired a tutor for some courses with his children. Nevertheless, in a rather amusing extract from a letter to a brother, Symington gives an indication of the degree of his own involvement:

> The evenings are devoted to family reading. Besides, I give
> the children a part of every forenoon and afternoon, and they

are already somewhat acquainted with the first principles of English grammar, geography, natural history, and arithmetic. Besides English reading and religious knowledge, they also write a little every day. Now that I have got into it, I do not dislike teaching them. This will be interesting to mother.[1]

Busy minister as he was, Symington's personal involvement in the education of his children can be noted as an indication of his family devotion.

In later years, the children were to write of their father's "eminently domestic" care with admiration. Two of his sons went on to become ministers in the Reformed Presbyterian Church, and one son became a Glasgow businessman. One of his daughters married William H. Goold, pastor of the Edinburgh RP congregation and later a professor at the Theological Hall, as well.

One of the seven children died in a most tragic childhood accident. While several of the children were playing in the yard outside the Stranraer manse, a stone sun-dial was somehow toppled. It fell on top of six-year-old Robert, who survived the initial accident, but the internal injuries were too severe. The horrified father, ever journaling, wrote sixteen pages of his intense emotion and wrestlings during the next thirty-six hours. Among those pages, the following record of Mrs. Symington's bedside communion with the dying six-year-old was preserved.

We might picture the teary-eyed mother, sitting at Robert's bedside, perhaps with a hand stroking his hair as she asks the six-year-old of his youthful faith. "Who redeems you, my sweet dear?" she queried. "Christ," Robert readily responded, perhaps looking up into his mother's eyes. "Would you like to go to Christ?" the mother further inquired, aware of what was now inevitable. "Yes," the boy answered. "Where do the righteous go at death, my dear?" the mother asked further. "To heaven," came the confident answer.

One can readily imagine how many times before she and her husband had asked their son such catechetical questions, never realizing the comfort which his early embrace of these truths, and ability to express them for himself, would bring in this hour. "Who are the righteous that go to heaven at death?" she continued. "Such as believe in Christ, love God, and hate evil," Robert answered.

---

1. "Memoir," xlix–l.

"Would you like to go to heaven?" "Yes." Mrs. Symington report-edly asked Robert one further question—"Would you not be sorry to leave us all?"—which Robert is said to have answered by "clasp-ing his arms around her neck and bidding her not to cry because he was going to be with Jesus."[2]

Robert died thirty-six hours after the accident and was buried in the Stranraer churchyard. His loss was a deep source of sorrow to the young minister and his wife, and one which (as will be later seen) directly contributed to Symington's close study of the atone-ment in his book on the subject. The Symingtons knew to turn to the cross for comfort.

This is also an incident which bears witness for us, who are privileged to peek into it, at the care with which these parents taught their children, from the youngest years, the Scriptures. Family life in the Symington household was not immune to the heartaches known to others. Nevertheless, one cannot fully appreciate the public minis-try of William Symington without equally appreciating the emphasis he placed on his private ministry as a husband and father.

Symington the Covenanter

It is also evident, from his early years, that Symington was disci-plined in the nurture of his own personal piety (that is, his personal walk with Christ). The importance of his devotional life is seen in his journals, which are filled with statements like: "O for more spiri-tuality and holiness!" and, "the leisure for [Bible] reading which I at present enjoy is delightful" and, "O that the spirit of all grace may enable me to cherish the spirit of prayer habitually."[3] Personal growth in holiness was important for Symington—and it was some-thing he believed he needed to be deliberate about.

It is in his approach to personal piety that Symington's view of what it means to be a "covenanter" has particular relevance. At this point, it might be worthwhile to make a distinction between *the* Covenanters (as those who were faithful to a particular series of National Covenants in Scotland), and *a* covenanter (as appli-cable to any Christian who responds, covenantally, to Christ). *The* Covenanters were also covenanters, but not all who practice the

---

2. "Memoir," lvii–lviii.

3. MS Journal, May 19, 1835; Jan. 15, 1835.

biblical discipline of covenanting are necessarily party to the Scottish National Covenants. Symington's devotional life reveals that he was not only a Covenanter, but he also took seriously the discipline of private covenanting.

As was seen in the previous chapter, Symington expressed his total surrender of himself to Christ during the summer of 1812 in a "solemn personal covenant." Throughout his life, he would regularly renew that "solemn personal covenant," verbalizing specific ways in which he needed to amend his life in order to respond more faithfully to Christ's Word.

For example, a few days before his ordination in Stranraer, Symington recorded in his journal that he had entered into such a renewal of his "solemn personal covenant." As part of that renewal, Symington worked out a schedule, or "plan" as he called it, for coordinating his new ministerial duties to the congregation with his personal, devotional duties before Christ. He was even so specific as to lay out projected times each day for private reading in Scripture, meditation, and prayer.[4] The demands of the ministry required flexibility and periodic adjustments in his schedule. Nonetheless, the plan represents the seriousness with which Symington took the Covenant of Redemption extended to him by Christ (in Scripture), and the need to respond to it self-consciously, thoughtfully, specifically, and covenantally. Such language as, "spent forenoon in devotion—engaged in renewal of covenant with God," was to be a frequent feature in his journal.[5] For Symington the Covenanter, covenanting was not just a practice incumbent upon nations, it was a discipline for private consecration (and personal reform) as well.

Sometimes, this idea of "covenanting" has been misunderstood. Some have mistakenly thought that the Covenanters supposed they could draft their own terms of relationship with God. That is not what covenanting, as practiced by the Scottish Covenanters, involves. Symington made this clear in a lecture on the subject:

> All other covenants, be it remembered, are founded on the covenant of grace, and can neither be acceptably entered into, nor stedfastly maintained, nor successfully prosecuted,

---

4. MS Journal, Aug. 8, 1819.

5. MS Journal, Apr. 2, 1850.

without faith in the mediator of that covenant which is ordered in all things and sure.[6]

Ultimately, the *only* covenant between man and God is the Covenant of Grace mediated by Jesus Christ. There are no other terms upon which a relationship with God can be entered into except those announced in the divine covenant in Scripture. The Covenanters had no concept of devising a new or revised covenant with God.

It was their conviction, nonetheless, that because God had chosen to extend his grace to men in terms of a covenant, it is incumbent upon men to respond covenantally. To enter or renew a covenant is merely to respond to God's offer of a relationship and to accept His terms. This acceptance of God's terms of covenant—chiefly meaning repentance and faith—ought to be specific, however. A nation, or a private individual, accepting God's covenant ought to indicate specific ways his repentance will be carried out, and what promises he has come to embrace by faith.

When Symington devoted a morning, or a full day, to renewing his "solemn personal covenant," he was reviewing his own faithfulness to Christ in the past, and any further ways he ought to be responding. One of Symington's sons described his father's practice of covenant renewal as "a solemn exercise of personal consecration."[7] Such consecrations came to be a regular practice on his birthday each year and, especially in the busier years later in his ministry, were increased to a regular, monthly exercise.

This clear sense of his *covenanted* obligation to Christ, and his need to respond to Christ *covenantally*, fueled Symington's lifelong spiritual development. The importance of this discipline to the active minister can be discerned in the following confession penned in his journal:

> I find it difficult amid the toil of incessant occupation, to keep alive the flame of inward devotion. It is not the secular business of the world only, but the more sacred business of a

---

6. William Symington, "The Nature and Obligation of Public Vows" (which is Lecture VII in: Andrew Symington, ed., *Lectures on the Principles of the Second Reformation* [Glasgow, 1841]), 48.

7. "Memoir," lxxxv.

minister's life, which is apt to trample down, or trample out, the fire of personal religion.[8]

Regular covenant renewals provided a way to review and refresh his Christian walk. Covenanting kept the obligatory nature of his care for his own soul poignantly before him, when other duties would threaten to interfere.

Symington also taught the discipline of personal covenanting to his family, by letting them each know of his having covenanted them to Christ. He dedicated each of his children to the Lord on the day of birth. Then, on each child's birthday from year to year, father Symington would renew this covenant-type dedication. Symington not only covenanted himself to Christ; to the extent that he, as a father, could "will" it, he was covenanting his family to the Lord.

Symington the Preacher

At the hour of eleven each Sabbath morning, Symington the preacher mounted the winding steps of the large Stranraer pulpit, with its rounded wings and over-hanging sounding board. A large man, tall, well-proportioned and erect, with large head and habitually grave expression, Symington presented a commanding appearance.

His expression, it is said, was generally stern, though he quickly brightened when speaking on a pleasant line. "His voice," according to one, was "soft" though "not disagreeable." His mannerisms also were "animated, varied, graceful." The source of these observations is John Smith, a contemporary who compiled descriptions of fifty-two of the leading Scottish preachers of that day, including Symington. Summarizing Symington's preaching abilities, Smith stated,

> His fame is by no means limited by denominational restriction.... He appears...among the most popular ministers of other sects. Whenever he preaches—and he has preached in churches of not a few denominations—eager crowds assemble, and, enraptured, listen to his eloquent prelections [i.e., public discourses].[9]

It was Symington's practice to write out his sermons (more or less) in full, reduce them to notes, and in prayer he prepared his

---

8. MS Journal, Jan. 10, 1848.

9. John Smith, *Our Scottish Clergy* (1848), 84.

Stranraer pulpit. The raised pulpit from which Symington preached in Stranraer. (Note the precentor's stand on the lower, front of the pulpit, and the overhead sounding board to project the preacher's voice.)

soul to deliver God's Word to the congregation. While his ability to captivate led many to regard him as an "orator," Symington himself was opposed to the trends in his day toward rhetorical flourish, and away from doctrinal substance, in preaching.

Preaching certainly ought to evoke the inward emotion: "[a] cold phlegmatic manner but ill harmonizes with the burning truth of inspiration," Symington insisted.[10] Nevertheless, he professed his own "decided predilection for the intellectual rather than for what has been appropriately styled the *baby* school of preaching." By this expression, "the *baby* school of preaching," Symington is not being derogatory. Rather, he is criticizing that approach to preaching which is so simplistic as to keep congregants constantly on the "milk" of the Word. Symington believed it the preacher's duty to lead the congregation into mature reasoning in the Scriptures. "The great doctrines of evangelical truth," he wrote, "both admit of and require a great amount of close and accurate thinking."[11]

It was a commitment to doctrinal instruction, and careful textual exposition, which characterized his preaching. His morning sermons were usually topical and followed some doctrinal theme or focus. His afternoon message (called, the "Lecture") ordinarily dealt with some book of the Bible, a biblical character, or a period of biblical church history. John Smith recalls how, in a message on "assurance" from Hebrews 6:11–12, Symington "first showed" how those verses fit within the context of the chapter, and "then proceeded to minutely analyse the subject of lecture, and to give the strict meaning of some of its original terms," finally bringing the text to bear on the assurance of the congregation.[12]

Another feature of Symington's preaching was his clear thinking about the centrality of the cross in all his sermons. According to Symington, "the sacrifice of Christ" must be "the chief article of [the preacher's] message, the burden of his doctrine, the central orb of the Christian system which gives to every part its living energy,

---

10. William Symington, *Charges Delivered at the Ordination of the Rev. James McGill, July 21, 1829* (Dumfries: D. Halliday, 1829), 12.

11. "Review: Lectures Delivered at Broadmead Chapel, Bristol: by John Foster," in *Scottish Presbyterian* (Mar., 1845), 69. In his Journal (Jan. 22, 1845), Symington identifies himself as the author of that review.

12. John Smith, *Our Scottish Clergy* (1848), 79.

and binds the whole together in sweet and indissoluble union."[13] Symington's book, *On the Atonement and Intercession of Jesus Christ*, shows that his commitment to the centrality of the cross was not simply pious rhetoric. Symington thought long and deeply on the place of the atonement in Scripture, in order to understand the natural, organic connections from every other Christian doctrine back to that one which is central. Symington's conscious recognition of the atonement as the keystone of the Christian faith influenced his preaching on every biblical text.

The fruit of Symington's preaching can be seen in the need, four years after his ordination, for a new facility to be built. A larger church building was finished a year later, yet it, too, continued to be filled to capacity. Symington's journal is occasioned by remarks like, "house crowded," "house oppressively crowded," or "immensely crowded audience, many strangers present." The number of actual members in the Stranraer congregation over the time of Symington's ministry there is difficult to assess, although a number around 400 seems to have been in membership by 1836. Perhaps more important than the figures for that single congregation where Symington pastored, however, is the remark of the Rev. James McGill. McGill was a thirteen-year-old lad in the Stranraer church when Symington first came there, and he went on to study for the ministry himself. Reflecting on the two decades Symington spent in Stranraer, McGill wrote,

> An impulse was given to the cause of religion in the whole district. A relish for evangelical preaching was widely and rapidly diffused, which not only caused his own church to be densely crowded, but which led to the erection of new churches and the settlement of additional ministers, in other denominations as well as our own.[14]

The words of Jesus to Nicodemus in John chapter 3 are certainly relevant at this point. "The wind bloweth where it listeth," Jesus explained, "and thou hearest the sound thereof, but canst not tell whence it cometh, and whither it goeth: so is every one that is born of the Spirit" (John 3:8). It would be a mistake to suppose that

---

13. William Symington, *On the Atonement and Intercession of Jesus Christ* (1834), 340.

14. "Memoir," lxii.

William Symington brought this "impulse" to the cause of religion in Stranraer. It was the Spirit of Christ who brought a certain measure of revival to the region.

Nevertheless, it must also be recognized that the Spirit uses the preaching of men as *His* means for saving the lost. It must certainly be acknowledged, therefore, that when Christ purposed to bring such an impulse to Stranraer, His raising up of the preacher William Symington was among His means to do so.

Symington the Pastor

Symington's devotion to his pulpit duties was complemented by his concern for visitation among the residents of his area. He regarded it as the duty of an "overseer" to know the state of the souls of those under his charge. What Symington viewed as his "charge," however, was much greater than the rolls of his particular congregation.

Although Symington was ordained at a time when the number of Reformed Presbyterian ministers was increasing, many Covenanter Societies remained without ministers. Symington felt it his duty to minister among the distant Society folk of southwest Scotland, and where possible to help them organize into new congregations able to call ministers.

To maintain his ministry among the distant Societies, Symington followed a regular, yearly program of pastoral visitation, leading him out sometimes for days on end. One contemporary vividly described the sight of Symington, riding through the heather astride his white pony, with a broad blue hat, long coat, corduroy knee-breeches, and gray plaid shirt, making some distant call.[15] A number of new preaching stations or new congregations can be connected with the itinerant ministry of Symington, most particularly those at Whithorn, Gatehouse of Fleet, Mainsriddle, Kilbirnie, Dumfries, Hightae, Dunscore, Sanquhar, and Eskdale-Ettrick.

Even these Societies did not form the whole of Symington's sense of pastoral duty, however. Speaking to a younger minister, Symington voiced his conviction this way: "As a minister you have a commission which knows no local limits but those of the earth.... Wherever you meet with a human soul, there you have an object of

---

15. S.R. Crockett's "Foreword" to: Patrick Walker, *Six Saints of the Covenant* (London: Hodder and Stoughton, 1901), 1.vii, ix.

your ministry."[16] The whole human race stood before Symington's eyes as within his charge.

Such devotion to both a strong pulpit ministry and commit- ted pastoral care was nothing short of exhausting. The limits of the man were not always equal to the needs before him. Certainly, there were heartaches and times of discouragement. A letter from Andrew Symington, the older brother and fellow RP minister, reflects on the discouragement William at times encountered. "My dear brother…," Andrew wrote,

> Every situation in which a minister can be placed has its difficulties…. Some success you may be permitted to see to encourage you, while there may be much to see hereafter, when you rest from your labours and your works follow you [Rev. 14:13]. But it cannot be all success now. We must have something to exercise faith. Without the enemy, where were the soldiers? Let us endure hardness as good soldiers of Jesus Christ [2 Tim. 2:3].[17]

These were hard years, and Symington's calling was a difficult one. Nonetheless, Christ was using Symington to extend the work of the Kingdom in Stranraer during those years; and he was using Stranraer to deepen the faith and spiritual disciplines of William Symington, the Covenanter minister.

---

16. William Symington, *Charges Delivered at the Ordination of the Rev. James McGill, July 21, 1829* (Dumfries: D. Halliday, 1829), 19.

17. "Memoir," liv.

CHAPTER 5

The Stranraer Years II:
Ministry of a Covenanter Pastor

The twenty years Symington spent in Stranraer left little room for idleness. With frequent petitions for divine grace in his journals, the Stranraer minister embraced an overwhelming measure of work by anyone's standard. In order to manage his many involvements, Symington found it necessary to maintain a carefully regulated schedule, and to guard his own need for consistent, private study.

Initially, Symington appointed a fairly regular schedule of daily activities: rising at 6:00 for Bible reading and prayer until breakfast; prayer for himself and the congregation from 10:00 to 11:00; theological study from 11:00 until 2:00; appointments from 2:00 until 3:00; and so on. "The above plan," he wrote in his journal as part of a personal, covenant renewal, "shall be as closely kept as circumstances will permit till I see cause to change it."[1]

Such causes to adjust his schedule were not slow to materialize. Nevertheless, Symington changed his schedule without abandoning his discipline of scheduling. "He owed much of his usefulness in life," one close associate in the ministry explained, "to what we may designate his peculiar love and faculty of order. His very study was the image of his thoughts—a place for everything and everything in its place."[2]

Once settled into the Stranraer pastorate, his activities settled into a fairly regular routine. Mondays came to be set aside for making calls. Tuesday was spent either in further calls or in reading. Wednesday was devoted to "close study," Thursday to sermon preparation, and Friday to preparation for the Sunday afternoon

---

1. MS Journal, Aug. 8, 1819.
2. William H. Goold, quoted in "Memoir," xcvii.

Stranraer Reformed Presbyterian Church building. The unassuming exterior (above) and two-level interior (below) of the church building built to handle the growing crowds which came to hear Symington preach during his pastorate in Stranraer. The building is still home to a Reformed Presbyterian congregation today.

"Lecture." Saturday was often described in his journals by the words, "preparations all day." Symington further divided his Tuesday and Wednesday study among a balanced diet of theology, biblical scholarship, and history. Special adjustments, such as his itinerant visitation periods, were thoughtfully worked in.

By God's grace, Symington was enabled to accomplish much in Stranraer. He also contributed in important ways to the wider church. He served faithfully in his presbytery; he lent his efforts to other Christian movements beyond the Reformed Presbyterian Church; and, in the latter half of his tenure in Stranraer, he began to write. It was Symington's writing which was most notably to spread his influence beyond the coasts of Scotland and the confines of his own time.

Symington the Presbyter

The Reformed Presbyterian Church was in a period of significant growth in Symington's day. Only as recently as 1743, the Covenanter Societies had had two ministers and had formed the first presbytery. By 1811, the church grew to thirteen ministers, eleven congregations, and three presbyteries. By the end of Symington's life (1862), the church would further grow to thirty-six ministers, forty-three congregations, and six presbyteries—more than doubling in size. Never before (or, to date, since) has the Reformed Presbyterian Church in Scotland seen such growth.

It fell to those gatherings of elders and ministers in presbyteries to guide the church through these times of growth. Stranraer was part of the Southern Reformed Presbytery. The influence Symington sought to bring through his work as a presbyter was one of firm defense of RP doctrine, yet readiness to accommodate old practices to new conditions where no compromise of doctrine was involved.

His firm adherence to RP doctrine can be illustrated in relation to a presbytery matter that arose in 1831. A church discipline issue was on the docket for that meeting. The individual under discipline was a minister named Osborne, charged with drunkenness and immorality. Osborne, however, appealed to the *civil* courts to block presbytery's meeting. Claiming that his *civil* rights were being infringed upon, Osborne succeeded in obtaining a government interdict against presbytery holding its appointed meeting. Here was a challenge to the church's doctrine, not only in statement, but in reality. The Covenanters understood the church to be directly ordained by Christ, and thus independent of the state's authority. The state had no right to interfere with a *(bona fide)* church discipline matter.

Symington was instrumental in the presbytery's response to Osborne and to the civil magistrates. In a carefully worded statement, the presbytery expressed its respect for the civil courts, yet defended their duty "firmly and conscientiously to resist every attempt to encroach upon their ecclesiastical rights or jurisdiction."[3] To proceed with the meeting could bring action from the government, but the presbytery was obliged by Scripture to carry out its Christ-appointed duties as a court of ecclesiastical discipline. Presbytery met at the appointed time and proceeded with the charges against Osborne, who was deposed from the ministry at that trial.

Thankfully, no further trouble followed from the civil courts. The magistrate involved acknowledged that Osborne had no civil grounds, after all, for his complaint. This was, nonetheless, a case that challenged in fact, not only in word, one of the doctrinal convictions of the church—with very real penalties that could have followed a failure to compromise. Symington pressed hard for the firm adherence to the doctrine of Christ's sole headship and rule over the church.

Though uncompromising in *principle,* Symington was, however, not inflexible in church *practices.* Symington was concerned to differentiate between doctrinal fidelity and flexibility on matters of practice—even long-standing practices which *did* have doctrinal importance in past circumstances, but no longer hold the same importance in present circumstances. Another presbytery matter will illustrate this side of Symington's influence within the wider church.

In another series of deliberations before presbytery, one minister argued staunchly for the old practices of "lining out" the Psalms in worship, and for requiring "an oath of adherence to the National Covenants."[4] While the church (and Symington) *did* uphold the continuing obligation of the National Covenant, it had been deemed no

---

3. MS "Reply" of the presbytery to the (civil) Court of Session, among the records of the Southern Reformed Presbytery in Trinity College Library, Glasgow.

4. MS "Minutes of the Southern Reformed Presbytery," Aug. 19, 1832.

longer necessary to require "an oath of adherence" to that Covenant as a condition for membership. Symington was appointed to a committee of three assigned to reason with the minister pressing these "ultra-conservative" issues. Symington defended these modified practices, because he saw them as a *continuation* of church doctrine with a willingness to adjust the way those doctrines were practically applied when warranted.

Times were different now from a few generations ago, when such measures were deemed practicable and important. Symington accepted, however, the need to adapt the old practices of the church to new conditions as warranted, so long as principles were not thereby abandoned.

Perhaps the most telling indication of Symington's labors on the presbytery level, however, are reflected in his itinerant visitation periods (noted in the previous chapter). Many of Symington's itinerancies were spent meeting with outlying Societies. Many of the Societies, far from locations with ministers and no longer feeling the pressure of persecution to hold them together, were beginning to disintegrate. Symington labored in his traveling visitation to hold these Societies together and see them organized as new congregations able to call ministers.

Symington recognized his responsibility as a minister, not only to pastor his appointed charge, but to support the growth of the church as a whole. His labors as a presbyter illustrate the carefulness of his labors to serve this growth, and to preserve the church's doctrinal testimony through her "growing pains."

Symington the Evangelical

Symington also labored as a churchman *beyond* the Reformed Presbyterian Church—interdenominationally. In his book, *Messiah the Prince,* Symington expressed his conviction concerning the fundamental unity of the church. Though operating in various denominations, there is ultimately only one King who has given one commission to His one church. Symington quotes with full agreement the following words from another Scottish theologian (George Hill):

> ...as every one who is baptized becomes a member of the catholic [i.e., universal] church, so every one who is ordained

by the laying on of the hands of the office-bearers of the church, becomes a minister of the church universal.[5]

Symington early came to recognize his own ordination as an appointment to serve Christ's church *from the platform* of the Reformed Presbyterian Church, but not in isolation to that particular denomination. One congregant described the Stranraer minister as one who "not unfrequently—nay, he very often—volunteered to preach" for evangelical causes outside the Reformed Presbyterian Church.[6] Some of the efforts in which Symington was particularly active included the Bible Societies, the Sabbath School Society, the Temperance Movement, and foreign missions.

The Bible Society was formed in 1804 to facilitate the publication and affordable sale of Bibles, at a time when purchasing a personal copy of the Bible was not always possible. Symington was enthusiastic for the extension of the work in Scotland and threw his support into the effort. Symington was also a constant advocate for the Sabbath School movement. His first published sermon, in fact, was a sermon preached in support of the Sabbath School movement in Stranraer ("The Evil of Ignorance, and Motives to Its Removal," preached in 1821).[7]

Symington's involvement with the Temperance Movement was motivated by the serious problem of drink in his own community. One period description speaks of Stranraer as having "too many retailers of whiskey, both licensed and unlicensed. The effects of it are…idleness, and the ruin of the health and morals [of the lower classes, especially]."[8] Symington helped to organize a Stranraer chapter of the Temperance Society, and encouraged similar developments in other areas of Scotland.

Foreign missions was, sadly, hardly heard of in Scottish churches in the early 1800s. At the beginning of the nineteenth century, foreign missions were considered a "utopian" and unrealistic idea. This attitude soon changed, however. By the middle of the same century, a

---

5. William Symington, *Messiah the Prince* (1839), 133.

6. The remark is from Rev. Thomas Liddell, cited in "Memoir," lxi.

7. William Symington, *The Evil of Ignorance and Motives to its Removal* (Glasgow: Young and Callie, 1821). Also reprinted in *Discourses on Public Occasions* (Glasgow: David Bryce, 1851), 1–28.

8. J. Sinclair, ed., *The (Old) Statistical Account of Scotland* (1791), 4.361.

widespread sense of obligation and excitement came to characterize the Scottish attitude toward missions. Symington's concern for missions was one of many various factors contributing to this change.

Symington's first public appearance on behalf of missions took place three years after his ordination. At that time, he spoke for the promotion of an interdenominational mission to the Jews. Evangelism among the Jews was a particular concern of Symington's throughout his ministry. Although such efforts were largely interdenominational in nature, Symington also encouraged more efforts in world missions from within the Reformed Presbyterian Church. Probably his greatest contribution to RP missions would take place during his years in Glasgow, and will thus be considered more fully in a later chapter on his Glasgow ministry. Nevertheless, an active concern for foreign missions can already be seen in the Stranraer years.

Symington saw the church universal as united under one King, thus vesting his own ordination with responsibility for the cause of the whole church, not just one branch of it. He therefore eagerly supported evangelical endeavors both inside and outside the Reformed Presbyterian Church. Perhaps nothing illustrates this so clearly as his hosting an 1837 meeting at the *Reformed Presbyterian Church* in Stranraer for a *Church of Scotland* extension project in that community. Theologically, there were important differences between the Reformed Presbyterian Church and the Church of Scotland, differences no one was more active than Symington to address. Nevertheless, this did not hinder Symington from supporting evangelical efforts by the Church of Scotland.

That being said, there is another side of Symington's interdenominational motivations which needs to be highlighted. Symington was not one who regarded doctrinal distinctives between his denomination and others as unimportant. On the contrary, it was *because* he saw the Reformed Presbyterian testimony as important that he believed interdenominational relationships needed to be built.

The Reformed Presbyterian Church, in Symington's view, had a particular doctrinal witness to bring to the church as a whole. The Covenanters had been compelled by Providence to define certain doctrines more fully than other branches of the Church. The Covenanters had worked out the doctrines of Christ's mediatorial kingship, Covenanting, and Christian civil government more fully than other branches of the Reformation heritage. It was the duty of

Reformed Presbyterians, therefore, not only to support the cause of evangelicalism *alongside* other churches, but also to strengthen interdenominational connections and her charitable witness *to* other churches and *in* other churches.

Symington did not hesitate—in his participation with the Sabbath School movement, Bible Society, and so forth—to show the basis in the *Crown of Christ* for these efforts. Because Symington saw the connection between the crown rights of Jesus and these other evangelical initiatives, he saw his involvement as a way to teach these (Covenanter) principles within the broader church. Symington's interdenominational activity, then, was bi-directional. On the one hand, it was his desire to involve the Reformed Presbyterian Church in various evangelical initiatives; on the other hand, he wanted to bring evangelicalism to a more firm grounding in the Reformation principles clarified by the Covenanters.

Symington was a broadly active evangelical, but he remained distinctly a *Covenanter* evangelical.

Symington the Covenanter Historian

Symington's interest in communicating the principles of the Covenanters also led him to speak frequently on the Covenanter martyrs, such as Richard Cameron and the two Margarets of Wigtown. Often these messages were delivered outdoors at the site where a certain martyr was killed. Some of these gatherings were attended by between 1,000 and 3,000 people, and lasted as long as four hours.

Symington's stated purpose for his martyr messages was to revive Scotland's attachment to the Scottish Reformation, to rescue their character and claims from those who were denigrating them, and furthermore to instruct the public in "the history and principles of that magnanimous struggle for religion and liberty."[9] He explained how the Covenanter martyrs were not flawless persons; they were, nonetheless, faithful believers who shed their blood in testimony for Jesus' rights as King of kings and Head of the church. Symington used their testimonies to instruct his own generation in those same biblical convictions.

---

9. William Symington, "The Character and Claims of the Scottish Covenanters" (in *Discourses on Public Occasions* [Glasgow: David Bryce, 1851]), 72.

The most extensive fruit of Symington's study in the old Covenanter sermons, writings, and martyrdoms, however, is in his own writings defending their claims—the books to be reviewed later in this volume.

Symington the Theologian and Author

Symington obviously could not continue "outputting" so much teaching without a regular discipline of "inputting" as well. He was, indeed, an avid reader, and he maintained a carefully managed routine of ongoing theological study. This was not easy to do in Stranraer. He felt keenly "the remoteness of his situation," as he described it, "at a distance from those stores of learning [i.e., libraries] to which he might otherwise have had access."[10] He therefore maintained a careful budget for building his own library, by visits to bookstores when in Glasgow or Edinburgh or by post.

With a striking note of humor, Symington described his "addiction" to books in an 1829 letter to a minister friend:

> The love of books is with me a perfect mania. When I see anything particular advertised, I immediately conceive a *wish* to have it—I persuade myself that really I *ought* to have it—and between the desire to have it and the reluctance to *pay* for it I am on the fidgets day and night. Then some demon or other whispers, "Your credit is good, it is a good while to the month of May, before then you will have had your purse replenished with next half year's stipend"—the *temptation* succeeds; and off goes a post letter for the desired article, all objections, financial as well as others, being unceremoniously sent about their business. In this way I have nearly ruined myself—and the worst of it is that I am nearly incorrigible. Unlike other sinners, misery does not lead me to repent—or if I do repent, I do not at all events *reform*. Can you tell me what is to become of me? The jail I suppose.[11]

The author would perhaps be embarrassed to find this heavily tongue-in-cheek specimen of his personal correspondence exposed

---

10. William Symington, *On the Atonement and Intercession of Jesus Christ* (Edinburgh: Whyte, 1834), vii.

11. MS Letter, dated Feb. 13, 1829, to "Rev. Gavin Rowatt, Whithorn," from "Wm. Symington," in Broughton House Museum, Dumfries.

to wide reading. He obviously exaggerates his condition, using the likeness of what he knows (all too well as a pastor) about the nature of addictions. In doing so, nonetheless, he gives us a glimpse at the interest with which he accumulated books for his continuing education.

Though remotely located, Symington continued to study with the leading theologians of the time through his reading. Furthermore, taking up his own pen, Symington was also to contribute to the printed conversation.

Early in his ministry, Symington began to publish pamphlets and individual sermons. His first published sermon (mentioned earlier in this chapter) was "The Evil of Ignorance," preached and printed in 1821. A sermon on "Charity to the Poor Explained and Enforced" was preached and published in Paisley in support of the Widow and Orphan Society there. Other sermons were preached and then put in print to support various evangelical movements. He also wrote pamphlets addressing social concerns in Stranraer, like, "The Profane Use of the Lot" (1827) and "Games of Chance" (1838) published to confront the gambling problem in town.

Symington's first book-length publication was a 164-page biography of a notorious lad of nearby Dumfries. Falling to severe illness and in that condition showing remarkable evidences of new life, John Williamson died professing faith in Christ. Symington's compilation of Williamson's testimony, *The Select Remains of John Williamson* (1827), was published as an effort to provide "something useful to the rising generation."[12]

Symington's first major theological work, however, was not to appear until 1834. After preaching a series of sermons on atonement, and being alarmed at certain doctrinal errors circulating within the Scottish church on the subject, Symington began to compose a comprehensive treatment of the doctrine. Begun in 1831, the work was interrupted by family illness. Then the tragic loss of his six-year-old son Robert in 1833 (noted in an earlier chapter), moved Symington to resume the project. In his grief at Robert's death, Symington's sole comfort was found in contemplating the atonement. He completed *On the Atonement and Intercession of Jesus Christ*

---

12. William Symington, *The Select Remains of John Williamson who Died at Dumfries, December 1826* (Dumfries: M'Dairmid, 1827).

almost as much as a balm for his own soul as for the benefit of the wider church. (The conditions of his writing it might be one reason for the warmth and pastoral concern which so many of its readers found in its pages.) This work went to press in May, 1834. There was wide interest in this work, and it underwent further editions both in Scotland and overseas.

Symington's well-known sequel to that book, namely *Messiah the Prince,* was begun in 1836. Again, family illness distracted the work. The Typhus epidemic of 1837 and 1838 brought suffering to the Symington household in Stranraer. (The same epidemic also claimed four lives in the Paisley home of William's older brother Andrew: Andrew's wife and three of his children died within two months time.) The Typhus epidemic had brought many of William's preaching and writing activities to a standstill. Nonetheless, by 1839, his most lasting volume was published.

The importance of *Messiah the Prince* (subtitled, *On the Mediatorial Dominion of Jesus Christ*) was immediately recognized. Literally within a week of its publication, the University of Edinburgh conferred on Symington a Doctor in Divinity degree—a move which was later found to have preempted a similar diploma already under preparation at the University of Glasgow. *Messiah the Prince* alone was not the impetus for this award, but was nonetheless a significant reason.

These two works in particular—*On the Atonement* and *Messiah the Prince*—will be examined in greater detail in later sections of the present book. These and other publications by Symington extended his ministry beyond his Stranraer pastorate—and continue to extend his ministry beyond his lifetime. Symington was by no means prolific, especially in comparison with some of the other writing ministers of his day. Nevertheless, his works have been enduring, especially his book *Messiah the Prince.*

Symington's desire for writing was clearly both theological and pastoral. He wrote with the acumen of theological distinction, but with the warmth and practicality of pastoral concern for the reader. He encouraged other Reformed Presbyterian ministers to write as well, seeing it as an important means for serving the cause of the church. At times, he even took liberty to write a fellow minister and suggest to him a subject needing attention. Symington recognized that the Covenanter Church had been entrusted by Christ with particular developments of Reformation theology which it was her divine duty to propagate. Writing was one way in which he believed the Scottish Reformers, though dead, might yet be given voice.

CHAPTER 6

The Glasgow Years I:
In the Great Hamilton Street Pulpit

The Great Hamilton Street Church was known as the "oldest" Reformed Presbyterian congregation. It had been organized in 1762 around several of the original Covenanter Societies, and those early Societies harked back to regular Covenanter assemblies as old as 1638 (the year of the National Covenant and the beginning of the Second Reformation). In other words, the Great Hamilton Street Church tangibly embodied the unbroken link between the RP Church and the whole of the Second Reformation.[1]

In addition to its distinguished age, Great Hamilton Street had also been associated with some of the leading ministers of the RP Church. The respected John Macmillan II had been their first minister, later joined by an associate, John Fairley. David Armstrong had been a strong minister serving that congregation from 1815 to 1838. In the latter years of Armstrong's pastorate, however, illness and other factors weakened the church's ministry. By the time of Armstrong's unexpected death, the Great Hamilton Street congregation was declining. The building then in use could accommodate 1100, but the membership had dropped to just over 300.

The congregation at Great Hamilton Street began their search for a new minister in 1838. The following year, a call was issued to William Symington.

It was not the first time Symington had been asked to leave his ministry in Stranraer for another congregation. The Dumfries Church had approached him in 1829, but Symington made it clear he was not open at that time to leaving Stranraer. Twice the West

---

1. See Thomas Binnie, *Sketch of the History of the First Reformed Presbyterian Congregation* (Paisley: J. and R. Parlane, 1888).

Campbell Street congregation in Glasgow had attempted to call
Symington to be their pastor. Symington's journal shows the seriousness with which he wrestled with the West Campbell Street call,
but in the end he declined. When the call came from Great Hamilton Street, however, the same reasons which led him to decline
other calls led him to accept this one.

This was to be a significant move, not only for Symington, but
for the whole RP Church in Scotland. Never before in the Reformed
Presbyterian Church had a minister, ordained in one congregation,
transferred to another. This "translation" (the term used at the time)
was unprecedented. Three sessions of a meeting of Synod were spent
debating the feasibility of such "translations" before Synod allowed
Symington's call to go forward. Symington's own final decision to
accept the call was also the cause of much personal anxiety. On the
day he announced his decision, Symington wrote in his journal:

> It was not without much painful agitation of mind that I came
> to the decision to change the scene of my labours.... May the
> Lord order it so that it may be for the good of the church, &
> may he watch over my poor people at Stranraer![2]

In the Synod's debate over Symington's "translation" to Great
Hamilton Street, the following reasons for finally arriving at a positive endorsement are recorded in the minutes:

> "...[1] in Glasgow...there is a University attended by the
> greater part of those youths who study for the Ministry
> in our Church.... [2] Members of country congregations
> are frequently moving to Glasgow.... [3] The cause of
> the Covenanter Reformation there ought to have the
> benefit of being advocated by men of...experience and
> accomplishments..., [4] and he has peculiar opportunities of
> promoting Missionary undertakings....[3]

In other words, in addition to the needs of that particular congregation calling Symington (Great Hamilton Street), there were
needs in Glasgow and in the RP Church more widely that required

---

2. MS Journal, May 16, 1839.

3. *Extracts of the Minutes of Synod of the Reformed Presbyterian Church*, May 1839,
Session IV.

a man of Symington's "experience and accomplishments" being located there.

A few basic facts will help capture the dynamics behind these reasons for Symington's "translation." The economic impact of the Industrial Revolution on Scotland has already been indicated in a previous chapter. Glasgow was sometimes called "The Second City of the Empire" because of its explosive growth and importance. A century before, Glasgow had been "a neat picturesque little town nestling on the banks of a humble stream."[4] By 1821, a census recorded its population at 147,000. By 1862 (the year of Symington's death), Glasgow had grown to over 395,000. Some of these moving into the city from the countryside would have been Society folk, or Covenanter youth coming into the University. All of them—Society folk or not—were in need of spiritual care.

Unfortunately, however, the mass migration of rural families into the factories was not well accommodated by the city's infrastructure. School systems were hopelessly overcrowded and outmoded. Child labor became common, exposing tender youth to hideous work conditions. Factory wages, though initially high enough to create the momentum of migration to the cities, subsequently fell and continued to decline. Housing conditions for the poor were deplorable. Disease epidemics were frequent. Not infrequently, factory uprisings broke out in the form of strikes or riots. The utopian dreams of industrial prosperity were beginning to face the cold reality of the new urban poverty.

Sadly, the church had been taken off-guard by the changes as well. Thomas Chalmers was one of the leading Church of Scotland ministers in Glasgow and was to become a close friend and associate of Symington's. In a study completed by him in 1817, Chalmers found that, "during a period of nearly one hundred years while the population [in Glasgow] had more than quadrupled, only two new [Church of Scotland] city churches had been built." As a result, as many as two-thirds of the population in some districts ceased

---

4. Sir Henry B. Craik, *A Century of Scottish History: From the Days Before '45 to those within Living Memory* (Edinburgh: William Blackwood, 1901), 2.433.

attending church upon their move into the city, "wholly cast[ing] off the very form and profession of Christianity."[5]

Furthermore, there was unrest within the Scottish church. In previous years, there had been a definite tendency toward liberalization within the National Church. Having been re-established after the Revolution Settlement of 1688 with a majority of its ministers being the unbelieving, "indulged curates" of the Killing Times, there had been an ongoing liberal (or, "moderate") momentum in the State Church. The early 1800's, however, brought a refreshing resurgence of evangelicalism within the Church of Scotland. A number of strong voices for evangelical reform within the mainline church (including Chalmers) were stirring in those days. Theological questions long neglected were being thrust back into the Church of Scotland courts, and the time seemed ripe for the Covenanter's witness to be promoted at the heart of these developments—in Glasgow.

Symington's excellent defense of both evangelical doctrine generally (in his first book, *On the Atonement),* and his articulation of Covenanter doctrine more specifically (in his second book, *On the Mediatorial Dominion),* had already begun to establish his name as an important voice of the RP Church in Scotland. It was natural, then, that Symington should be "translated" to Glasgow, to the pulpit of Great Hamilton Street, to contribute to the needed social and theological reform of the time.

As Symington himself had stated in a sermon before Synod in 1835—four years prior to his move to Glasgow—

> The times in which our lot is cast are *reforming times.* A spirit has sprung up to correct abuses, theoretical and practical, political, moral, and religious.... We see it in questions that have been entertained in the high councils of the nation; we see it in measures that have been agitated in ecclesiastical assemblies;... These are favourable indications...to which, surely, they cannot be indifferent on whose ecclesiastical banner the word *reform* holds so conspicuous a place.[6]

---

5. William Hanna, *Memoirs of Thomas Chalmers* (Edinburgh: T. Constable. 1854), 1.454–455.

6. William Symington, "The Rebuilding of Jerusalem" (in *Discourses on Public Occasions* [Glasgow: David Bryce, 1851]), 154–155.

Four years after that sermon before Synod, Synod affirmed these same sentiments and forwarded to Symington a call to the Great Hamilton Street Church. The Glasgow-born and Glasgow-reared minister, after labored prayer and contemplation, accepted and moved his family from Stranraer. On July 14, 1839, he entered the pulpit of his new charge and preached from 2 Corinthians 4:2–3: "...by manifestation of the truth [we are] commending ourselves to every man's conscience in the sight of God. But if our gospel be hid, it is hid to them that are lost."

In the Great Hamilton Street Pulpit

Symington's call to Glasgow was to have implications far wider than the members in the church where he pastored. Nonetheless, it was the congregation of the Great Hamilton Street Church which had called him to be their minister, and it was there that he focused his ministry.

The Glasgow manse. Today the residences on Annfield Place have been renovated and converted into business establishments, but number 15 was the Symington home during his pastorate in Glasgow.

The same careful attention to sermon preparation and delivery, which had characterized his ministry in Stranraer, was continued in Glasgow. Certainly, he had natural gifts of oratory which were put to good use. Nonetheless, those close to Symington attest to his lively study of Scripture, his regular system of reading in theological works, and his love for the gospel which brought a constant freshness and vividness to his sermons. It was not long after Symington relocated to Glasgow before faces strange to the Great Hamilton Street congregation began to appear in their midst for Sabbath services.

Four months after settling, Symington began a monthly lecture series, conducted on Sabbath evenings, which was to prove particularly significant. His first series began in the Book of Daniel. Within three or four lectures, the evening attendance was filling the 1100-seat hall to capacity. After six lectures, the overcrowding began to cause problems. Members of the congregation were finding "their" pews occupied by strangers and were thus complaining about being unable to attend these lectures themselves. Symington was compelled, from his seventh evening lecture onward, to deliver these addresses twice each: first on the Sabbath afternoon and repeated in the evening. One entry in Symington's journal, from March 1, 1840, gives a tragic indication of the ongoing eagerness with which these lectures were received:

> The crowd at evening lecture most overwhelming: many hurt in getting in: hundreds not able to find admission: house filled in five minutes after door opened.

The Daniel series continued for three years. It was followed by a series on Joseph, and after that a five-year series on the Book of Revelation. It was only in 1850, due to Symington's taking new responsibilities as a lecturer at the RP Theological Hall, that the monthly lecture series at the church ended. The value which these evening expositions brought to the wider community can be discerned by the following notice on Symington's lectures from a local newspaper, *The Glasgow Examiner,* on January 25, 1845:

> We are happy that his instructive course of lectures continues and the interest still increases. To the youth of our town they offer an excellent opportunity of acquiring a correct and concise system of religion and morals.

Such outreach to urbanized youth was, of course, one of the reasons Symington engaged upon the pastorate in industrial Glasgow. Nonetheless, Symington was particularly earnest to insure that solid biblical instruction was being provided for the families and Covenanter youth of his congregation.

"Side by side with preaching," his sons were later to say of Symington's Glasgow ministry, "there went faithful and very exhausting pastoral work."[7] Symington made regular house visits, he called on the sick, and he gathered the young people of the congregation for classes and prayer meetings. A devoted circle of elders worked closely with their new minister. The congregation was divided into geographical areas, with an elder assigned to each. Symington led the elders in keeping written records of the members (and their addresses) in their respective areas, along with a written accounting of their visitations which were then reviewed twice each year. It was important that the congregation receive personal, pastoral care from their minister and the elders.

Symington also published another book while in Glasgow, which he addressed primarily to his congregation. The volume was a compilation of sermons preached by Symington in his Stranraer years, which were thus unknown to the Glasgow congregation. *Discourses on Public Occasions* was published in 1851 with a prefatory dedication—

> principally for the use of my own congregation.... That the whole may be made a means of confirming my readers in general in the faith...and of ripening them for a higher and brighter state of being.... To the people of my own ministerial charge in particular, I dedicate the volume, with much affection and pastoral solicitude....[8]

Symington's influence on the wider church in Scotland, and the RP Church denominationally, is what makes his life particularly interesting for the attention of later generations. Church historian J.R. Fleming speaks of him as among the important religious lead-

---

7. "Memoir," lxxiii.

8. William Symington, *Discourses on Public Occasions* (Glasgow: David Bryce, 1851), v–vii.

ers of Scotland at an "epoch making time."[9] However, this extended influence should not be allowed to overshadow Symington's pastoral devotion to his own congregation. That 1851 publication just noted offers an apt indication of the man. Symington was one who shepherded the sheep charged to his care—the Great Hamilton Street congregation—but did so in such a way that permitted a much wider circle to benefit (e.g., to "read along") as well.

Indeed, as Symington's ministry did widen, so did the number of those who sought membership in the congregation at the heart of his instruction and prayer. Three months after Symington undertook the Glasgow pastorate, sixty-five new names were added to the membership rolls in connection with the communion season. Over subsequent years, the bi-annual communion seasons (each April and October) seldom saw fewer than forty new members being added. Some of these are recorded as members from other congregations moving to the Great Hamilton Street Church, such as Society folk moving to the city from the countryside. Nevertheless, the majority of names on the lists do not have certificates of reference from other congregations indicated. At least a good number of the new members seem to have been the unchurched being brought to Christ. By April, 1853, the membership numbered 993 and Symington began to call for dividing that number and daughtering a new congregation.

It should be recalled that these were times of evangelical renewal more widely than the RP Church. Other Glasgow ministers (like Thomas Chalmers, already mentioned) saw significant growth during the same period. Nonetheless, such developments were by no means universal. They were wrought by Christ through the earnest efforts of capable ministers and faithful congregations. Symington, and the Great Hamilton Street RP Church, was one such means of evangelism in nineteenth-century Glasgow.

Sabbath School and Day School Programs

Under Symington's leadership, the congregation at Great Hamilton Street undertook an aggressive missionary effort within Glasgow. At the forefront of the church's outreach was the development of

---

9. J.R. Fleming, *A History of the Church in Scotland: 1834–1874* (Edinburgh: T&T Clark, 1927), 14–15.

several educational initiatives addressed to the needs of the poor in the city.

In his early months at Great Hamilton Street, Symington instigated a survey of families in the area. From that study, Symington later remarked,

> It was found that from indifference, inability, or unwillingness of many parents…the sanctification of the Sabbath and the religious instruction of the rising generation were sadly neglected by thousands. Hence Sabbath evening schools were reckoned…absolutely necessary.[10]

The church promptly rented rooms on Risk Street and began to offer religious education classes for children, every Sabbath evening, from 5:15 to 7:15. By the end of its opening year, there were 260 children attending this instruction, and in 1849, the following report by one of the Sabbath School leaders was made:

> The number of Teachers at present employed in the Sabbath School is 30, and the number of children receiving instruction is 591…. What is still better, we are not without the cheering conviction that they are growing not only in knowledge, but also in grace. My heart is gladdened from time to time in seeing some of those who were lately pupils in some of the classes, taking their part as Teachers in the School. Still more, at every communion season, several of them have taken their places at the table of the Lord, and thus given testimony to their desire to honour and obey the Saviour.[11]

In other words, the Sabbath school instruction was not only bearing fruit, but was multiplying itself as children saved and trained in that program went on to become teachers themselves.

The nature of the Sabbath School instruction was, however, strictly religious. The Sabbath School was a course in biblical, doctrinal, and religious education intended for children whose parents either did not desire to, or were not able to, provide religious education at home. Nevertheless, it quickly became obvious that such

---

10. William Symington, "The History and Importance of Sabbath Schools," (which is Lecture I in *A Course of Lectures on Sabbath Schools* [Glasgow: Collins, 1841]), 5.

11. "Reports of the Different Societies Connected with the First Reformed Presbyterian Congregation," in *Scottish Presbyterian 1849–1850*, vol. 2.

religious education could not be effectively pursued without also tending to the general lack of education among the urban youth.

Finding that many of the children in the Sabbath School classes were not able to read their Bibles, it was deemed important to begin reading classes, as well as other basic courses of education. Because instruction in reading was not a *religious* study, and thus not suitable for a *Sabbath* School, the church determined to open weekday courses in practical subjects.

The first Day School opened on September 22, 1840. Because many of the children needing this instruction were employed in the factories during the day, an Evening School soon followed as well. By January of 1842, there were one-hundred children receiving instruction in the Day School, and sixty in the Evening School. In addition to basic academics, one of the church members, a Miss Robertson by name, organized a dozen other women into a "School of Industry." Sixty to seventy girls a year were enrolled in this School of Industry, where they learned how to sew, knit, and so forth. Another member of the congregation, skilled in music, offered to teach the children sacred music one night a week.

(It is perhaps worth note that Miss Robertson later married, and the teaching experience she gained at Great Hamilton Street found new outlet in her role as a mother. A son reared under her own "home mission," Clarence McCartney, became one of the leading presbyterian ministers in America in the late nineteenth century. In his biography, McCartney is said to have spoken of his mother's "Friday-night Bible class for mill girls," and her other memories recounted to him of her spiritual nurture under Symington's pastorate.[12] Only heaven will reveal the full influence Symington had through such congregants, nurtured under his preaching and mentored for ministry through the Great Hamilton Street ministries.)

By 1850, the Sabbath, Day, and Evening School ministries had expanded to such a point that the church began to explore purchasing a building for them. In January 1852, a vacant Methodist Church building was purchased on Green Street and renovated.

Symington aggressively supported the Sabbath School movement (and church-sponsored education generally), not only in his own congregation but in alliance with other churches and organi-

---

12. Clarence E. McCartney, *The Making of a Minister* (1961), 38.

zations. This has been indicated by all that has been documented above. Nevertheless, there is a further dimension of Symington's interest in the Sabbath School movement crucial to note. It is another indication of the minister's carefulness to differentiate between *principles* and *practices,* and to zealously pursue certain practices only as means to establishing a clearly perceived principle.

In the case of the Sabbath School movement, Symington made it clear that he viewed this movement as a temporary expedient. He taught that,

> The parent is the natural guardian of his children in religious matters, nor ought he, if adequate himself—and every parent ought to be adequate—to yield up the matter to a stranger. Every Christian family ought to be a Sabbath school. Nevertheless, while there are so many parents who are either unable or unwilling to superintend the religious instruction of their children, it is every way proper, rather than that these children should be neglected, to provide for them by a public institution [i.e., the church Sabbath School]. In conducting such institutions, however, every attention ought to be paid, that nothing be done to relax the exertions of the natural instructors [the parents]; and everything should be managed with the express design of bringing matters to their proper state.[13]

In other words, Symington recognized that the very program which served as the necessary support of a principle in one generation, might very readily become the enemy of that principle in the next. Thus the practice of running Sabbath Schools was not, in and of itself, a cause to promote. Rather, the education of children in religious knowledge, and the equipping of parents (and future parents) to take a leading role in that work in their homes, was a principle worth devoting every energy to achieve. The Sabbath School movement was, in Symington's day, a means towards that end.

City Missions and Church Planting
The Sabbath School ministry, and the other Day and Evening School efforts, were an important avenue for reaching out into the needs of

---

13. William Symington, "The Evil of Ignorance, and Motives to its Removal," in *Discourses on Public Occasions* (Glasgow: David Bryce, 1851), 26.

east Glasgow. Not content with this means of outreach alone, however, the Great Hamilton Street Church Session began to discuss further ways to expand its community evangelism. In 1847, while the Sabbath School program was in its early stages, attention turned to the idea of employing a full-time "home missionary."

The first home missionary appointed was a man by the name of Cochran. However, Mr. Cochran's services were not satisfactory and he was soon dismissed. Urgent prayer followed for some time, until a new home missionary was identified and appointed on March 27, 1850. The young man's name was John G. Paton. Later, Paton's name would gain renown as a missionary to the New Hebrides.[14] However, his early education in missions took place through his work with Symington and the Great Hamilton Street congregation's Home Missions program.

When the Green Street facility was purchased in 1852, various rooms in the building were converted for school classes (as previously noted), but the main sanctuary was devoted to Paton's missionary meetings. The Green Street mission (or, "rescue work," as it was often termed) saw numerous conversions. Paton eventually left Glasgow for the foreign mission field, at which time his brother, Walter Paton, was hired to continue the Green Street mission. Walter also went on to pursue full theological studies and eventually resigned the mission work to accept a call into the regular pastorate.

The next home missionary hired was a student of Symington's named John Edgar. Under Edgar's energetic labors, ten prayer meetings were organized in various locations around Green Street, involving roughly thirty members of the Great Hamilton Street congregation in leading them and 125 unchurched Glaswegians in attendance. By 1862, the Green Street mission had achieved sufficient strength to organize as a congregation, with John Edgar as its first minister.

The new church, however, did not remain at the Green Street facilities. As soon as possible a new building was erected on Landressy Street for the fledgling congregation, and the Green Street facility was returned to a home missions and Sabbath School base

---

14. John G. Paton, *Missionary to the New Hebrides: An Autobiography* (London: Banner of Truth Trust, 1965).

for the Great Hamilton Street congregation. Meanwhile, in addition to the new church planted through Green Street, another new congregation was daughtered (in 1853) on the south side of Glasgow, and a third congregation was formed on the west side of the city through a cooperative effort with another Glasgow congregation (the West Campbell Street RP Church).

Some years later, reflecting on the significance of the Green Street ministry, one of the sons of the congregation (Thomas Binnie) offered the following description:

> There was work suitable for every one, and there are comparatively few members of the Congregation who have not in some way or other taken part in the work in Green Street.... Now there are scattered far and wide, in every quarter of the globe, earnest Christian workers, who received their early training in that mission field.[15]

World Missions

Closely connected to the Great Hamilton Street Church's emphasis on *home* missions was its emphasis on *world* missions. Though already involved in some missionary endeavors, Symington's enthusiasm for world missions received a marked boost in 1837 (in his closing years at Stranraer).

It had been in that year, in Stranraer, that Symington went to hear Alexander Duff preach at a local gathering. Duff was a prominent Scottish missionary to India who had, for the first time, succeeded in bringing the gospel to the upper class Hindus and Muslims of India. Previous missionaries had seen conversions among the lower caste in India—a ministry of no little importance. Nonetheless, Duff had arrived in India in 1830 with a desire to further extend the gospel's impact among the Hindu and Muslim communities there. To do so, Duff developed what was then an unprecedented approach: He set up a school. By bringing English language education (and other rudimentary and advanced studies) to India, Duff was able to open the doors for biblical instruction to the unreached upper castes.

Declining health had forced Duff to return to Scotland in 1834, where he became an outspoken advocate for foreign missions. Sym-

---

15. Thomas Binnie, *Sketch of the History of the First Reformed Presbyterian Congregation* (Paisley: J. and R. Parlane, 1888), 130.

ington attended one of Duff's messages when the latter was traveling through Stranraer in 1837. The message Symington heard that night profoundly impacted him. Reflecting on what he heard that night in his journal, Symington wrote, "May it be blessed for increasing my zeal for the conversion of the heathen."[16]

The next January (still in Stranraer), Symington began the new year with an emphasis on foreign missions. In particular, he conducted a youth meeting where he spoke to the young people about missions, forming among them a juvenile missionary society. Sixty youth joined the society and a collection of £10 (a significant sum in those days) was raised from children's coppers for the support of missionary endeavors overseas. "May this," Symington prayed, "be the commencement of a mission to the heathen from the Reformed Presbyterian Church!"[17]

Symington's interest in foreign missions—and the pursuit of this aim by the Reformed Presbyterian Church—had actually been developing for some years prior to that point. As seen in a previous chapter, Symington had been supporting missions to the Jews from his early days at Stranraer. Furthermore, in 1830 (seven years before Symington's meeting with Duff), the RP Synod had already established its first Foreign Missions Committee. Nevertheless, the RP foreign mission program had thus far focused on the sending of three missionaries to America. Symington's growing passion was to see missionaries sent "to the heathen"—that is, to lands where the gospel was not yet known.

His journal indicates that the promotion of world missions was one of the reasons he accepted the call to Great Hamilton Street. And he was not slow to make this concern known. At the same meeting of Synod where his call to the Great Hamilton Street Church was approved, Symington introduced a motion that Synod should expand its missionary endeavors beyond "the colonies" (America) and more actively pursue missions to unreached corners of the globe. This motion met with warm agreement, and Synod appointed Symington to a seat on the Foreign Missions Committee to help facilitate that purpose.

---

16. "Memoir," lxvii.
17. "Memoir," lxvii.

The Great Hamilton Street congregation was soon to share Symington's vision for world missions as they were active with him in local missions.

In 1840, a Reformed Presbyterian named James Duncan and his wife offered themselves for overseas missions. They began training with Symington toward that end. Symington thought it wise to send two, if possible, and soon a second man offered himself as a partner. This latter volunteer was a "pious young mechanic" in Symington's congregation, and Symington immediately saw the potential for his aiding both in catechetical instruction and in teaching practical skills.[18] In November, 1842, Duncan was ordained and the first missions team was sent to labor among the indigenous Maori peoples of New Zealand. This early mission was to achieve great success, planting a church and also establishing a school for teaching the Maori to read, to write, and to do math, weights, and measures.

No sooner had Duncan and his associate left than another young man training for the ministry offered himself (accompanied by his wife) for the mission field. Symington began to work with Mr. and Mrs. John Inglis in October, 1842, and conducted John's ordination service in September, 1843. By summer, 1844, the Inglis family was also in New Zealand. The Inglises came to be particularly known, however, for their pioneering work in the South Pacific island chain, the New Hebrides (present day Vanuatu). John and his wife undertook a mission to Aneityum, the southernmost island of the New Hebrides, in 1852. Another missionary named John Geddie and his wife (sent from a Presbyterian church in Nova Scotia) had been landed on the opposite side of the same island four years before. Previous missionaries to the New Hebrides had often been killed by the native cannibals, so that this undertaking was no light matter. Nonetheless, between the Geddies' labors from one side of Aneityum, and the harmonious labors of the Inglises on the other side of the island, almost the whole island—some 3500 inhabitants—was marvelously converted from idolatry to Christ.

"We have nearly sixty native teachers," Inglis was later to report, "every native is within fifteen minutes' walk of a school and within about an hour's walk of a place of public worship on the Sab-

18. *Extracts of the Minutes of Synod of the Reformed Presbyterian Church,* May 10, 1841, Session VII.

bath."[19] From Aneityum, the gospel was to spread to other islands of the New Hebrides, and further missionaries were to join the effort.

Perhaps the most well-known missionary to come from the Great Hamilton Street Church (and the Reformed Presbyterian Church in Scotland) was John G. Paton. As seen in the earlier discussion of the congregation's *home* missions efforts, Paton began his missionary labors as part of the Green Street "rescue work." Paton also served as an elder on the Great Hamilton Street Session.

In his autobiography, Paton tells of his presence at a meeting of Synod in 1856 where the desperate need for another missionary to join Inglis in the New Hebrides was discussed.[20] For two years, the Foreign Mission Committee had aggressively sought another missionary to send to no avail. Yet so keen was the Synod's conviction that another missionary was needed that they agreed even to release, there and then, one of the currently serving ministers to go. Each of the Synod members wrote down the names of three among them whom they believed most suited for such a calling, and then the slips of papers were gathered and tallied. It had been agreed that, should one (or two) among them be most clearly confirmed by this method, he (or they) would be released to go to the New Hebrides. With solemn prayer, the votes were counted. The sad conclusion was announced that no decisive choice had thereby emerged.

Although the slips collected in that vote failed to produce a clear candidate, the process itself succeeded to impress upon Paton the critical need in the New Hebrides. He retired to his apartment to pray about volunteering himself for such a venture. He had already devoted himself to the ministry. In addition to his mission work, he was both studying at the Theological Hall and studying medicine at the University. Surely such a background in medicine and theology would be useful on the foreign field. After much prayer, Paton volunteered himself for the New Hebrides mission. His roommate—Joseph Copeland, who had labored side-by-side with Paton in Glasgow missions—decided to offer himself also, and continue co-laboring with his friend on the foreign field. The Synod now had two missionaries to send.

---

19. John Inglis, *In the New Hebrides* (London: T. Nelson, 1887), 113.

20. John G. Paton, *Missionary to the New Hebrides: An Autobiography* (London: Banner of Truth Trust, 1965), ch. 4.

Understandably, Symington was reluctant to see Paton go. The work at Green Street was flourishing, and Paton was personally and pastorally involved in the lives of so many there. It was going to be a severe loss to the home mission work to lose Paton. Nonetheless, the Lord did raise up qualified replacements at Green Street (Walter Paton, and then John Edgar), and Symington preached the commissioning sermon for sending Paton and Copeland to the New Hebrides. Symington's choice of text for that sermon—"Come over...and help us" (Acts 16:9)—was undoubtedly expressive of his own resolve to send his beloved coworkers, as it was also a charge to Paton and his companion to go.

The work in the New Hebrides—involving Inglis, Copeland, Paton, and ministers from other denominations—became one of the remarkable chapters in nineteenth-century missions. The Great Hamilton Street congregation had not only contributed several of the key missionaries to that field from their own number, but the congregation contributed generously toward that ministry and other foreign missions over the years. Furthermore, it is no coincidence that the New Hebrides mission featured the establishment of churches and schools along a similar pattern to that taking place in the Great Hamilton Street home mission programs. These men had been trained by Symington through their involvement in the Glasgow ministry.

Perhaps the most touching indication of Symington's impact on foreign missions is an account told by Symington's sons some years later. After the early years of ministry on Aneityum in the New Hebrides, Inglis and others began to work on a translation of the Bible into the local language. The native Christians began to cultivate arrowroot as a transportable crop which could be sold back in Scotland to pay for the printing of this Bible. In connection with this project, Inglis returned to Scotland with one of the native elders of the new church in Aneityum. This "first fruit" of their mission was introduced to the Synod in Scotland by his Christian name, "William." On his conversion and baptism, he had been given the new name "William" in honor of Symington, whose labors had so significantly contributed to the mission to that land.[21]

---

21. "Memoir," lxviii.

Additional missions to Belgium, France, Switzerland, and a mission to the Jews in London, were also undertaken by the Reformed Presbyterian Church during those years. Symington was an active contributor to these efforts as well. Furthermore, as in those early days at Stranraer when Symington had rallied the children into a juvenile missions society, so Symington continued to keep foreign missions before the youth of the congregation in Glasgow. Children from the various school programs were known to help pack missionary boxes, and to raise money for such endeavors as Chinese Bibles for the Far East or jaw-harps for children in the New Hebrides.

In such ways, Symington was not only involving the congregation in foreign missions, but he was also nurturing a heart for missions among them. And indeed, several in the congregation took up the mantle of overseas work themselves.

Training Men for Ministry

Another facet of Symington's ministry at Great Hamilton Street is woven through all the above-noted areas. In the midst of his pulpit work, his Sabbath and Day School labors, his missionary initiatives near and far, and his church planting work, Symington was actively mentoring men for ministry. His journal for those Glasgow years records frequent expressions like, "young men at tea," "students," and other indications of his involvement with young men in his congregation.

James McGill was one such young man under Symington's care, who went on to become a pastor in the RP Church. McGill wrote this recollection of his relationship with Symington during those years when he was beginning to study for the ministry:

> ...He treated me with every possible kindness, admitting me to his study, showing me whatever work he was engaged with, conversing freely on every subject which he thought would interest me, and, without seeming to exercise the least authority, really guiding my thoughts and directing my studies.[22]

---

22. "Memoir," lxxxviii.

Such concern to impart whatever he could of his own learning and experience to young men in his congregation—especially those who might themselves pursue the ministry—was characteristic of Symington. "I am not the only one," McGill expressly affirmed, "[others] might have made a similar confession."

William Binnie was another young man in the Great Hamilton Street Church who went on to a fruitful career in the ministry. Binnie eventually filled a professorship at the Free Church College in Aberdeen, a post in which he became widely distinguished. He spoke warmly of his memories of Symington's personal influence on him as a young man. "I can never forget," Binnie wrote,

> a parting visit I paid him in his study one day in the autumn of 1845. I was going off to spend a winter on the continent. He made me kneel along with him, and commended me to God in a prayer which affected me far more than any public prayer of his had ever done....[23]

Such scenes offer an important insight into the reason why more than a dozen young men went on to pursue the ministry from Symington's Glasgow congregation. Four young men can be accounted for from Stranraer during Symington's years there, as well. Symington was, of course, committed to the spiritual growth of all the youth in his church, several indications of which have previously been noted. Nonetheless, he also recognized his particular, biblical responsibility as a minister for the equipping of future ministers, and he took this charge seriously. The fruit of his investments to prepare young men for the ministry, both in formal instruction and informally involving them in his own labors and studies, is evident in the generation of missionaries and ministers that came out of the Great Hamilton Street and Stranraer congregations.

Undergirding and overflowing from all Symington's many endeavors in the Great Hamilton Street congregation is the enthusiasm and confidence of a man fully persuaded that his Savior is on the Throne—and that it is a Throne over a vast dominion. Writing for the *Reformed Presbyterian Magazine* in 1859, Symington made this vision behind his labors explicit:

The grand distinctive point for which we have long been

---

23. "Memoir," lxxxix.

testifying is the royalty of Jesus Christ as the heaven-ordained ruler of men, and we cannot but think that we are in the most practical manner working out that testimony when, in our different spheres, we labour to bring everyone around us under the government of Him whose enthronement in the minds of men will make righteousness and praise spring forth before all nations.[24]

Symington was not seeking church growth, or social welfare, or even world missions as ends in and of themselves. Symington had fixed his heart clearly and decisively to "seek ye first the kingdom" (Matt. 6:33). Deep reflection upon the universality and redemptive purposes of Christ's reign had kindled within his soul a love for seeing Messiah's royal prerogatives pressed into all these fields and more. And thus "seeking first the kingdom," indeed, "all these things [were] added" to Symington and the Great Hamilton Street congregation.

---

24. *Reformed Presbyterian Magazine,* June 1859, 194.

CHAPTER 7

The Glasgow Years II:
Ambassador for Christ's Crown

Symington was called to Great Hamilton Street because *that congregation* needed a minister with his gifts. He was also relocated to that place, however, because *the Reformed Presbyterian Church as a whole* needed a spokesman, teacher, and theologian of his caliber. From Glasgow, Symington would be able more effectively to provide leadership to the Reformed Presbyterian Church as a whole; and in Glasgow, Symington would be able to represent the Covenanter claims in dialog with other ecclesiastical and political leaders of the age.

In the previous chapter, aspects of Symington's ministry within the Great Hamilton Street congregation have been reviewed. The impact of that ministry has already been seen to have extended, literally, around the globe.

Symington was also keen, moreover, to encourage other churches in their development of similar ministry at home and abroad. Based on the Sabbath School work of his own congregation, for example, Symington was a keynote speaker for the Glasgow Sabbath School Union, helping churches of various denominations in similar efforts. Furthermore, reports of the Green Street ministry were published in the *Reformed Presbyterian Magazine,* and others of Symington's sermons were occasionally printed in pamphlet or book form for wider circulation among RP churches and other denominations. Lectures by Symington on such subjects as "Covenants," "Sabbath Schools," and "Amusements for Young Men" were frequently requested in other churches—Reformed Presbyterian, Church of Scotland, Congregationalist, and more widely—around Glasgow and in Edinburgh.

In addition to Symington's labors within the Great Hamilton Street congregation (indeed, in many ways because of them), the Covenanter churchman and theologian had extended influence throughout the RP Church, into the Christian church more broadly, and across contemporary society. Several aspects of this wider outreach of his ministry will be the focus of the present chapter.

Addressing Political Issues

One of the particular claims of the Covenanters during the Second Reformation was, of course, the independence of the church from state control (and, likewise, the state from church control). However, this mutual independence was never perceived as indicating *separation* (as has become the dominant dogma of present-day democracies). On the contrary, both church and state are ordained by Christ to serve harmoniously under His crown. The church is accountable to Christ, and so is the state. With a common King, church and state also enjoy *complementary* (even if different) commissions. Their harmonious cooperation *in shared submission to Christ*, therefore, is the norm which the Covenanters of Symington's day continued to assert.

Symington's best known book, *Messiah the Prince or, On the Mediatorial Dominion of Jesus Christ*, is a thorough articulation of this doctrine. This was not merely a doctrine Symington wrote about, however. He "practiced what he preached," and his ministry included attention to matters of political concern.

In his private relations, Symington maintained connections with various men of public and political influence, such as Sir Andrew Agnew (who later became a champion of Sabbath reform in Parliament), the Earl of Galloway, Sir James Hay, and General Andrew McDowell (whose conversion was connected to Symington's preaching).

In his public ministry, Symington spoke regularly to public issues, including legislation or judicial acts where the state needed to be reminded of its obligations under Christ. When, for instance, the Edinburgh and Glasgow Railway was to inaugurate regular Sabbath Day rail service (in 1842), Symington spoke in opposition to it, one of his speeches being published in the *Scottish Guardian* newspaper and later in pamphlet form. When Parliament passed legislation in 1845, establishing a government subsidy for the Roman

Catholic seminary at Maynooth, Symington and others spoke and published tracts calling for its repeal. On one occasion, Symington could be found speaking at a City Hall gathering against British treaties on the slave trade; on other occasions, Symington addressed the political entrenchment of slavery in America. Important court decisions like the 1859 Cardross Case, and important legislative measures like education reform bills, alcohol reform, Sabbath mail operation, and so forth, were topics of his busy speaking schedule outside the church hall. Because the state, too, is subject to Christ, although the church has no power to lord over the state, she does have a place to admonish and encourage government in its respect to Christ's laws.

A closer look at two of these public issues will help to clarify the distinctive character of Symington's approach to political activity. Take, for instance, the slavery issue. In a speech delivered by Symington at the Glasgow City Hall on the subject, he stated matter-of-factly,

> ...*that all Slavery is sinful*.... It is not in those cases in which the slaves are worked, flogged, and branded like beasts, that it is sinful, but even when they are treated gently and kindly.... Observe, also, that I say "sinful," not impolitic merely, not inexpedient, but *sinful,*—necessarily and essentially sinful...."[1]

What Symington was endeavoring to stress is that slavery must be governmentally opposed, not on political or pragmatic reasons alone, but on religious (i.e., explicitly biblical) grounds. Many anti-slavery proponents preferred to argue against slavery merely because of its physical and emotional cruelty. Symington, however, insisted that slavery is wrong even where conducted in the utmost gentleness and kindness. Some would oppose slavery because it is politically wrong; that is, slavery denies basic human rights. Symington insisted that slavery is "not impolitic merely," but it is sin. Government ought to outlaw slavery *because it is sin*, and for this reason plainly and frankly.

---

1. William Symington, "Rev. Professor Symington on American Slavery" (a speech delivered at the Glasgow City Hall in Nov., 1860, and printed in *Reformed Presbyterian Magazine*, Dec. 1860), 392.

"Man, I grant you," Symington continued in the same speech, "is property; but whose? The property of his Maker, and of his Maker alone. And for man to claim property in man, amounts to sacrilegious invasion of the rights of Deity—a daring robbery of heaven!"[2] Government should legislate against slavery, not merely because it is "immoral" or "inhumane" (which it is), but because it is sinful. It is a violation of the law of Christ, to which governments also are to be self-consciously subject. It is only by legislating against slavery *as biblically wrong* that a state thus legislates in submission to Christ's command.

Does this mean that governments are to pass laws against every sin? No, of course not. Much sin is a matter of the human heart, and government has no jurisdiction over the human heart. The church is that institution charged by Christ to address the conscience. Nevertheless, to the extent that issues which *are* within the jurisdiction of the state have sinful implications, the government ought to regulate accordingly. Slavery is not wrong merely because it violates political rights or is pragmatically harmful; it is wrong because it is sin. A government under King Jesus ought to regulate in submission to King Jesus' laws.

Symington advanced similar arguments in regard to Sabbath Day laws. Many of Symington's contemporaries who opposed the running of trains, the post, or businesses on the Sabbath Day sought to establish such legislation on purely secular and practical grounds. It was argued, by some, that it was necessary for health and social reasons for laborers to have a day of rest each week. It was argued, likewise, that it was economically beneficial for the nation to maintain a universal off-day. Other such pragmatic and secular arguments were apt to be advanced for the "wisdom" of legislating one day of rest in seven.

Symington insisted, in contrast to these, that the state, too, is obliged to the Ten Commandments (including the fourth, to "keep the Sabbath"). The state cannot enforce the *spiritual* observance of the Sabbath in individual hearts, and ought not suppose to try. Nonetheless, the state is obliged, as an agent of Christ, to

---

2. William Symington, "Rev. Professor Symington on American Slavery" (a speech delivered at the Glasgow City Hall in Nov., 1860, and printed in *Reformed Presbyterian Magazine*, Dec. 1860), 392.

enforce the cessation of public business in order to facilitate Sabbath observance. This ought to be done, not under guise of "pragmatic benefits" for the citizens or the economy (though of these there may be many). Rather, a state is obliged to honor the Sabbath Day in submission to her King.[3]

Such views have often been misunderstood as an "imposition of religion" on unwilling citizens of a nation. None would be quicker than Symington to oppose religious persecution, or attempts to coerce faith, by the state. Nevertheless, Symington insists,

> It is quite a mistake to say, that the magistrate's giving his countenance to one set of religious opinions in preference to others, involves the essence of persecution.... The legislature does not, in any sense, dictate to the subject what his religion shall be. It only determines what system of religious belief shall be taught with the aid and countenance of the state.[4]

There is a vast difference between, on the one hand, forcing the conscience to embrace a certain creed, and on the other hand, legally limiting business activity. The state has no power nor right to constrain the conscience, or to impose a certain profession on its inhabitants. Nonetheless, the state *does* have every duty to regulate commerce, and every state does just that according to some standard or another. Symington sees no reason why a state, which acknowledges the reign of Christ as a reality, cannot regulate commerce in submission to Christ's laws. Britain (for example) had, in the Solemn League and Covenant, legally professed national submission to the reign of Jesus. Symington accordingly confronted political policies which needed to be reconciled with Christ's laws.

The full explanation of Symington's views on Christ's crown applied to the state are to be found in chapters 8 and 9 of his book, *Messiah the Prince*. These matters will be reviewed in some greater detail, at the appropriate place in this volume. Here, however, it should be noted that Symington "practiced what he preached," and not without significant impact. One historian, contemporary with Symington, wrote of his speeches on public issues: "on the plat-

---

3. William Symington, *Messiah the Prince* (Philadelphia: The Christian Statesman, 1884), 289–298.

4. William Symington, *Messiah the Prince* (Philadelphia: The Christian Statesman, 1884), 288–289.

forms of our city…few speakers command more general attention, and elicit more rapturous applause."[5]

More important than public effectiveness, however, Symington was satisfied to know he was attesting to the reign of Christ over all affairs of men, including his right to be King *of kings*, and Lord *of lords* (Rev. 19:16).

Resolving Political Involvement Questions

One political issue of the day was especially sticky for the Covenanters. That issue was the "franchise," as it was then called, or the extension of voting rights to the general public.

Prior to 1832, only certain landowners were permitted to vote for members to the House of Commons. Only about five percent of the population were eligible to vote, and even when these did vote, they voted in open meetings by a show of hands. Consequently, even those who did vote could be pressured by a smaller number of powerful aristocrats (who could easily note which hands were raised against their "preferred" candidate, and make life "difficult" for those voting "wrongly"). The actual circle of electing power was probably even smaller than that five percent.

Another problem with the old system was that members of the Commons received no pay for their work, so only men of significant private means were able to hold office. Additionally, the list of cities allotted seats in the Commons had been drawn up in 1682. Many of the new industrial cities of the nineteenth century had no representation, while some of the towns which were important in medieval times but were now tiny villages had several representatives.

While the old election system had worked for medieval England, it was proving badly outmoded for Britain in the Industrial Age. The rising middle class had little influence on elections and the poor had none. Both inequities in an outdated system, and its corrupt abuses, made reform a rising cry of the nineteenth century. A series of election reforms took place throughout the nineteenth century, beginning with the Reform Act of 1832.

In that first Great Reform Act, the right to vote was extended to include more of the middle class. Later legislation would further introduce the secret ballot, compensation for elected officers, and

---

5. John Smith, *Our Scottish Clergy* (Edinburgh: Oliver and Boyd, 1848), 83.

added extensions of voting privileges to all (male) heads of house-holds and eventually to all men age twenty-one and over. Further lowering the age and enfranchising women in the vote would be developments of the early twentieth century.

These reforms forced a difficult, but important, debate into the forefront of the Reformed Presbyterian Church. Should Reformed Presbyterians vote? The answer, in a nineteenth-century Scottish context, is not so simple as it might appear to modern Christians. Many Christians today have learned to regard voting as something of a "salt and light" obligation. Today, voting is often perceived as a means for having a Christian influence on government. But there is another side to the citizen-government relationship entailed in voting.

By voting, the citizen—to some extent—becomes part of the government. By voting, a citizen is sending *a representative* to carry out governmental duties *on his behalf*—in *representation*. The voting citizen becomes party, through his representative, to the government. The Covenanters, it will be recalled, regarded it as biblically necessary (e.g., Ps. 2:12) for governments to submit to Jesus Christ and His crown, both in word and in deed. A government which fails to do so is sinfully constituted, a sin particularly aggravated where that nation (as was the case in Britain) had once already confessed Christ but now rejected His crown. Once these two facts are considered—that voting makes one party to the operation of government, and that governments not confessing Christ are in sin—the morality of voting becomes a serious question.

Would voting for representatives to a non-Christian government implicate the voter in that government's guilt for rejecting Christ's crown? Would voting in nineteenth-century Britain be a compromise to the long-standing Covenanter testimony "For Christ's Crown and Covenant"?

During the persecution years, many of the Covenanters had been killed for refusing to incorporate with the king's disloyalty to Christ by taking the oath of allegiance. Eighteen-year-old Margaret Wilson, the famous young martyr of Wigtown, is one well-known example. She was ordered by the anti-Covenanter soldiers to declare her allegiance to the king (and his government) or perish. She reportedly answered, "God save the king if He will, for it is his salvation that I desire."[6] However, she would not take the oath of allegiance to a king who was himself not in allegiance to Christ. To do so would be to swear to rebellion against *the* King. Margaret was drowned in the waters of the Solway Firth, as many martyrs were slain for not taking the oath.

The powerful witness of thousands of such martyrdoms could not be rashly ignored when the nineteenth-century election reform suddenly invited participation in government. Does voting make one a participant in—and thus sharing guilt with—a government constituted in rejection of Christ's crown? This was the vexing issue pressed upon the Covenanter church by nineteenth-century election reforms, and Symington found himself in the midst of many years of debate over the matter.

Just after the Reform Act of 1832 extended voting into the middle classes, a question about it came up in one of the Presbyteries. The question was promptly forwarded to Synod for the attention of the whole denomination. Although no Parliamentary elections had yet been held under the new law, an initial encouragement was published to abstain from voting until the matter could be carefully considered and resolved.

In the Synod meeting of 1833, an Overture was drafted stating the Synod's understanding of the issue. In that Overture, Synod affirmed the rightness of the popular vote in principle: "it confers an important political right on a large body of the people."[7] However, Synod also recognized that the government then in power was still ignoring its Covenanted obligation to Christ. Therefore, in that situation, voting seemed to be "inconsistent" with membership in the Reformed Presbyterian Church.

That statement was not intended to be the end of the discussion, however. It was an "Overture," which means it was a statement expressing the understanding of Synod, but which would be forwarded to the Sessions of each individual congregation for their further review. Oddly, however, there is no record of that Overture actually being sent to the congregations. There was, nonetheless, an outpouring of submissions from the various local Sessions to Synod

---

6. Alexander Smellie, *Men of the Covenants* (London: Banner of Truth Trust, 1960), 419.

7. *Minutes of Synod*, Feb. 1833.

requesting either clarification, or reconsideration, of that Overture. Furthermore, as elections were held in subsequent years, some Reformed Presbyterians did vote—and even in cases ran for office. Some churches exercised discipline against such activity, while other churches did not find reason to bring discipline.

Symington's own position in these early years of the debate is not easy to discern. On the one hand, his name can be found among certain committees charged to author statements of the church's position. Two such statements, including the aforementioned Overture, maintained that voting did indeed implicate the voter in the sinful condition of the government constitution. Symington would appear to have been party to that view early on. On the other hand, it was Symington's own congregation (Great Hamilton Street) which was particularly accused of being negligent on the issue. One of the members of that congregation, a David McCubbin by name, ran for the Glasgow City Council two or three years in a row, and was elected. Some brought charges against Symington and the Session for not disciplining McCubbin. From evidence such as this, it would seem Symington was not so strongly opposed to the vote.

Probably the best interpretation of Symington's activity during those early years is that he himself was not clear on the issue. He was clear on the principles involved. Indeed, he had already authored his magisterial work, *Messiah the Prince*, outlining the doctrine of church–state relationships. Without a doubt, Symington saw the state as obligated to profess Christ and serve His crown. A government constituted without reference to Christ was in sin. What was not clear, however, was whether *voting* made a citizen party to that sin. During a Synod debate on the subject, Symington put the question this way: "None of us doubt that there is a breach of our principles in incorporation with the British Constitution; but the question is—is voting an incorporation with the British Constitution?"[8]

Until this question was resolved, Symington favored forbearance. He did not encourage congregations to take discipline against members who voted, or even ran for office. Thus the Great Hamilton Street Session did not see fit to discipline David McCubbins. After

---

8. *Our Testimony Compromised: A Full Report of the Discussion in the Reformed Presbyterian Synod Regarding the Use of the Elective Franchise* (Glasgow, 1869), 31.

one discussion of the issue in Synod in 1858, Symington recorded in his journal, "Spoke my mind openly on the side of forbearance."[9] In the end, Symington did come to recognize voting in a non-Christian nation as not only acceptable, but a means of Christian influence.

When voting a representative into office, Symington was to say, "I don't ask him to take an oath, and I am free of taking it. It is an accessory and accidental fact that does not reduplicate upon the individual."[10] In other words, even though an elected official must take an oath of allegiance to the national constitution, the *voter* does not take that oath. Voting is not the same thing as taking an oath of incorporation with the state, and does not bring guilt upon the individual for the nation's sins.

Furthermore, even in regard to the taking of an oath of office, Symington was to say, "If the oath [of office] merely binds the one who takes it to the adoption of no unconstitutional means for changing the constitution, then the question is forever settled."[11] Even running for office is permissible with a clear conscience. The martyrs had rightly resisted swearing allegiance to the existing constitution because of the king's defiance of Christ. In the new political arrangement of Symington's day, however, an elected officer was actually *permitted to challenge* the existing constitution of the state. He simply swore to employ "constitutional means" for bringing about change. This was a profound realization on Symington's part.

For many Christians in America and Britain today, voting and running for office are readily seen as ways to exert a Christian influence on government. Prior to the franchise, however, officers of the state were always officers of the king. The whole system was top-down. To become incorporated with the state was to become an implementer (more or less) of the king's agenda. Initially, the Covenanter church in Scotland would only have been able to see voting and running for office as enrolling them as agents of the existing (sinful) arrangement of the state.

---

9. MS Journal, June 5, 1858.

10. *Our Testimony Compromised: A Full Report of the Discussion in the Reformed Presbyterian Synod Regarding the Use of the Elective Franchise* (Glasgow, 1869), 31.

11. *Our Testimony Compromised: A Full Report of the Discussion in the Reformed Presbyterian Synod Regarding the Use of the Elective Franchise* (Glasgow, 1869), 31.

Symington, however, was among those who began to realize that the elective franchise was actually something very different. God was opening a way for citizens to influence the state. The oath, in this new arrangement, was no longer an oath to uphold the existing constitution. It was merely an oath to employ orderly and constitutional means for *changing* the state wherever needed. The franchise was, in God's providence, opening an unexpected avenue to continue the Covenanter labors for political reformation.

Unfortunately, Symington died before the debate was finally settled within the Reformed Presbyterian Church. Nonetheless, in his last recorded comment on the matter, he wrote his opinion on the 1861 Synod decision to overturn the 1833 Overture. After Synod thereby repealed the earlier "no-voting" position, Symington recorded in his journal, "A right conclusion carried by a large majority."[12]

Symington's death in January, 1862, removed him from the tumult which followed. The 1861 synod decision to countenance voting brought reactions from some within the church. It became evident in subsequent debate that the majority decision of the church would remain "pro-voting." In 1863, three ministers and four elders separated from the RP Church in dissent. These dissenters subsequently organized themselves as *another* Reformed Presbyterian Church in Scotland. Sadly, the Reformed Presbyterian Church had, for the first time, divided.

Symington's own position on the voting controversy paralleled, and likely influenced, the gradual movement of the majority in the RP Synod to accept the opportunity to vote (and run for office). Initially, the debate had focused on guarding the extent of the Christian's participation in national sin. Gradually, however, it became clear that the vote provided an unexpected avenue for advancing the cause of Christian civil government. The oath of allegiance was no longer a declaration of abject loyalty to a current government order. Rather, a way was now being opened to confront and correct those errors which persisted in the civil order. Without denying the remaining presence of national sin, Symington and others became interested in the extent to which Christian citizens

---

12. MS Journal, May 7, 1861.

could use their new political rights to press for the reformation of civil government.

The question of voting (and running for office) continued to be controversial in some Reformed Presbyterian circles. It is actually from the "anti-voting" minority Synod (which split from the "pro-voting" Synod in 1863) that the RP Church in Scotland, today, derives. The "pro-voting" RP Church merged into the Free Church of Scotland in 1876. Whether the time and conditions were right for that union is another question. Nonetheless, in God's providence, because of the split over the voting issue in 1863, a small RP Church remained to uphold the Covenanter testimony in Scotland thereafter.

Nurturing Interdenominational Relationships

While it is Symington's writings on Christ's reign over the *state* that has garnered the most attention over the years, Symington himself spent more of his energy to see Christ's reign over the *church* acknowledged. One of the ways he pursued the wider church's response to Christ's crown was through his interdenominational activity. Such interdenominational work was being done as early as his Stranraer years.

Once in Glasgow, Symington's concern for the wider church found broader scope for activity. He became an outspoken advocate for greater unity among Christian denominations. Because these churches are all under one King, there ought to be a greater expression of that unity than often seemed to be practiced. In pursuing such inter-church unity, Symington saw himself as standing firmly in the heritage of the Covenants. In the first obligation of the Solemn League and Covenant (1643), the churches of Great Britain had sworn:

> That we shall sincerely, really, and constantly...endeavor [after]...the preservation of the reformed religion in the Church of Scotland...; the reformation of religion in the kingdoms of England and Ireland...; and shall endeavour to bring the Churches of God in the three kingdoms to the nearest conjunction and uniformity in religion....

The Westminster Assembly (1643–1649), with Scottish commissioners in attendance, was an implementation of this Covenanted pursuit of unity. The Westminster Standards—among the most important unifying documents of Reformed churches around the world—were its fruit. Although much had happened in the years after the Solemn League and Covenant, resulting in widespread divisions throughout Britain, church union remained an important duty of those upholding the continuing obligation of the Covenants. Symington was a prominent and aggressive advocate of the continued pursuit of this Covenanted cause.

One important distinction ought to be noted up front, however—a distinction between this effort for unity in the Covenanter heritage and that which has come to characterize the well-known, modern ecumenical movements. Symington himself expressed the distinction in this way:

> We candidly avow that we have no taste whatever for the sentimental cant of the day, which would go to reduce all differences of religious profession to some vague levelling scheme of indiscriminate communion. The maintenance of truth, the support of discipline, the preservation of ecclesiastical order, we humbly deem matters of moment....[13]

Whereas it was already becoming popular to speak of interdenominational *union* as an aim in itself, Symington insisted rather on the pursuit of interdenominational *unity*. That is, the important doctrinal questions that separate churches do not need to be abandoned (at least not without due study and reform). Rather, because all true churches are under one and the same King, even though they remain distinct denominations, churches can and ought to manifest a warm and real unity. Symington expressed the importance of co-laboring between genuine branches of the church in this way:

> The man has good reason to question his christianity altogether who would hesitate to say, "Grace be with all them that love our Lord Jesus Christ in sincerity" [Eph. 6:24]. We may surely wish one another well without lending our countenance to error; we may surely seek one another's good without making a compromise of truth.... By kindness, by candour, by forbearance, by prayer, and by cheerful co-operation in common efforts for the support and extension

---

13. William Symington, "Love One Another" (in *Discourses on Public Occasions* [Glasgow: David Bryce, 1851]), 195.

of religion, let us show that we can combine firm adherence to principle with warmth of love to the brethren.[14]

There are certainly many ways in which evangelical branches of the church can lovingly co-labor without ignoring (or abandoning) important differences. In fact, it might even be regarded as especially incumbent on churches like the Covenanter congregations, which strongly adhere to the importance of doctrinal precision, to all the more insure that they also adhere to the importance of charity in word and deed to all fellow servants of King Jesus. Such loving cooperation between denominations in basic gospel efforts was the first implication of the call to unity taught by Symington.

There is moreover a second aspect of church unity urged by Symington. Once (and only as) that unity already described is being lived out, it then becomes feasible to engage in the kinds of deliberations envisioned in the Solemn League and Covenant, and actually exemplified by Westminster. As inter-church unity is more keenly perceived and enjoyed, then the important doctrinal differences between churches can be charitably addressed. Symington urged,

> Let us show a willingness to meet, on the arena of frank and friendly consultation, [with] brethren of other churches, and to discuss with them our points of difference in a spirit of Christian candour and charity. The friends of the Redeemer are surely not always to be separated and divided. The reign of disunion is not to be forever. There is "one Lord, one faith, one baptism, one God and Father of all.... There is one body, and one Spirit" [Eph. 4:5–6, 4a]. And believing that these statements of sacred writ are destined to receive *visible* as well as an *invisible* fulfillment, we must hold Christians bound to use all lawful means for bringing this about.[15]

In Symington's view, such co-laboring and attention to differences were not only an explicit expectation of the Solemn League and Covenant (for the UK), but a universal consequence for the whole church as under the crown of Christ.

---

14. William Symington, "Love One Another" (in *Discourses on Public Occasions* [Glasgow: David Bryce, 1851]), 196.

15. William Symington, "Love One Another" (in *Discourses on Public Occasions* [Glasgow: David Bryce, 1851]), 203.

Some indication of Symington's own cooperation with Christians outside Covenanter circles has already been noted in reference to his Stranraer years. Symington spoke widely in support of Bible Societies, Sabbath School movements, Temperance meetings, non-RP missions meetings, and he preached in other denominational pulpits as well. Such activities continued, and increased, during his Glasgow years. His journal gives record of his frequent preaching in Church of Scotland pulpits, Congregational churches, Free Church services, Burgher Churches, Relief Churches, and among other evangelical congregations. Symington also served as a secretary for the National Bible Society of Scotland for some years, and he labored on behalf of the Old Men's Charity, the Boy's House of Refuge, and other institutions of Christian concern.

Of particular significance, however, is Symington's exercise of that second facet of the pursuit of unity: the charitable confrontation of differences. In one sense, it was through his interdenominational activity that Symington *demonstrated* the mutuality of his love for Christ with that of other believers. It was on the foundation of this real and practiced mutual love, then, that *doctrinal discussion* could also be pursued. And it was through this latter effort that Symington labored to improve the unity of a sadly divided church.

Much of Symington's doctrinal dialog with other denominational leaders took place in informal ways. The dinner table was a common site for such discussions, either with ministers from other churches sharing at Symington's table, or with Symington hosted in others' homes.

More formal discussions were also arranged. For instance, the following conference with leaders of the Original Seceder Church (a body which had separated from the National Church in 1733) is described in this journal entry for January 7–9, 1846:

> 7. Mr. McCrie & Mr. Goold [of the Original Seceder Church] with us all night. 8. A very pleasant meeting with Original Seceders. Conferences conducted in best spirit. Forenoon spent in devotion and talking over the state of matters in our respective churches. In the evening talked over the points on wh[ich] supposed to differ. Found substantial agreement on extent of Mediatorial Dominion, & on the evils of Rev'n Settlement. Differences on recognition of British Gov't explained on both sides. Several of the brethren dined with

me between meetings. All parted in harmony. 9. Mr. McCrie
left us after breakfast.

Such informal and small group, interchurch discussions might
well be considered the most important of Symington's contributions
toward church unity. Personal discussion, in charity, is probably
more fruitful in many respects than mass appeal. Nonetheless,
Symington contributed to larger ecumenical efforts as well. In fact,
Symington was one of the founding proponents of the World Evangelical Alliance (WEA).

The WEA was the first of the modern international ecumenical
organizations, and continues to be one of the largest. It is markedly different today, however, from its original form. Symington's
enthusiasm for the WEA's organization in the nineteenth century
would not necessarily indicate his endorsement of the WEA as it
exists today. Present-day critics of the WEA (and similar organizations) often note a lack of commitment to the *precise doctrinal unity*
that was Symington's (and others') concern. One can certainly note
the broad inclusiveness of the WEA's present Statement of Faith in
marked contrast to the Alliance's original Credal Basis drawn up
with Symington's participation. Nonetheless, Symington's involvement with that Alliance illustrates his concern to promote broad,
evangelical confrontation of doctrinal differences.

The impetus for the WEA's formation can be traced, in part, to
the Bicentennial Celebration of the Westminster Assembly in 1843.
A gathering of leaders from various Scottish churches holding to the
Westminster Standards met in Edinburgh on July 11 of that year.
Symington was asked to deliver the opening address. "Not the
least interesting," Symington stated in his opening remarks, "and...
not the least *appropriate*, feature of the present meeting is, that it is
composed of persons of different denominations."[16] Despite the dis-
union which had come to characterize recent events in the Scottish
churches, Symington took the occasion of that gathering to emphasize the actual measure of unity that still existed among the various
Reformed denominations—a unity of common doctrinal standards
all too often overlooked or undervalued.

---

16. William Symington, "Love One Another" (in *Discourses on Public Occasions*
[Glasgow: David Bryce, 1851]), 185.

Symington chose, therefore, as his text for that opening sermon, John 13:34: "A new commandment I give unto you, That ye love one another...." In that message, Symington traced out the "high road" to church-wide unity through, on the one hand, a love that is genuinely warm and cooperative toward *all* who truly belong to Christ, and, on the other hand, a love that does not despair to continue the labors for doctrinal unity so profoundly undertaken by the Westminster divines. In regard to the Westminster Assembly, Symington remarked,

> They contemplated, besides a religious uniformity in the three kingdoms [of England, Ireland, and Scotland], a great Protestant union among the nations of Christendom.... No sectarian prejudice, no weak partiality of kindred or of country, was permitted to freeze or confine [their efforts].... They opened correspondence with foreign churches, and in the largeness and warmth of their affection, formed schemes of co-operation and intercourse.... The [documents] they framed were so constructed as to exhibit a generous and catholic bearing, being equally adapted to the church in Britain, on the continent of Europe, in the Republican States of America, in the Islands of the South Pacific, the plains of Hindustan, the deserts of Africa, the West Indies, and New Zealand....
>
> May the present commemorative services be blessed of God for leading to movements that shall issue in putting an end to existing dissentions and divisions!...[17]

Symington was not alone in these sentiments. Other speakers at the Westminster Bicentenary shared a similar interest to see the work of doctrinal unity begun at Westminster continued in the British church of the nineteenth century. Symington joined a group of Scottish ministers (which included six other Reformed Presbyterians), to publish an invitation to "the evangelical churches of England, Wales, and Ireland" to attend an exploratory conference in Liverpool, England, in October 1845. Symington, unfortunately, fell ill and was unable to attend that Liverpool conference. He did

---

17. William Symington, "Love One Another" (in *Discourses on Public Occasions* [Glasgow: David Bryce, 1851]), 201–203.

attend the follow-on meeting in London the next year, however, which meeting was attended by representatives from ten countries.

In a letter which he sent to his wife during the meetings, Symington reported, "A motion of mine to have introduced into the Basis [of Alliance] a recognition of the Universal Mediatorial Dominion of Christ occasioned a discussion of nearly three hours...."[18] One of those present in that discussion was Edward Bickersteth, a rector in the Church of England. Taking the floor, Bickersteth admitted that he "felt at first some hesitation in making the addition" proposed by Symington. But he simply had not comprehended "the largeness of our work"—that is the scope of what Christ's universal dominion entailed. "My Scotch Brethren and my American Brethren," Bickersteth continued, "have helped me here," and he moved the adoption of Symington's amendment, which carried.[19]

Bickersteth's remarks indicate something of the educational nature of those early Alliance assemblies. Symington's statement on Christ's mediatorial dominion was an occasion for instructing others not acquainted with that doctrine. Whether this forum would prove extremely effective for such doctrinal instruction remained to be seen.

"We make slow progress," Symington wrote home in another letter, "but this is inevitable seeing there are so many different denominations who have so much to explain."[20] Not everything needing to be addressed would or could be covered in that London conference, of course. Nonetheless, sufficient headway was made to formally establish the World Evangelical Alliance that year (1846), as an effort toward interdenominational unity of labor and doctrinal reform. In one of the "summarizing" resolutions coming out of that meeting, which Symington was charged to present, the Covenanter churchman exhorted the WEA assembly:

> There may be some danger of individuals going away with the impression, that they are to keep up their differences of opinion for ever. Now, one of the things which, from the very commencement, has commended this movement to my

---

18. MS Letter, dated Aug. 18, 1846.

19. *Evangelical Alliance, Being a Report of the Proceedings of the Conference of 1846* (London: Simkin, 1847), 79.

20. MS Letter, dated Aug. 22, 1846.

mind, has been, that it holds out to me a prospect—I grant, but a very distant one—that our differences of opinion will be got over...[not] *forgetting* our differences, [or] *banishing* our differences, [or]...*merging* our differences...[but] I want the differences to be done away with altogether [that is, resolved]....[21]

Standing with the hindsight of more than two centuries, it is now possible to see how the great ecumenical organizations have tended more toward the "forgetting...banishing...[or] merging" of sectarian differences rather than facilitating their resolution. Perhaps time has shown that the informal and smaller gatherings are more fruitful than the mass alliances and conference hall "negotiations." Before drawing this conclusion too far, however, one would have to take into consideration the numerous "Edward Bickersteths" who, in the course of the early WEA forums, may have experienced important doctrinal reform in one point or another. Nonetheless, the ecumenical movement has clearly gone a different direction from that envisioned by the likes of William Symington.

Symington had readily observed, as just quoted, that the success of the WEA was a long shot ("a very distant prospect"). Nonetheless, his faith in the reality and universality of Christ's reign led him to eagerly do all he could to promote doctrinal reform, rather than forever despairing the many unlikelihoods that often discourage any efforts. As he had written many years before,

> Christians are apt to feel discouraged when they reflect on the extensive prevalence of error compared with the limited success of the true religion and despairingly to inquire, "By whom shall Jacob arise? for he is small." [Amos 7:2] But if they can only have faith in the mediatorial dominion, they may dismiss their fears, and confidently rely in, not merely the preservation, but the triumphant success and universal establishment, of the church.[22]

Symington understood the seeming futility of, in fact, *any* church effort when the prevalence of sin and the hardness of human

---

21. *Evangelical Alliance, Being a Report of the Proceedings of the Conference of 1846* (London: Simkin, 1847), 196.

22. William Symington, *Messiah the Prince* (Philadelphia: The Christian Statesman, 1884), 187.

hearts is considered. But he also observed the real and inevitable success of the church in *all* her duties when the absolute dominion of her King is taken into account. Because of the crown of Christ, Symington labored at the dining room table and in London conference halls to uphold the church's biblical obligation (and, indeed in the UK, nationally covenanted promise): "That we shall sincerely, really, and constantly...endeavour to bring the churches of God in the three kingdoms to the nearest conjunction and uniformity in religion...."

Before leaving this subject, it ought be noted that Symington's "ecumenical" efforts were not without critics. For many long generations, the Covenanters had strictly avoided participation with the established church, in particular. During the days of the United Societies, the Covenanters had condemned any "occasional hearing" of ministers in the national church. There were those in Symington's day who felt absolute separation from other denominations remained a necessary practice.

Early in Symington's ministry in Stranraer—a ministry already characterized by interdenominational activity—one of the Societies under Symington's care had forwarded a question to Presbytery: "Is attendance on [a] sermon preached on behalf of Bible Societies and such like institutions by Ministers of other denominations but of Evangelical principles, an offence which should be subjected to the discipline of the Church?"[23] A few years later, additional petitions from within Symington's congregation came before Presbytery. Included was a request from several members of the Stranraer Session for help resolving "a diversity both of sentiment and practice... on the subject of what is usually called occasional hearing."[24]

Later, when Symington entered his labors at Great Hamilton Street in Glasgow, another Glasgow congregation (West Campbell Street) submitted a request to Synod: "That this Court enjoin both ministers and sessions under their charge to adhere to the practice of the church in bygone times, in regard to the interchange of pulpits with ministers of other denominations...."[25]

---

23. MS *Minutes of the Southern Reformed Presbytery,* Sept. 13, 1826.
24. MS *Minutes of the Synod of the Reformed Presbyterian Church,* Apr. 29, 1831.
25. *Extracts of Synod Minutes,* May 6, 1859, Session VIII.

There were those who frowned upon Symington's broad involvements. Furthermore, there clearly *was* a change of practice taking place in Symington's interdenominational activities in comparison to the closedness of the old Societies. Nonetheless, the church courts responded to these questions about Symington's activities in his favor. He was by no means opening RP pulpits to liberal or unbelieving preachers. Nor was he attending upon apostate preaching himself. Such activities would have been disciplineable. Symington's interdenominational activities were clearly evangelical and Christian, not liberal, moderate, or compromising.

Furthermore, the closedness of the old Societies was not inconsistent with interdenominational fellowship of the later RP churches. Symington wrote in a pamphlet touching on the subject:

> ...I quite vindicate our forefathers in keeping up their fellowship Societies rather than hear the indulged [i.e., government sanctioned (and often unbelieving)] curates that constituted the Assembly at that time; and I think that they were quite right in refusing them, and I would not have heard them in the circumstances. They could not have made out their position of dissent from the Revolution Settlement had they not done so. I still think there is no case made out to-day to show us that the practice is now such as to call for interference.[26]

Symington further cited the actions of the early Scottish Covenanters, who had sent one of their young men (James Renwick) to Holland for education and ordination before his returning to preach and administer sacraments among the Covenanters. In other words, strict closedness was not in itself a doctrine of the Covenanters. Rather, under the conditions of the Revolution Settlement, it became necessary to remain separate from the newly (and wrongly) established church. Strict separation was a necessary application of principle in those conditions, but separation was not the Covenanter's principle in itself.

Now that the Covenanters were no longer mere Societies, but had become an organized church, the same principle called for different practice. Rather than standing outside the Scottish church, the

---

26. *Our Testimony Compromised: A Full Report of the Discussion in the Reformed Presbyterian Synod Regarding the Use of the Elective Franchise* (Glasgow, 1869), 60.

Lord had brought the Covenanters inside the wider Scottish church, and Symington saw it as a Covenanter duty to interact as brothers among them (even if they be brothers with important differences to resolve). To suppose that isolation was, itself, a Covenanter doctrine was to ignore the frank denunciation by the old Covenanters in their early testimony: "We hold, That Schism...[is] a very heinous, hateful, and hurtful Sin."[27]

There is again, in this instance, an example of Symington's careful effort to distinguish between *principles* (which do not change) and *practices* (which sometimes require amendment). Although some in the RP Church continued to be unhappy with the growing degree of interaction with other denominations, the majority in the church courts concurred with Symington.

Seeking Reform in the Established Church

The Covenanters refused to join the post-Revolution national church because of its Erastian constitution. (*Erastianism* is the formal term used to describe those churches which are subject to state authority. The term comes from the name Thomas Erastus, who was a prominent proponent of the idea in the sixteenth century.) In the Revolution Settlement of 1688, as seen in an earlier chapter, William and Mary granted Scotland a Presbyterian church; but they also maintained that it was the king who granted legitimacy to the church. The state could regulate her activities, making her an Erastian church, rather than a church under Christ's sole and direct rule.

It was chiefly for this reason that the Covenanters refused to join the national church of the Revolution Settlement. Instead, they organized into Societies for temporary gospel fellowship outside the state church, while continuing to call for church reform according to the Covenants. When the Societies were later able to organize

---

27. James Renwick and Alexander Shiells, *An Informatory Vindication of a Poor, Wasted, Misrepresented Remnant, of the Suffering, Anti-Popish, Anti-Prelatic, Anti-Erastian, Anti-Sectarian, True Presbyterian Church of Christ in Scotland, United Together in a General Correspondence, By Way of Reply to Various Accusations, in Letters, Informations and Conferences Given forth Against Them* (Edinburgh: R. Drummond, 1744 [reprinted from original edition, 1687]), 27–28.

as a church with their own ministers and courts, they by no means ceased to look for the reform of the national church.

In addition to Symington's interdenominational activities generally speaking (considered in the previous section), his participation in that ongoing call for reform within the national church—with a surprising measure of success—deserves special notice.

The Covenanters' opposition to the Revolution Settlement was, in many respects, vindicated in subsequent years. One of the most troublesome, and frequent, infringements of the state on the established church in subsequent years was in the appointment of ministers. The civil government retained a measure of control over the manner of appointing ministers to open pulpits. In 1712, most notably, the British Parliament passed legislation confirming the rights of certain aristocrats (patrons) to nominate the ministers who would fill pulpits in their parishes. This regulation was put in place despite the fact that the Scottish church, as far back as the days of John Knox, had recognized the biblical right of congregations to nominate their own ministers.

This was not the only kind of state imposition upon the national church that followed the Revolution Settlement. Nonetheless, this matter of "patronage" was to prove especially divisive. And it also was to contribute to the predominance of unbelieving, politically chosen ministers (and a smaller number of gospel preaching ministers) in the national church.

In 1733, a small body separated from the national church over the rights of congregations to choose their own ministers. These dissenters later became known as the "Original Seceders," and are one of the denominations with whom Symington held extensive dialog, as noted earlier. Another division over the "patronage" issue took place in 1761. At that time, a small group separated from the national church to form the Relief Church, "for Christians oppressed in their Church privileges."

In addition to these splits resulting in new denominations, it was not unheard of for individual congregations to leave the national church and join one of these dissenting bodies. If a congregation did not want the minister nominated by the patron, but wanted another, they might readily join a dissenting body which allowed them to elect their own choice. The selection of ministers was not the only problem arising from state interference with church affairs, but it was probably the most volatile.

Prior to the nineteenth century, however, the resulting divisions had been limited in their effect. For the most part, the national church remained unified in its Erastian order. But there were changes underway. More specifically, the Spirit was at work in the late 1700's, converting more and more national church ministers. The majority of the national church ministers after the Revolution Settlement had been moderates and unbelievers. They preached on morality, but rarely on the gospel.

Toward the end of the eighteenth century, however, a greater number of national church ministers came under the power of the gospel themselves. The number of believing ministers was on the rise, leading to the Evangelical movement in nineteenth-century Scotland. One of the most influential evangelicals in the early nineteenth-century Church of Scotland was Thomas Chalmers. Chalmers had been in the ministry for seven years before his conversion. Although for decades the minority evangelicals in the national church had labored within their congregations without prospect of changing the overall church, Chalmers was probably the key influence in organizing the evangelical ministers, beginning in the 1830's, into a movement for national church reform.

It is partly due to these significant developments taking place in the established church that Symington, in his sermon to Synod at the time of his translation to Glasgow, had stated, "The times in which our lot is cast are reforming times" (see p. 72 above). Symington was optimistic that the long desired reformation of the National Church might well be within reach.

It was not long after Symington's settlement in Glasgow before he and Chalmers were developing a close friendship. Symington was already becoming well known, and respected, among national church evangelicals for his book, *Messiah the Prince*. Symington's clear articulation of the biblical relationship between church and state, as hammered out in the Scottish Reformation, offered a profound alternative to that which the evangelical ministers of the established church presently endured. Symington eagerly built bridges with the evangelical ministers in the Church of Scotland in order to do all he could to encourage reform.

As Chalmers organized the evangelicals and they increased in momentum, significant changes began to take place. Chalmers introduced a Church Extension program which would lead to the planting of two hundred new churches during the 1830s. Many of those churches were in neglected areas outside the legally authorized parish system. In response to the long-standing "patronage" system, the evangelical body also managed to push a "Veto Act" through the General Assembly of the church. This Veto Act, accepted in 1834, recognized the right of individual congregations to veto the minister nominated by their local patron. This ruling was to prove significant, for it was a ruling by the *church* which directly contradicted an existing statute of Parliament on the same matter. Who had the right to regulate the appointment of ministers?

Other changes were also instituted during those years. It was, nonetheless, the "patronage" issue which was to bring things to a head. Lord Fife, patron for the parish church in Marnoch, nominated a Mr. Edwards to fill the pulpit there. Under the new Veto Act, however, the congregation at Marnoch refused him, and the Presbytery therefore refrained from examining and installing him. The flint of a great controversy had been kindled, for Lord Fife and Edwards appealed to the civil courts under the 1712 statute of Parliament empowering patronage. The ensuing case was to be a test of authority over national church affairs—whether the established church was independent of state interference, or would continue as an Erastian church.

A series of interdicts were imposed by the civil authorities, blocking the church's exercise of the Veto Act. Presbytery appealed directly to Parliament, and even to Queen Victoria, to hold off this government intrusion on affairs of the church. In the end, after extensive involvement by courts, a hearing before Parliament (in London), and the attention of various ministers of state, it became evident that the government would not budge. Although there was a significant movement within the church to reform, the state was not yet willing to reform and acknowledge Christ's sole headship over the church.

The determination of the prime minister, Sir Robert Peel, expressed the resolve of the government: "The establishment of an ecclesiastical domination, in defiance of law, could not be acceded to without the utmost ultimate danger...."[28] If the Church of Scotland was going to continue to hold her status as the officially established national church, she would have to remain under the regulation of the state.

Naturally, Symington watched these proceedings with great interest (especially since his book had been at least one means of influence for national church ministers thinking more clearly about Christ's rule over the church). In May of 1843, Symington made his way to Edinburgh to attend the Church of Scotland General Assembly. At that Assembly, the government's final ultimatum was to be answered. Symington's journal gives these short, but vivid, remarks:

> 18. Witnessed the Disruption in the Church of Scotland—a splendid sight. Worth living a century to behold. The meeting at Canonmills immense, & proceedings full of deepest interest. 19. Attended Free Assembly....

The "Disruption" took place on May 18, with Symington observing. Submitting a protest on the floor of the General Assembly, a large number of national church ministers declared this intrusion by the civil government into church affairs "inconsistent with Christian liberty, and with the authority which the Head of the church hath conferred on the church alone."[29] So long as government establishment meant government control, these ministers would surrender the rights of establishment rather than abandon their allegiance to Christ as sole King and Head of the church.

After issuing their written protest with an initial tally of 169 signatures, these protestors left the General Assembly. Ultimately, a full third of the Church of Scotland clergy (474 ministers) left the national church and reorganized themselves as the Free Church of Scotland. They were not dissenting to the principle of national church establishment. The Free Church continued to uphold (as did Symington and the Reformed Presbyterian Church) that there ought

---

28. Sir Thomas Erskine May, *The Constitutional History of England since the Accession of George the Third: 1760–1860* (London: Longmans, Green, & Co., 1875), 3.251.

29. Sir Thomas Erskine May, *The Constitutional History of England since the Accession of George the Third: 1760–1860* (London: Longmans, Green, & Co., 1875), 3.251.

to be a state established and supported church. Nonetheless, until the state was ready to reform, those faithful to Christ's sole rule over the church would have to operate without such state recognition.

There was great personal sacrifice entailed in this act. Ministers who left the national church lost their manses, their incomes, and their church buildings. The Free Church ministers, and the congregations that came with them, had to meet in barns and fields in many places. Some found other churches willing to help. Symington, for example, opened the Great Hamilton Street facilities for use by one of the building-less Free Church congregations until they could obtain property. Symington also packaged up a collection of books to donate for the Free Church's establishment of a new Theological Hall.

Although, sadly, the whole Church of Scotland had not yet been freed from its yoke to civil intrusion, and the state itself continued to resist reform in this point, a remarkable proportion of the once Erastian churches in Scotland had now been reformed. The long and patient witness of the Covenanters over the generations, including the defense of Christ's mediatorial dominion in his book on the subject, had not been in vain. Symington counted himself privileged to have witnessed the embrace of this Covenanted objective—Christ's sole rule over the church—in so impressive an event as the Disruption of May 18, 1843.

It is not insignificant that this event took place just a matter of weeks before Symington made his plea for greater church unity at the Westminster Assembly Bicentennial Celebrations. Although the Disruption had meant a division within the state church, it was nonetheless a movement toward greater church unity in doctrinal terms. It meant that 474 ministers and their congregations now shared markedly greater unity of doctrine with those churches faithful to the Reformation standards (such as the Reformation Presbyterians). The division of the national church was nothing to take pleasure in—far better it would have been for the entire Church of Scotland to have reformed, and the state as well. Nonetheless, reformation in one-third of the Church of Scotland churches was itself a major contribution toward greater doctrinal unity. That event must have heartily encouraged Symington's hopes for further doctrinal dialog among evangelical churches, as he joined the World Evangelical Alliance effort that same year.

All that being so, nonetheless there was certainly no hasty effort to establish organizational union between the Reformed Presbyterian Church and the Free Church. There remained still other doctrinal differences which would have to be addressed before visible union could be contemplated.

Someone asked Symington, seeing his excitement at the events of 1843, why he did not join the Free Church himself. Symington replied in humor, "Nay, for with a great sum you have purchased this freedom, but we were free-born!"[30] (cf. Acts 22:28). On a more serious tone, Symington took the occasion of the Disruption to preach to the Great Hamilton Street congregation on Christ's sole headship over the church and the error of "patronage." And he also preached a sermon on "some distinctions betwixt the RP Church & Free Church," which would yet need to be resolved before visible union could be contemplated.[31]

Some years after Symington's death, in 1876, a union would take place between the Free Church and the *larger* Reformed Presbyterian Synod. It should be recalled that a small number of RP congregations separated over the voting controversy in 1863. That smaller, "no-voting" RP Church would continue as a distinct body, although the "pro-voting" RP Church merged into the Free Church in 1876. Whether Symington would have considered union appropriate in 1876 is not clear. Unquestionably, he was agreeable to union if all the important doctrinal differences were resolved. His earlier noted comments on the subject, nonetheless, also show his readiness to wait patiently until such conditions actually existed. There does seem to be reason to question whether union in 1876 may have been premature. That, at least, is the question raised by the following article published by another church (the Original Seceders) watching the terms of that union from the outside:

> It is not altogether unnoticeable here that the Reformed Presbyterian Synod's Committee, though the representatives of those who so long claimed to be Covenanters, *par excellence*, has entirely ignored the Covenants, and the doctrine of covenant obligation, in their statement of principles given in

---

30. "Memoir," lxxviii.
31. MS Journal, July 13, 1843.

to the Joint-Committee [i.e., as principles requiring agreement for union]....[32]

It seems doubtful that Symington would have voted in favor of a union that "ignored" the principle of covenanting itself, and the continuing obligation of the National Covenants engaged by Scotland. That, however, is another question not necessary to resolve in this place. In God's providence, nonetheless, the RP Church split over the voting issue in 1863 meant that a body still existed in Scotland to testify to the covenanting principle. What is remarkable here, is that so large a number of congregations from the national church had now embraced the crown rights of Jesus so that union in 1876 was even conceivable. To at least some measure, the living and written witness of William Symington to the doctrine of Christ's mediatorial dominion must be regarded as an important factor in bringing that about.

As all that has preceded has made manifest, Symington was committed to the biblical (and in Britain, at least, the Covenanted) obligation of the church to pursue doctrinal unity under the universal rule of King Jesus. This commitment led him to address complex and difficult questions of church practice, both within the RP Church (like voting) and in relation to other churches. His basis for examining and drawing conclusions on each of those concerns serves to highlight the profound importance, and practicality, which he found in the doctrine of Christ's mediatorial dominion.

---

32. An article in the *Original Seceeder Magazine*, in: John C. Johnston, *Treasury of the Scottish Covenant* (Edinburgh: Andrew Elliot, 1887), 220; cf., also 232.

CHAPTER 8

The Final Years:
A Covenanter Testimony

As Symington moved into his later years, illness and weakening vigor became more regular companions. He also enjoyed, nonetheless, the pleasure of reflecting on a rich experience of Christ over the years, and a deepened knowledge of God's Word and His ways, matured through a lifetime of piety and service. Though compelled to slow down in some respects, Symington continued his active ministry in Glasgow until Christ received him to his eternal reward. He even shouldered new responsibilities.

It was only natural, when the professor's chair at the Theological Hall fell vacant in 1853, that the Synod would turn to Symington to fill it. It was only natural to ask this seasoned minister to invest his years of wisdom in the upcoming generation of church leaders.

Symington was in his fifty-ninth year (1854) when the appointment was set before him. He spent a restless night in prayer before responding to the request. In part, he was sobered by the seriousness of the task and the added weight it would place upon his ongoing pastoral duties in his later years. (Improvements in health standards today allow a much longer life expectancy than was normal in the nineteenth century.) A further cause of his sobriety at this appointment was a consciousness of the shoes he would be filling.

Andrew Symington, William's older brother, had been the professor at the Hall for the past thirty-four years. The close friendship of these two brothers, the "second father" that Andrew had been to William, and the co-laborer Andrew had been in the ministry, all served to render the elder brother's death the previous autumn a painful loss for William. Now William was being asked to take up his brother's place at the Theological Hall.

Historically, the RP Theological Hall had always had a one-man faculty. The divinity students in those days only met for eight weeks each autumn, during which time the professor provided a rigorous course of lectures and assignments. As one Synod report at the time put it, "the maximum of work in the minimum of time was the rule in this seminary."[1] Synod provided other ministers to cover preaching for the professor's home congregation during that eight-week session, but the seminary instructor continued in the full-time pastorate throughout the remainder of the year. In between the autumn sessions, students were occupied in internships, preaching, research assignments, and study.

Due to the increasing numbers of men training for ministry, the Synod determined to appoint two professors to the faculty to replace Andrew Symington. William was asked to teach systematic theology, although he would also end up shouldering other subjects as well, especially homiletics. Dr. William Goold was asked to teach church history and biblical literature. (Goold was an RP minister from Edinburgh. He also happens to have married one of William Symington's daughters, and thus was Symington's son-in-law.) Both men accepted their appointments.

The Great Hamilton Street congregation made physical re-arrangements to the church property in order to allow the Theological Hall to meet there, and Symington's journal for the period indicates a significant amount of work being expended in preparation for his lectures the coming autumn. "Although he maintained his habitual cheerfulness," Symington's sons were later to recount, "…the double work of minister and professor was carried on at serious expense of vital energy."[2] The vast extent of Symington's labors was taking its toll on his strength, but his journals indicate a man still thoroughly absorbed—and delighted—in the work.

In 1855, Symington asked his congregation to find a "colleague and successor" to share with him in the pastoral duties of the church. The congregation seemed reluctant to introduce another minister into their cherished relationship with Symington. It was not until 1857 that active steps to obtain an associate minister began. In 1859, Symington's son William was called to be the associate pastor at

---

1. *Reformed Presbyterian Magazine* (Nov. 1855), 369.
2. "Memoir," xciv.

Great Hamilton Street. The younger William had been pastor of the RP Church in Castle Douglas for thirteen years, and was to prove a great help as associate minister to his father during the last three years of his life.

Mrs. Symington's health was also showing marks of decline, and the busy minister seems to have been attuned to the importance of this changing season of life. The family home at Annfield Place, so long the scene of six children and a busy household, was now occupied only by "the old folk" (a favorite self-reference for Symington in family conversation in those years). They also retained their faithful housekeeper of many years, Sarah, who lived with them. Nevertheless, Symington is said by his sons to have "spen[t] less time in the study" in those days "that he might spend more with our mother." The same family memoir tells of an aging minister and wife who "laughingly said they were beginning life again, and renewing the happiness of a youth forty years past."[3] Theirs was a happy marriage through many fruitful years.

Even in his elder years, nonetheless, Symington continued to exercise his wide-ranging interest in the dominion of Christ and its application in every sphere. On January 1, 1861, Symington looked ahead into the year and wrote,

> January 1, 1861. The state of affairs in Italy, Syria, and the Southern States of America is pregnant with interest; well calculated to arrest the attention of all who would observe the doings of the Lord, and fitted to keep the eye of faith directed to the reigning Governor of the nations, and Prince of the Kings of the earth. Thy kingdom come, O Lord; for thine is the kingdom, and the power, and the glory. Amen.[4]

The same faith in the reigning Christ, reflected in those lines of global interest, was expressed in concerns closer to home on New Year's Day, one year later:

> January 1, 1862.—The year which has just closed, like its predecessors, has been a chequered one. The last month the darkest of all, from illness first of my son and latterly

---

3. "Memoir," xcviii.

4. As quoted by William H. Goold in: *Reformed Presbyterian Magazine* (Sept. 1, 1862), 339.

of my wife. The amount of anxiety, distress, and watching compressed into the last four or five weeks has been all but overwhelming. The Lord, however, has upheld me. And now the invalids are both in a state of promising convalescence.... Blessed be His gracious name! May we be prepared for whatever shall fall out during this period on which we have entered! We would rest on the Lord and wait patiently for Him....[5]

The same entry actually goes on to observe global events of the new year, as well. But it was Symington's own translation to heaven that was closer at hand than he realized, as he thus surrendered himself and his family into the Lord's grace "for whatever shall fall out during this period on which we have entered."

Symington preached, as normal, on the first Lord's Days of 1862. On Friday, January 10, he suffered a bout of illness—what seemed to be a flu—but was in the pulpit again on the 12th. His morning text, that Lord's Day, was Matthew 6:19–21: "Lay not up for yourselves treasures upon earth, where moth and rust doth corrupt, and where thieves break through and steal: but lay up for yourselves treasures in heaven, where neither moth nor rust doth corrupt, and where thieves do not break through nor steal: for where your treasure is, there will your heart be also." In the afternoon, Symington preached from Lamentations 3:22: "It is of the LORD's mercies that we are not consumed, because his compassions fail not."

"He appeared feeble in the forenoon [i.e., the morning service]," his son was later to recall, "but had much of his old fire and unction in the afternoon."[6]

The next morning, Symington wrote to his youngest son in Dumfries who was already planning to preach at Great Hamilton Street the following Lord's Day. Symington wrote to ask that he prepare to take the Young Men's Society lecture as well. The unwell father expected that his "cold" would hinder him from doing so, personally.

Symington's strength continued, mysteriously, to drain from him. On January 14, the last entry in his journal simply reads, "Still weak as ever." He was not to rise from his bed again after the 14th.

---

5. "Memoir," xcix.

6. "Memoir," c.

Two of Symington's good Christian friends who were doctors tended to him during the week. They realized that his condition was more serious than initially thought, and likely terminal. For two weeks, Symington lay in great weakness. It was only after his death that the doctors determined he was suffering from an aneurysm in his knee, and his weakness was due to the gradual loss of blood.[7]

As various members of the family would sit with him, Symington often requested a particular Psalm, or some other certain passage of Scripture, to be read. One of the lay leaders in the Great Hamilton Street congregation, Robert Walker, called on Symington in those closing weeks, from which the following conversation has been preserved:

"Robert," Symington asked, "have you ever had any desire to depart from this world?... I had sweet meditations last night on departing hence." "Save for the friends you hold so dear," Robert answered. "Oh, yes," Symington was quick to acknowledge, "but it is my dear old wife that I am thinking of: the children are all settled in their own families...."[8]

By that point, Symington recognized that his course was almost done. Although he sorrowed for the pain his death would bring to his wife, he was ready to go and be with the Savior he had served through so many joyful years. That moment came on January 28, 1862. His last words, just prior to his final translation to the arms of his Savior, were the quotation of a promise from Scripture: "There remaineth a rest to the people of God" (i.e., Heb. 4:9). It was a promise Symington was claiming with his last breath in this world, only to cross the threshold to its fulfillment in the next.

Mrs. Symington, as already noted, had herself been seriously unwell just the previous month. Her health had recovered sufficiently to tend to her husband in his final weeks; nevertheless, she was not left long to grieve his death. A few months later, the Lord took Agnes Symington home as well. She, too, however, professed her faith in Christ to the end: "My anchor was cast long ago," she remarked close to the end, "and it is holding firm now."[9]

---

7. "Memoir," ci; *Reformed Presbyterian Magazine* (March, 1862), 87.

8. "Memoir," ci.

9. "Memoir," xcix.

A striking example of both parents' living and dying faith can be found in the written wills which they each left for their families after them.

Mrs. Symington, the Christian mother and grandmother, had penned her dying wish during a serious bout of illness a few years prior to her death. The whole expression of her dying wish was expressed in these lines:

> May, 1858.—Should it be the Lord's will to take me away suddenly and soon, I add my wish that every grandchild may get a Bible as my dying gift, and marked so; and that they may read it daily and make it the rule of their life. And, oh! may their heavenly Father pour out His Spirit upon them, opening their eyes to see clearly His great love, and thus drawing them unto Him through Jesus Christ their Lord.[10]

More than twenty Bibles were accordingly obtained for Mrs. Symington's many grandchildren. This paragraph was copied into the front of each of them as a constant and continuing reminder of a grandmother's longing prayer for her family.

The father's last will and testament had been composed while he was still in the prime of his strength (dated 1845), and similarly reflects the spiritual nature of his most important desires—his "will"—for his children. Symington's first wish was stated as follows:

> *First,* That my wife and children shall continue to walk in the ways of truth and godliness, resting their hopes of eternal salvation on the finished righteousness of Jesus Christ the Son of God and the alone Saviour of sinners, adhering to the visible fellowship of that church which shall appear to them, on diligent, conscientious examination, to possess the firmest basis of scriptural authority, and choosing as their companions, whether permanent or occasional, only such as give evidence that they fear God and keep His commandments.[11]

At the close of his will, then, Symington assigned a particular piece of household furniture to each of the children by name, concluding with this final paragraph:

---

10. "Memoir," xcviii–ix.
11. "Memoir," lxxx–xxxi.

Burial monument. This monument was erected by Symington's congregation to mark his, and his wife's, burial place in the Glasgow necropolis. (A round decorative piece, which would have adorned the front, is missing.)

These individual bequests I make that my children may possess a memorial of the love and esteem of their affectionate father, who, having dedicated them often to the Lord in prayer, and recorded many supplications on their behalf at the throne of grace, through the merit and grace of the blessed Jesus cherishes the good hope of meeting them all in the Father's House, in which are many mansions, there to resume social intercourse and to enjoy throughout the ages the blessings of an inheritance that is incorruptible, undefiled, and that fadeth not away.[12]

These written memorials of William and Agnes Symington testify, not only to that faith which they desired more than anything for their children, but also to that faith which was their own stronghold and hope throughout life—and in the face of death.

It might not be inappropriate to likewise regard Symington's two most important books as memorials left by him to his family in Christ. These two works—*On the Atonement* and *Messiah the Prince*—might be regarded as a theological testament, left by this able minister for the encouragement of the whole family of the church in succeeding generations. These are the guiding doctrines of Christ's work as our Priest and King which he longed to see understood and embraced by all who name the name of Christ. In this respect, Symington was writing as a penman for all the Scottish Covenanters.

Just as John Calvin had been the penman who systematically preserved the doctrines of the Continental Reformers, so William Symington stood at the crossroads between eras and preserved the fruits of the Second Reformation in Scotland. Symington was, in many ways, the one who put the voice of the Second Reformation into a comprehensive theology. His two principal works, therefore, can be regarded as a theological testament bequeathed from the Second Reformation Covenanters to their heirs and all serious-minded Christians.

---

12. "Memoir," lxxxi.

WRITINGS:

On the Atonement and Intercession of Jesus Christ (1834)

CHAPTER 9

Introduction to

On the Atonement and Intercession of Jesus Christ (1834)

Symington wrote his book, *On the Atonement and Intercession of Jesus Christ,* when he was in the Stranraer pastorate. It was published in May, 1834. The book was well received in Scotland and underwent a second printing within that same year. Within two years, the book had made its way across the Atlantic. A New York printer named Robert Carter issued its first American printing in 1836. *On the Atonement* came to be so widely circulated in America that Carter was able to substantially expand his business around that title, running four editions by 1858. The Reformed Presbyterian Church of North America formed its own publishing board in 1838 and, in the first year of its operation, printed three tracts using portions from Symington's book. All three of those tracts were later bound together and reprinted again in 1842.

The United Presbyterian Church of North America also showed interest in Symington's work, publishing a title of their own called, *Symington on Atonement.* By 1864, the United Presbyterians had run their fifth printing of that book and, in 1868, began another edition of it. The "Presbyterian Tract and Sunday School Society," likewise, reproduced and distributed portions of Symington's book. By the mid-ninteenth century, Symington's *On the Atonement* had become one of the standard works in the field. Even as far away as southeast India, students for the ministry were trained with Symington's *On the Atonement* as a primary text. Recently, Symington's *On the Atonement* has been reprinted by Reformation Heritage Books in Grand Rapids (in 2006), and several services specializing in digitizing and reprinting out-of-print books have also made it available (such as Kessinger Publishing in Whitefish, Mont., in 2008, and Bibliolife in Charleston, S.C., also in 2008).

One of the reasons for this broad interest in Symington's book was the author's ability to make doctrine practical. Symington's writing reflects his keen awareness that these truths have direct implications for human hope and human life. It was this practical emphasis in his work which contributed to its broad appeal.

Symington had not set out with the conscious intent to write a "practical" piece. On the first page of his text, the author wrote:

> To prevent disappointment, it may be remarked, that it was not so much the Author's intention to treat [these doctrines] practically, as to explain, establish, and vindicate them, as grand leading *truths* of the gospel of the Son of God, which are, unhappily, much misunderstood, neglected, and impugned in the present day. (p. iii)[1]

Symington knew that he would have to write an exegetically, philosophically, and logically sophisticated work in order to disentangle doctrinal truth from the errors then circulating. He was conscious he would have to contend with theologians—at a scholarly level—to accomplish his end of defending the biblical faith. Nonetheless, he wrote with the layman in his heart. His pastoral concern for lay Christians—and even to those unbelievers he addressed as "serious and anxious inquirers" (p. iii)—about the practical implications of the truths being discussed. For example, after one section of intricate theological discourse, Symington issues the appeal:

> It may be proper to remind the reader...[that] care ought to be taken to view the subject as one, not of speculative research, but of practical and awful importance; affecting the very foundation of a sinner's hopes; the bond of Christian doctrine; the heart and life blood of the religion of Jesus. (p. 19)

Symington was urgently concerned that his readers not only

---

1. All page references in these chapters, not otherwise identified with a source, are taken from Symington's *On the Atonement and Intercession of Jesus Christ* (New York: Robert Carter & Brothers, 1863; reprint, Grand Rapids: Reformation Heritage Books, 2006).

think about the atonement, but *embrace* Christ's atonement. Even his opening apology, confessing the lack of practicality which he felt the subject could and should receive, reveals the pastor in Symington. It was this pastoral concern, echoing in and between profoundly learned arguments, that made Symington's book a widely read text, not only among theologians and seminarians, but among laity and "the serious and anxious inquirers" he desired to reach as well. The result of this blend of theological sophistication and pastoral earnest was a work that became at once both a standard text for theological study and a source for gospel tracts and devotional reading.

By providing, on the following pages, a review of Symington's *On the Atonement and Intercession of Jesus Christ*, it is hoped that similar ends might be encouraged for modern readers. As his book divides into two parts (Part One: *On the Atonement*; Part Two: *On the Intercession*), the following introduction will likewise be presented in two chapters. Such a two-chapter overview can never hope to bring out the full wealth of Symington's 308-page book, but it is hoped that a summary of this nature will provide a useful introduction to Symington's articulation of the atonement, as well as a means of benefit for the reader's edification.

It will therefore be worthwhile to repeat once again, by way of introduction to Symington's *On the Atonement*, his own exhortation:

> It may be proper to remind the reader...[that] care ought to be taken to view the subject as one, not of speculative research, but of practical and awful importance; affecting the very foundation of a sinner's hopes; the bond of Christian doctrine; the heart and life blood of the religion of Jesus. (p. 19)

CHAPTER 10

On the Atonement of Jesus Christ

The Bible teaches us that God created a beautiful world—a world endowed with every blessing; a world unstained by any sorrow (Gen. 1). After the creation was finished, God showed Himself earnest to provide for every need of His creation in order to insure the ongoing joy and prosperity of mankind and the world (Gen. 1:26–27; 2:15, 18). The proper relationship between God, man, and the earth is one of perfect harmony and cooperative benefit.

Why, then, is there such pain and sorrow in the world today? What "broke" the harmonious relationships God established at the first? Why does the world no longer know the same comprehensive blessings of God? And, most importantly, can the "break" between God and man be corrected?

There is, Scripture assures us, a solution. There is a way to be made "at one" with God again. It is that solution, taught in the Bible, which theologians refer to as *atonement* (literally, "at-onement"). It is that hope of atonement with God—and the restoration of all His blessings—that Symington wrote about in his first book. Before we would consider the solution to the problem, however, we must first fully appreciate the problem itself.

Scripture teaches us that the reason for this tragic "breakdown" in the God–man relationship is *human sin* (Gen. 3). This is how the prophet Isaiah explained it:

> Behold, the LORD's hand is not shortened, that it cannot save; neither his ear heavy, that it cannot hear: but *your iniquities have seperated* between you and your God, and your sins have hid his face from you, that he will not hear (Isa. 59:1–2).

God has not turned His back on the world. Humanity—by our sin against God's holy standards—has turned away from God. By rebelling against God's moral standards, and by failing to love and worship Him as our Creator, mankind has broken the original God–man relationship. Human troubles in the world are not because God's arm is "too short" that He cannot help us, but because humanity has turned its back on God by choosing our own way.

None of us can plead individual innocence, either. The God who searches every heart and knows every secret has already announced His verdict: "For *all* have sinned, and come short of the glory of God" (Rom. 3:23; cf. 1 John 1:10; Rev. 2:23). Not everyone is "as bad as Hitler," but all mankind sin. And all sin is black against the holiness of God.

The result of our sins is what Isaiah called "a separation between you and your God." That gulf has deprived us of God's loving care and provision—not only *now*, but there are *eternal* ramifications as well. Even more fearful than the present sorrow of the world's condition is the Bible's warning of *an eternal judgment* that awaits all mankind. We read, for example, in the last book of the Bible:

> But the fearful [i.e., those ashamed of Christ], and unbelieving, and the abominable, and murderers, and whoremongers, and sorcerers, and idolaters, and all liars, shall have their part in the lake which burneth with fire and brimstone: which is the second death (Rev. 21:8).

In our culture, "hell" is more often the butt of jokes than a serious topic of concern. Hell is often painted as a cartoon fantasy, or a superstitious illusion. But that "lake of burning fire" is no laughing matter in Scripture. God's Word warns us that hell is a real destination and, consequently, a matter of serious urgency.

Some of the terms used in the above verse to describe those condemned to that eternal punishment are rather extreme. Severe terms like "abominable" and "murderers" are used. Other terms, however, are much more mild—like "all liars" and, perhaps, "unbelieving." Such a grouping together of "major" and "minor" sins shows how seriously God regards *every* sin, big or small. They all have their due in eternal judgment. As Jesus taught in His "Sermon on the Mount":

> Ye have heard that it was said by them of old time, Thou shalt not kill; and whosoever shall kill shall be in danger of the judgment: but I say unto you, That whosoever is angry

with his brother without a cause shall be in danger of the judgment: and whosoever shall say to his brother, Raca, shall be in danger of the council: but whosoever shall say, Thou fool, shall be in danger of hell fire (Matt. 5:21–22).

Whether one literally murders another or "simply" despises him in his heart; whether one literally commits sexual immorality or "simply" lusts in his heart (Matt. 5:27–28); all sins, in deed or thought, are grievous violations against the holiness of God. Sin is a serious problem that has created a huge gulf between the world and the Creator. Sin is a serious crime in which all humanity are complicit, and for which all mankind (without a solution) have a burning, eternal punishment to anticipate.

This is the grievous problem which faces humanity. It is a cause more urgent than all the political, economic, educational, and other social problems facing our race. It is, however, a need for which God Himself *has* provided the solution. The solution to this "separation" between man and God is what the doctrine of *atonement* is all about. *There is a way to be reconciled, to be made "at-one," with God*—with all the blessings of God's favor restored for eternity. "For the wages of sin is death; but the gift of God is eternal life through Jesus Christ our Lord" (Rom. 6:23).

It is this most important of truths—the way of atonement— that William Symington wrote his first book to expound from Scripture.

Of course, many have written on the subject, both prior to Symington and since. The Reformation period had been full of the joyous proclamation of the atonement as taught in Scripture. As is often the case, however, with so much attention there is bound to be a lot of *mis*-teaching as well. In Symington's day, theories about the atonement were circulating which were inconsistent with the actual teachings of Scripture. With so much at stake, such errors could not be allowed to go unanswered. Symington took up his pen to defend and promote a *biblical* understanding of Christ's atonement.

He began his work by getting right to the heart of the problem. Symington wrote,

All who believe the Scriptures, profess to regard the work of Christ as the only remedy for moral evil. They all agree... that He is...the only Saviour of men from sin and wrath. But by those who agree thus far very different views are taken respecting the *nature* of the remedy Christ has provided. (p. 10)

In other words, people in the church agree that atonement *is available* through Jesus. There is confusion, however, about *what kind* of atonement Jesus provides. According to Symington, other misunderstandings about the atonement generally derive from a mistake here, in one's view of "the *nature* of the remedy Christ has provided."

The Nature of Christ's Atonement: Penal Substitution

There are many ways in which we, as human beings, are accustomed to reconciling after a relationship breakdown. For example, we are familiar with the "forgive and forget" approach to reconciliation. Some people make amends after a disagreement simply by not talking about the problem anymore. "It's in the past. What's done is done. Let's just forget about it and move on." The problem is brushed under the carpet, and we pretend it never happened.

Another kind of reconciliation we often employ in human relationships is what might be termed the "I'll make it up to you" approach. After some problem has disrupted a relationship, one person decides "to make up for the problem" by going out of his way to do something extra nice for the other. Maybe he buys an expensive gift. Maybe he does a special favor. He hopes that, by doing something extra good, the other person will forgive the wrong and reconcile.

In our human experience, we are familiar with numerous different *kinds* of reconciliation efforts. What kind of reconciliation is it that Jesus accomplishes for us? What is the *nature* of the atonement He makes between us and God? There are three different kinds of atonement which have generally been taught by theologians, but only one of them is biblically sound. Symington begins his book by comparing each of these three "schools" on the atonement to show which one accords with Scripture.

1. The Moral Influence School—The first position which Symington confronts is the so-called "Moral Influence Theory" of atonement. This same view has also been called "Socinianism" (because it was popularized by the sixteenth-century teacher, Faustus Socinus). Though labeled with such obscure titles, this view of Jesus' atonement essentially boils down to the familiar "forgive and forget" approach to reconciliation commonly employed in human relationships. "The abettors of this opinion," Symington explains, "represent [God] as ready to forgive the sins of His creatures, simply on their repentance" (p. 10).

It is true that God forgives sins. It is also true that He cleanses our record. He, in a manner of speaking, "forgets" our sins once forgiven (Isa. 43:25). He does not, however, simply brush them aside. As Symington points out, the Scriptures are abundantly clear that *a great price had to be paid* in order to purchase forgiveness. Jesus had to shed His blood in order to make atonement possible. The Moral Influence view of atonement ignores this vital fact and is therefore inconsistent with scriptural teaching.

The Apostle Paul wrote concerning Jesus' death, "In whom we have redemption *through his blood,* the forgiveness of sins..." (Eph. 1:7). Why did Jesus have to die if, as the Moral Influence theologians would have us believe, God simply "forgives and forgets"? The Socinians do not completely overlook the importance of Jesus' death. However, His death is regarded as a role model for us, not a payment for sin. Here is how Symington explains their position on Jesus' death:

> When it is said, Christ 'died for us,' the meaning [according to the Moral Influence view] is, that He died for our benefit.... He 'saves men from sin' by the influence of His precepts and His example, in leading men to the practice of holiness. (p. 10)

In other words, we receive forgiveness (for past sins) simply for asking. Jesus' death has nothing to do with the forgiveness of past sins. We learn how to stop sinning (in the future) by imitating Jesus' self-sacrificial love. Jesus' death is a role model—a "moral influence"—to help us cease from sinning. That is the Moral Influence view of the atonement.

There is a degree of truth in this position. Jesus' life and death *are* a pattern of perfect love for our imitation (1 Peter 2:21). However, His death was so much more than a moral example: it was a sacrifice for atonement. Jesus, Symington reminds us, is constantly identified in Scripture as our High Priest who offered His own body as a sacrifice *to purchase* atonement. As the author of Hebrews informs us,

> But Christ being come an high priest.... by his own blood
> he entered in once into the holy place, having obtained
> eternal redemption for us.... without shedding of blood is no
> remission (Heb. 9:11–12, 22).

In the Moral Influence school's view of Christ, Symington writes, "His priestly office is obliterated" (p. 10). Jesus is only a Prophet who announces forgiveness, not a Priest who *secures* forgiveness by sacrifice. This view is, in Symington's words, "inconsistent" and "utterly irreconcilable" with the teachings of Scripture (p. 11). Christ's atonement is not of the simple "forgive and forget" variety. God does not simply brush sin under the carpet. Something had to be done to satisfy divine justice against our sin.

2. The Governmental School — A second view of the atonement that Symington confronted is what theologians call the "Governmental Theory" of atonement. (In Symington's day, the title "Middle System" was also used.) To explain this position, it might be helpful to consider another human method of reconciliation with which we are familiar.

Sometimes, when two people have a falling out that is particularly pernicious, it takes a "middle man" to sort things out. Because neither of the opposing parties are willing to talk to one another, a "middle man" steps in. He must be a person in good standing with both sides. He endeavors to use his good standing with each side to broker their reconciliation. "For my sake," he pleads with one or the other, "For *my* sake, let go of your anger against so-and-so...." We might call this the "middle-man" approach to reconciliation.

According to the Governmental (or "Middle") school of atonement, Jesus had to become such a "middle-man" to broker our reconciliation with God. He became one of us by the incarnation. Furthermore, as a man, Jesus perfectly obeyed all God's laws, even to the point of dying on the cross in His innocence. All this, according to this school of atonement, was simply to establish Jesus' good standing with the Father. His obedience unto death was Jesus' means of establishing His own good standing with the Father. Having done so, Jesus now acts as a "middle-man" to appeal to the Father to forgive sinful men "for My sake."

"This scheme," Symington writes, "may be thought nearer the truth than the former" (p. 11). The Governmental Theory rightly emphasizes the *mediatorial* nature of Jesus' role in atonement. Furthermore, this school regards the cross as truly necessary for atonement. At least in this school it is recognized that Jesus had to die in order for atonement to be possible. In these points, this view is better than the "forgive and forget" position of the Moral Influence school. However, this view is also, in Symington's words, "open to some substantial objections."

Most pointedly, just like the previous view (Moral Influence), the present approach "discards the idea of anything being done to procure pardon" (p. 11). That is, this school rightly acknowledges that Jesus had to die, but it gives the wrong reason. In this view, Jesus died *to secure His own standing* with the Father. This position fails to recognize that Jesus' death was necessary *in order to purchase our forgiveness.*

In the end, this teaching falls to the same problem as the former: "The friends of this system…allow that God could freely forgive the sins of His creatures without any satisfaction [being paid]" (p. 11). The biblical teaching that Jesus, as our Priest, purchased our forgiveness *by sacrifice* is neglected. This "middle-man" view of the atonement is also inadequate.

The Good Works School—Before considering the third view of the atonement (and the one Symington defends as biblical), one other common approach might be noted. It is the approach which we might call the "Good Works" view of atonement.

Unfortunately, it is all too common for people to see God as a "heavenly accountant" who keeps a log of a person's good and bad deeds throughout life. At the end of life, it is assumed that the "numbers" of good and bad deeds will be tallied. If a person has done enough good to outweigh the bad, his overall account is "in the black." He goes (presumably) to heaven. If the person has done more bad than good, his account is "in the red," and eternal judgment is imposed. This view of atonement is rather like the familiar "I'll make it up to you" method so common in human relationships.

The view that one can make atonement with God through good works is, however, so completely unbiblical that Symington did not even discuss it in his book. His concern was to correct misunderstandings about *Christian* atonement—that is, views of atonement which "profess regard to Christ as the only remedy for moral evil"

(p. 10). The "Good Works" approach is really not dependent on Christ at all. Under this school of thought, *we* are expected to be *our own* saviors. It is assumed, by this view, that we can make up for our sins ourselves.

The Good Works approach to atonement is, therefore, not really a *Christian* view of atonement at all (though, sadly, even some inside the church teach this way). There are no biblical grounds for atonement by good works. From the earliest pages of Scripture, atonement has always required *sacrificial payment* (e.g., Gen. 3:15; 4:4; Lev.). Even our best efforts to "make it up" to God are wholly inadequate.

The prophet Isaiah wrote, "But we are all as an unclean thing, and all our righteousnesses are as filthy rags" (Isa. 64:6). Note what Isaiah is teaching in that verse. *We* have become unclean by our sin. The problem is not just a matter of bad deeds, but of *having become* filthy ourselves. The problem is like that of the neighborhood bully who digs up the rose garden and makes a huge muddy mess of himself. Even though he takes a few of the plucked roses in hand when he walks into his mother's kitchen, even the flowers are wilted and muddied. The analogy is not perfect, but it illustrates the point. Isaiah says that "*we* have become unclean" by sin. As a result, even "our righteous deeds" are dirtied by the hands that perform them. To speak more precisely: we carry out even our good deeds with the sins of pride, selfishness, and lack of love for God still in our hearts.

The problem is not so simple as balancing out good and bad deeds in life. The problem is what we have become inside because of our sins, not just what we do with our hands. The inside must be cleansed, and "good works" atonement can never wash the inside.

Jesus said, "I am the way, the truth, and the life: no man cometh unto the Father, *but by me*" (John 14:6). He is the only way to reconciliation with God. We cannot atone for ourselves. Scripture does not teach an "I'll make it up to you" approach to atonement.

3. The Penal Substitution School—The view of atonement which Symington shows to be biblically sound is that which theologians call, "Penal Substitution." This is the orthodox doctrine of atonement, having "been held by the great body of Christians since the days of the apostles" (p. 12). It is not because of the longstanding historicity of the doctrine, however, that Symington supports it, but because of its biblical accuracy.

In this view, Jesus is understood to have become our Priest, who approached the Father on our behalf with a sacrifice—the sacrifice of His own flesh.

A priest must be holy in order to approach God. Jesus alone, of all humanity, lived a perfect, sinless life. He alone could approach the holy God on His own merits. He alone did *not* deserve to suffer or die. Nevertheless, He *did* suffer and die. Why? To take upon Himself the penalty that others deserve. Jesus not only became our Priest to approach God on our behalf, but He became our sacrifice *to die for our sins.* Jesus presented His own body as a sacrifice to pay for our sins. This is what the Apostle Peter wrote: "For Christ also hath once suffered for sins, the just for the unjust, that he might bring us to God" (1 Peter 3:18).

Atonement between men and God is accomplished through Jesus' suffering and dying in our place. This is the meaning of the term, "penal substitution." Jesus' suffering was *penal*—that is, He was fulfilling a *penalty.* God did not merely brush sin aside, or ignore it for the sake of Jesus' goodness. The penalty for human sin must be exacted, and such a penalty was exacted upon Christ. It was not, however, Jesus' own penalty. Rather, Jesus bore that penalty *on behalf of others*—it was *substitutionary.* Hence the term, "penal substitution."

The Penal Substitutionary view of atonement, writes Symington,

> ...is founded on the principle that God is just as well as merciful. It maintains that the pardon of sin is procured by the work of Christ, by which He gave satisfaction to the justice of God on behalf of those to be redeemed. (p. 12)

God does not simply excuse sin. He does exact its full penalty. Christ offered Himself as a substitute for those who trust in Him. It is "penal substitution" that resolves the break between God and man imposed by sin. It is "penal substitution" that achieves atonement and restores man to the present love of God—and the promise of eternal joy.

The rest of Symington's work on the atonement rises from this beginning point—that "The Nature of Christ's Atonement" is penal substitutionary. It was as a *Priest* that Jesus accomplished our atonement—a Priest offering *a substitutionary sacrifice.* From this foundational conviction (and, indeed, to further establish this position), Symington proceeded, in the rest of his book, to expound on the "hows, whys, whens, and whats" of Christ's priestly sacrifice:

• The Necessity of Atonement	*Why "penal substitution"? Couldn't God have done it some other way?*
• The Reality of Atonement	*This is all good theory, but how do I know it is something real I can stake my life upon?*
• The Substance of Atonement	*What exactly was it about Jesus' work that brought about atonement?*
• The Value of Atonement	*How do I know that the payment of this one man was enough to secure atonement for so many?*
• The Extent of Atonement	*If Jesus' sacrifice was "substitutionary," substitutionary for who? Who receives the benefits?*
• The Results of Atonement	*What, in fact, are the benefits secured by atonement?*

The Necessity of Christ's Atonement: Holy Love

Why was it necessary for Jesus to die in order for sins to be forgiven? Couldn't atonement have been achieved some other way?

After all, Genesis 1 shows us that God created everything that exists by simple commands. "Let there be light," He said, "and there was light" (Gen. 1:3). "Let the waters bring forth abundantly the moving creature that hath life," He said, and the waters teemed with new life (Gen. 1:20–21). And so on. The God of the Bible is a God of absolute authority. He only has to speak, and it is (Ps. 33:6–9).

The simplicity of such creation-by-fiat stands in stark contrast to the duration, cost, and agony expended to work out the atonement. If God wields such authority as to speak the universe into existence, why was atonement a work of such great expense (and, frankly, of such brutality)? Symington's section on "The Necessity of Atonement" seeks to show why it was necessary that atonement took place as it did—by penal substitution.

Symington makes it clear up front, however, that God had no obligation to save mankind in the first place. That is, it was not necessary for God to save mankind. It is only because God *did* decide to save men that penal substitution was the necessary method for doing so.

Some theologians have taught that God had no choice but to save. It has often been said, even by the most orthodox of Bible scholars, that God *was obliged* to make a way of salvation for sinners though He did not desire to do so. Francis Turretin, for example, had taught, "God neither has willed, nor could have willed to forgive sins, without...satisfaction made to His justice."[1] In other words, according to Turretin it was only because Jesus atoned for sin that God came to desire reconciliation with man. He did not desire to save man apart from the cross.

Symington believed it important to correct this view. Such a view undermines the clear testimony of Scripture that *love* is the motivating cause of salvation. Symington countered,

> The true view of the matter is this, that divine love is the cause of the atonement, and not that atonement is the cause of divine love.... In the estimation of the inspired writers, the gift of His Son is ever regarded as the most perfect manifestation of the riches of God's grace. 'For God so loved the world, that he gave his only begotten Son....' (pp. 21–22; quoting John 3:16)

Perhaps the following diagram will help contrast the subtle, but important, distinction between these two positions:

---

1. Francis Turretin, "On The Atonement," 133. In James A. Willson, *A Historical Sketch of Opinions on the Atonement, Interspersed with Biographical Notices of the Leading Doctors, and Outlines of the Sections of the Church in North America, From the Introduction of Christianity into that Country to the Year 1817. With Translations from Francis Turretin on The Atonement* (Paisley, 1827), 133–287.

Symington:
(*God loved,*
therefore He saved)

Turretin:
(*God saved,*
therefore He loved)

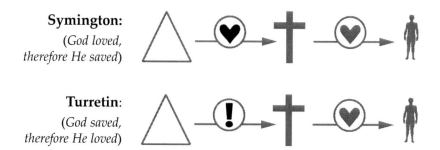

Symington (top) taught that God's love ❤ motivated *both* His decision to save *and* the application of that salvation to men.

Turretin (bottom) taught that the just God could not have *wanted* to save sinners. Some other obligation (such as His own holiness) made it necessary to do so. Some other obligation ❢ motivated God's decision to save, and His great love ❤ for man became possible as a result.

Symington was not the first to emphasize the free love of God behind His decision to save. John Calvin (himself following Augustine) had taught similarly. "In a manner wondrous and divine," Calvin wrote, "He loved even when He hated us."[2] There is a mystery behind God's loving desire to save sinful men (as repugnant as sin is to Him), but He was under no obligation to do so. He saves because He loved.

Symington reasserts this important point, at the beginning of his study on the "Necessity of Christ's Atonement," for two reasons. First, he believed it more faithful to Scripture to keep the wonder of God's free love at the forefront of the atonement. It is divine love (not divine obligation) that saves. Second, this point clarifies what we mean when we speak of the "necessity" of atonement. There was **no** "*absolute* necessity" for atonement. When we speak of the "necessity" of atonement, we do not mean that God was obliged to save. We simply understand that, because God *does* save, it was "*morally* necessary" for it to happen by Christ's sacrifice. If it was going to happen, it had to happen this way. It is this *moral* necessity for *this* atonement that Symington has in view when he speaks of the "Necessity of Christ's Atonement."

---

2. Calvin, *Institutes*, 2.16.4.

Symington offers four kinds of evidence to establish the moral necessity for penal substitution. It had to happen this way, and here are four sets of reasons why:

- *The Perfections of God*—God is just. His character is one of majesty, truth, holiness, justice, and goodness. This being the case, He will never excuse sin without penalty. This is what God Himself declared to Moses when He revealed His nature as "merciful and gracious, longsuffering, and abundant in goodness and truth..., forgiving iniquity and transgression and sin, *and that will by no means clear the guilty...*" (Ex. 34:6–7). Because God is "abundant in goodness," He *does* provide forgiveness. However, because He is just, He will "by no means" do so by ignoring guilt. Symington writes,

  > It is quite a mistake to regard God as acting...at one time according to mercy, and at another according to justice. He acts agreeably to both at all times. The exercise of the one never supposes the suspension of the other. When He punishes the guilty, it is not at the expense of mercy; when He pardons the transgressor, it is not at the expense of justice. Mercy must, therefore, proceed on a principle which is agreeable to justice. (p. 23)

  It is the *penal substitution* of Christ, alone, that could express both the mercy and justice of God together. It is only by this means that God can be both perfectly just *and* perfectly merciful. (Cf. Josh. 24:19; Pss. 5:4, 7:11; Nah. 1:2, 6; Rom. 3:5; Heb. 12:29)

- *The Terms of God's Declared Law*—Upon creating mankind, God established perfect obedience as the basis for the God–man relationship. He also established the penalty of death for disobedience. We find this principle first announced in the Garden of Eden: "And the LORD God commanded the man, saying, ...of the tree of the knowledge of good and evil, thou shalt not eat of it, for in the day that thou eatest thereof thou shalt surely die" (Gen. 2:16–17). This being the declared principle of divine government, *the penalty must be exacted.* Only the principle of penal substitution offers a way of satisfying that penalty on behalf of sinners, thereby allowing their disobedience to be forgiven. (Cf. Ex. 18:20; Deut. 27:26; Matt. 5:18; Gal. 3:10)

- *The Inability of All Other Means*—The above reasons are adequate to demonstrate the necessity for *some* means like penal substitution to be provided. But is there any other means that also would satisfy the nature and law of God? Symington answers with a resounding no. Scripture makes it clear that there is nothing else that would work. Neither apologies, nor spirituality, nor any amount of other efforts can achieve atonement. "No man cometh unto the Father, *but by me*," Jesus said (John 14:6). The Bible shows us no other way whereby a man could be atoned for, *except* the substitutionary death of Christ. (Cf. Rom. 3:20; 11:6; Gal. 3:10; Eph. 2:9)

- *The Scriptures Say It Was Necessary*—The preceding points show various *reasons* why we ought to conclude that penal substitution was necessary. Not only is this a reasonable conclusion, but it is also the explicit statement of Scripture. Lest there be any remaining question about the necessity of Christ's substitutionary atonement, Symington marshals Scriptures that plainly state this to be the case. For example, Jesus told His disciples after the resurrection, "Ought not Christ to have suffered these things...?" (Luke 24:26; cf. Heb. 2:10; 8:3; 9:22–23)

There was no compunction upon God requiring that sinners be saved. Symington would have us beware of ever supposing that God had any obligation to save. "There was nothing in His own character that rendered it absolutely imperative to take any steps whatever toward the remission of iniquity..." (p. 47). (In fact, even the fact that God is *loving* did not oblige Him to save men. He might just as readily have expressed His love by saving the rest of the creation from the sorrow brought through human sin, by purging all mankind. [Cf. Lev. 26:33–34; Prov. 12:10; John 4:11; Rom. 8:20–22]) The atonement was not necessary.

Nevertheless, since God *did* lovingly (and wondrously) choose to save men, a penal substitute was necessary. Symington summarizes,

"The Lord is a jealous God, he will not forgive [i.e., excuse] your
transgressions nor your sins" [Josh. 24:19].... Sin cannot go
unpunished; it cannot be pardoned without satisfaction;
God cannot but take vengeance on iniquity.... Just He is, and
just He ever must be; and there is only one way, that of an
atoning sacrifice, by which He can be at once "a just God and
a Saviour" [Isa. 45:21]. (pp. 51–52)

In the face of so expensive a salvation, unobligingly bestowed,
every Christian can only marvel. Every saint can only praise God
and rejoice that He, "who is rich in mercy, for his great love wherewith he loved us, even when we were dead in sins, hath quickened
us together with Christ (by grace ye are saved)" (Eph. 2:4–5).

The Reality of Christ's Atonement: The Altar and the Cross

"Hitherto," Symington wrote at the opening of this next section,

we have been occupied with what may be reckoned prelimi-
nary matter. It was necessary to explain the nature of atonement...and to evince the necessity [of it].... But these do not
prove the fact of atonement. (pp. 66–67)

We have thus far been like people gathered at the gate of
heaven, examining the lock on the front gate. We can see, from the
lock, what *kind* of key would be required to get in. We can see, by
the construction of the gate, that there is *no other way* to get through
it but to find the right key. But does the right key exist? Has God, in
fact, provided the atonement needed to get in?

The short answer is, "Yes!" The announcement of Scripture is
that God *did*, in fact, "so [love] the world, that he gave his only
begotten Son, that whosoever believeth in him should not perish, but
have everlasting life" (John 3:16). It is to elaborate upon this wonderful truth that Symington wrote on "The *Reality* of Atonement."
The needed "key" *has* been provided. In this section, Symington
also seeks to demonstrate that mankind had *a real promise* to hope
upon, even before the cross. Mankind was not left to wish for the
right "key" to fit the "lock," only to be surprised by its provision.
From the beginning of history, man possessed a real promise from
God of a penal substitute.

In considering the "reality" of Christ's atonement, therefore, we are concerned with the factuality of the *promise,* and the factuality of the *provision,* of a penal substitute.

Symington's evidence can be summarized as follows:

- *The Antiquity and Universality of Sacrifices*—After the very first sin was committed (Adam's fall), God promised a penal substitute. He promised that one would come to take "the bruise" of sin on Himself in order to remove sin once and for all (Gen. 3:15). Indications in the context show that Adam (and his descendants) understood this as a promise of penal substitutionary atonement (e.g., Gen. 3:20; 4:4).

  This account is not mere myth. It indicates a real, historical promise from heaven to all humanity. To show the factuality of this promise, Symington shows how all humanity, from the earliest times, shared a common doctrine of penal substitutionary atonement. Not only Scripture, but writings and artifacts from all ancient peoples attest to the use of sacrifices. As the ancient Roman author Pliny wrote, "All the world have agreed in them [sacrifices], although enemies or strangers to one another" (p. 70).

  Apart from Scripture, one would have to marvel at such an amazing uniformity across the otherwise diverse peoples of the ancient world. Penal substitution bears every mark of a doctrine tracing back to the earliest humans. Scripture, moreover, leaves us no doubt as to the reason for this humanity-wide doctrine. From the time of Adam, and his sacrificing sons Cain and Abel, blood sacrifice for atonement was taught by God. (Cf. Gen. 3:21; 4:4; 8:20–21; 22:13; Ex. 29:14; 30:10; Lev. 9:24; Job 1:5; 42:8–9)

- *The Hebrew Sacrifices and Prophets*—From Adam (and later, Noah), *all* humanity received a common hope of atonement through sacrifice. Not just any sacrifice would do, however. In Israel, God revealed the need for a certain sacrifice—one to be offered through this people. The Levitical laws of sacrifice carefully define the kind of sacrifice God requires—and the kind of sacrifice *He would provide.*

Symington is urgent to show that the ancient believers in Israel *understood* that the animal sacrifices at the temple were anticipatory. They were not themselves the means of actual atonement, but were sacraments by which they laid claim to a promise yet to be fulfilled. Symington points, for instance, to Isaiah's clear description of "the man of sorrows" who would give Himself "like a lamb that is led to the slaughter" to make "intercession for the transgressors" (Isa. 53). King David also wrote of one who would offer His own body as the sacrifice that fulfills God's law (Ps. 40:6–8; cf. Heb. 10:1–10; Ps. 16:10; Acts 2:31). Daniel also prophesied of the coming Prince who would *finally* "atone for iniquity" by His own death (Dan. 9:24–27).

Symington focused his attention on these statements from the prophets due to their particular clarity. We might nonetheless add notice of expressions within the Pentateuch itself showing the anticipatory nature of the Hebrew sacrifices. In Genesis 22, for example, God called Abraham to offer *his son* as a blood sacrifice (i.e., a penal substitute). Abraham was stopped from actually killing Isaac and was given a ram instead. The lesson of that event, nonetheless, is recorded by the text: "it is said to this day, In the mount of the LORD it shall be seen [provided]" (Gen. 22:14). The ram seems to be provided for Abraham as a sacramental seal of that *coming* provision, while Isaac (the heir) indicates the kind of sacrifice "God will provide" (v. 8). In any case, Moses evidently recognized that the sins of Israel ultimately required the personal sacrifice of a righteous substitute. After the golden calf travesty (Ex. 32), Moses offered *himself* to "make an atonement" for sin (Ex. 32:30–34). Even Moses, however, was not adequate to be this needed substitute.

From such material within the Old Testament it can be seen that the author of Hebrews expressed what ancient believers had long known: "For the law having a shadow of good things to come…for it is not possible that the blood of bulls and of goats should take away sins…" (Heb. 10:1–4; cf. Ps. 40:6; 51:16). The sacrifices of the Old Testament were not themselves the means of atonement. They were, however, tangible seals to the factuality of God's promise—"In the mount of the LORD it shall be seen [provided]" (Gen. 22:14; cf. Acts 3:18; 17:3; 26:23; 1 Peter 1:11).

- *The Sufferings of Christ*—The preceding evidence attests to the reality of God's promise to provide a penal substitute for sin. The greatest proof of the atonement's reality is, however, its actual fulfillment. In discussing the sufferings and death of Christ, Symington is not merely concerned that they happened. He is also concerned to show that Christ's death could have had no other reason than atonement. Because Jesus is shown by Scripture to have been without sin, it must have been gross injustice on God's part to bring such sufferings and death against Him—*unless* Jesus died as a penal substitute. For anyone who takes the witness of Scripture seriously, there is no alternative: "For Christ also hath once suffered for sins, the just for the unjust, that he might bring us to God!" [1 Peter 3:18] (p. 135; Cf. Matt. 26–27; Mark 14–15; Luke 22–23; John 18–19; Heb. 5:7; 13:12)

- *The Apostolic Writings*—In his final section on "The Reality of Atonement," Symington works through the statements of the Apostles which explicitly assure us that atonement is not just a need or an ideal, but a fact historically accomplished by the cross. (Cf. Matt. 20:28; Rom. 3:24–25; 4:25; 8:32; 1 Cor. 15:3; 2 Cor. 5:18–21; Gal. 1:4; Eph. 5:2; 1 Thess. 5:10; 1 Tim. 2:6; Titus 2:14; Heb. 9:15, 26; 1 Peter 1:18–19, 2:21, 3:18; 1 John 3:16, 4:10)

We stand at the "gate" of heaven examining the "lock." We do not ponder in vain about the kind of "key" necessary to open it. Not only does Scripture teach us the *kind* of atonement we need, and the *necessity* of that atonement and no other, but we also have every assurance that God *really promised and provided it* in Jesus Christ.

The Substance of Christ's Atonement: His Sufferings

The next question Symington poses is the *how* question: How did Jesus accomplish our atonement? On one hand, the answer is obvious. Jesus atoned for sin *by His sufferings and death* in our place. He is our *penal*—that is, penalty-bearing—substitute. It was by bearing the *penalty* in our place that Jesus made reconciliation between men and God. This is what the Scriptures teach us. For example, we read in Hebrews:

> Without shedding of blood there is no remission.... Where-fore Jesus also, that he might sanctify the people with his own blood, suffered without the gate (Heb. 9:22; 13:12).

It is the consistent testimony of the Scriptures that Jesus *suffered* in order to reconcile us to God (e.g., Rom. 3:24–25, 5:10; Col. 1:20; Heb. 9:14; 1 Peter 3:18; 1 John 1:7).

Some closer examination is necessary, however, for this reason: suffering is not the only thing Jesus did for our redemption. Jesus not only suffered the penalty for breaking God's law, *He also perfectly obeyed the whole law of God*. His perfect obedience on our behalf was also necessary for salvation. We read, for instance, in Paul's epistle to the Romans:

> For as by one man's [Adam's] disobedience many were made sinners, so by the obedience of one [Jesus] shall many be made righteous (Rom. 5:19).

Not only did Jesus *suffer* for us, but He also *obeyed* for us. Theologians often speak of these two aspects of Jesus' work as His "preceptive" and "penal" (or, His "active" and "passive") fulfill-ment of God's law. The preceptive (or active) demands of God's law are its positive requirements to love God and love one another (Matt. 22:37–40; cf. Gal. 5:14). The penal (or passive) demands of God's law are its negative punishments for all law-breakers—ulti-mately death (Gen. 2:17; Rom. 6:23). Jesus fulfilled both the precepts and penalties of God's law.

Symington fully concurs that we needed Jesus to both suffer *and* obey for us. However, Symington drew a careful distinction other theologians had not generally recognized. Although both Jesus' sufferings and obedience are necessary for our full salvation, Symington insists that it is *only* His sufferings that accomplished our *atonement*: "Christ made atonement by His sufferings alone" (p. 149).[3] What is Symington seeking to highlight by this point?

---

3. Symington insisted that theologians must be careful not to confuse the pre-cise terms used in Scripture for different facets, or emphases, within the scope of redemption. He devoted a section at the start of his book to defining the terms

First of all, Scripture itself, as earlier noted, consistently speaks of Christ's *blood* and His *sufferings* as the grounds for our reconciliation. What Symington seeks to point out is that reconciliation is not the whole work of our salvation. "If by the atonement of Christ," he writes, "is meant only a particular department of the work performed by Him for our salvation, correct thinking will require us to restrict our view of its matter [its cause] to His sufferings alone" (p. 150). The Apostle Paul makes such a distinction when he writes,

> For if, when we were enemies, we were reconciled to God by the death of his Son, much more, being reconciled, we shall be saved by his life.... By the obedience of one shall many be made righteous (Rom. 5:10, 19)

It was the sufferings of Jesus that brought about our reconciliation. Nonetheless, we need more than reconciliation with God to be saved. Symington writes,

> The work of Christ...is to be viewed in two lights—as satisfaction to the federal [or, preceptive] demands of the law, and as a compliance with its penal sanction. The former is necessary to give man a title to the life promised in the covenant, and is effected by [Jesus'] positive obedience to the whole precepts of the law. The latter is necessary to free man from the death or curse denounced in the covenant on human disobedience, and is effected by suffering the whole amount of the penalty. Now, it is the last of these objects which is contemplated by the atonement.... (p. 152)

Understanding this distinction will be helped by considering Adam in the Garden of Eden. When God created Adam, he was already in good standing with God. Adam was already in God's favor, for he had never sinned. He was already "at one" with God, enjoying all God's care and blessings. Nonetheless, Adam also had a charge to fulfill which he had not yet fulfilled. God appointed Adam to order the whole earth as a reflection of God's glory (Gen. 1:26–30; 2:5–7, 15, 18–24). That was to be a huge task—a task he would need the help of a whole human family to carry out (Gen.

---

atonement, reconciliation, redemption, propitiation, satisfaction, substitution, vicarious, and *expiation* (pp. 13–19).

2:18–24). Although Adam was already "at one" with God, he still had a task to lead the human race into completion for God.

When Adam sinned, he not only lost his good standing with God, he also brought a curse on the earth, rendering mankind's positive duties even more difficult (Gen. 3:16–19). In order to fulfill our task before God as a race, we need a Savior who can both atone for our loss of God's favor and who can sovereignly bring about the fulfillment of God's glory in the earth. These are the two aspects of God's law—its penalties *and* its preceptive tasks—which Jesus fulfills .

Jesus, by His blood, restores us to God's favor. He makes us "at one" again with the Father. He washes away the sins that placed us outside of divine blessing. In a sense, His atonement restores us to the status of Adam before his fall. The positive task incumbent upon us remains, nonetheless. We not only need Jesus to restore us to God's favor, but we also need Him (as the Second Adam) to lead us into fulfillment of all God's purposes for us. It is in Jesus' obedience to the law, as our new Head, that this further need is also accomplished.

Why is this distinction important? Because it is central to granting Christ full esteem as both our Priest *and our King*. In making this distinction, Symington is preparing the way for his later work on the *kingship* of Christ. It is as our *Priest* that Jesus offered the atoning sacrifice that reconciles men to God. We rightly ascribe the atonement to His labors for us *as our sacrificing Priest*. It is as our *King*, moreover, that Jesus fulfills the righteousness of the law for us. When we fail to carefully ascribe the sufferings alone to Jesus' priestly atonement, and suppose that His obedience also belongs to this priestly work, we are in danger of diminishing the kingly work of Jesus.

In the Old Testament order, it was the temple priests who were charged with the duty of bringing sacrifices before God. It was the duty of the king to establish righteousness in the land. It was the duty of the king of Israel to practice God's law personally (Deut. 18:18–20), and to enforce it and sponsor its teaching publicly (2 Kings 23; 2 Chron. 17:6–9; Ps. 72). When Israel had a righteous king on the throne, the nation prospered under his rule (e.g., 1 Chron. 28:8; 2 Chron. 26:3–15). When Israel had a lawbreaking

king on the throne, the nation shared in and suffered for his rebellion (e.g., 1 Kings 11:9–13; 2 Kings 15:26, 30, 34).

Symington's carefulness to distinguish Jesus' sufferings—and only His sufferings—as the grounds of *atonement* is due to his particular sensitivity to insure that Jesus' *kingly* office is not diminished, nor its importance for our salvation overlooked. As Scripture consistently connects the atonement with Jesus' sufferings, so Symington notes a particular connection between Jesus' obedience and His reign. For example, the Apostle Paul has written,

> Being found in fashion as a man, [Jesus] humbled himself, and *became obedient.... Wherefore God also hath highly exalted him,* and given him a name which is above every name.... (Phil. 2:8, 9)

We can summarize the distinction as follows:

Office	Activity	Result
As our High Priest	Jesus **suffered** the law's penalty (*suffering and death*)	thereby **removing the law's curse** (*divine disfavor unto eternal death*).
As our King	Jesus **obeyed** the law's precepts (*perfect love to God and neighbor*)	thereby **securing the law's blessings** (*divine favor unto eternal life*).

One caution from Symington should be noted. Symington maintains the importance of *conceptually* distinguishing between Jesus' priestly and kingly functions (because Scripture itself teaches us to do so). Nonetheless, Symington also warns against going so far as to suppose that Jesus' *specific activities* could ever be categorized as strictly belonging to one or the other office. He writes,

> It is not to be understood, that, in making this distinction between the positive obedience and penal sufferings of Christ, it is meant to be insinuated that these were ever actually separated from one another.... While He suffered He obeyed, and while He obeyed He suffered; He became *"obedient unto death"* [Phil. 2:8]. (pp. 152–153)

In other words, although Jesus was both our law-satisfying Priest and our law-fulfilling King, He conducted both these offices *in perfect unity* as our Priest-king. Indeed, He also served as our Prophet (revealing God's law) concurrently with His priesthood and kingship (satisfying and fulfilling God's law). As Symington elsewhere explained,

> When [Jesus] taught His disciples, He acted not only as a prophet, but also as a priest and a king; inasmuch as the doctrine He taught brought fully to view His sacerdotal character, and the authority with which His instructions were enforced distinctly recognised His regal power. Again, when as a priest He offered Himself a spotless sacrifice to God, He gave to the world as a prophet a new revelation of the character of God…[and] as a king He triumphed gloriously over His enemies. In like manner, His royal achievements not only manifest His majesty and His power, but serve to publish the clemency of His grace, and to recognise the merit of His atoning sacrifice.…[4]

Jesus is not at once a Prophet, at another time a Priest, and later a King: He is at all times our Prophet-Priest-King. It is for this reason that we can take comfort that everyone whom Jesus convicts (as Prophet), He also atones for (as Priest) and secures in eternal glory (as King). Symington states reassuringly,

> No one ever reaps the fruits of the one, without reaping also those of the other; whoever is delivered from death [by Jesus' penal substitution], is made a partaker also of life [earned by His obedience]; whoever is freed from condemnation, is put in possession of a valid title to glory; whoever receives *forgiveness of sins,* obtains, at the same time, *inheritance among them who are sanctified.* (p. 153)

Jesus neither achieved our redemption "one office at a time," nor do we receive His benefits "one office at a time." Nevertheless, as seamlessly as these offices are fulfilled by Jesus, it is Scripture that teaches us to conceive of Christ's work with these distinctions in view (e.g., Ps. 2:6; Acts 3:22; Heb. 5:6). Properly ascribing these offices to Christ is important for our accurate understanding of redemption.[5]

---

4. Symington, *Messiah the Prince,* 2.

5. For these offices of Christ as recognized in the various Reformed standards, see *Heidelberg Catechism* 31; *Westminster Confession of Faith* ch 8; *Westminster Shorter Catechism* 23–26; *Westminster Larger Catechism* 43–45.

Symington's careful ascription of Jesus' sufferings to His priestly atonement, and His obedience to His royalty, was one of the important emphases of his book. Few had drawn this distinction quite so clearly before. The Continental Reformers—men like Martin Luther and John Calvin—had labored for a proper understanding of Jesus' priestly work. They by no means overlooked His kingly office, but the kingship of Christ did not receive the same degree of attention prior to the Scottish Second Reformation. As Dutch theologian Willem Visser 't Hooft remarked,

> Protestantism stands in a theological tradition in which the priestly and prophetic ministries of Christ have been strongly worked out but in which the kingly office has been obscured.... The Reformers are more reserved in their teaching concerning the Kingship of Christ than they are about His other offices.[6]

It was in the so-called "Second Reformation" in Scotland that Christ's mediatorial reign came to be more fully explored (see pp. 7–19, above). In Symington's handling of the "Substance of Christ's Atonement," we find one of his particular contributions as penman of the Scottish Covenanters. By restricting the atonement to that which was accomplished by Christ's sufferings, Symington is opening the way for a full appreciation of His law-fulfilling, kingdom-building work as *Messiah the Prince*.

The Value of Christ's Atonement: The Worth of the Lamb

When someone bumps a glass from the edge of a table, we know what the outcome will be. Unless someone is there to catch it, it will fall to the floor and very likely break. When a family member walks into the room laughing, we are prone to ask, "What happened?" Something must have tickled his or her funny bone to prompt such laughter. When a fire breaks out somewhere in town, investigators endeavor to find out how it started. What caused the fire?

Each of these scenarios illustrates the everyday operation of causes and effects. We are so familiar with the law of cause and effect, that it has become common sense. For every effect—whether

---

6. Visser 't Hooft, 1948: 14.

a broken glass on the floor, a person's laughter, or a fire—we expect to find a cause behind it.

We also expect there to be a measure of equality between causes and effects. Sir Isaac Newton famously expressed it this way: "For every action there is an equal and opposite reaction." In other words, to lift a *ten* pound weight, one has to exert *ten* pounds of force; to lift a *fifty* pound weight, one must exert *fifty* pounds of force. To put the same principle into financial terms, it is not possible to pay off a $600 bank overdraft with a $50 check. For every effect desired (wiping out a $600 debt), there must be a cause equal to it (a $600 payment).

The principle of cause and effect has had significant influence on how people understand the sufferings of Christ. If Jesus' sufferings atoned for vast myriads of sinful men and women, the question can hardly be avoided. Were the sufferings of one man sufficient to pay the penalty for so many? The *effect* of His atonement is immeasurably great. Is the *cause*—one man's bleeding and dying—really equal to so great an effect?

This is the question behind a study of the "value" of Christ's atonement. And because of the principle of equality between causes and effects, theologians have often felt compelled to ascribe to Christ suffering equivalent to a myriad eternities. If one were to put a "pain thermometer" to Jesus' lips while He was on the cross, and a "pain thermometer" into the eternal sufferings due to the vast millions of saved humanity, some have assumed there would need to have been a literal equivalence. Jesus' sufferings on the cross, it has sometimes been taught, were equal to the sum total of all the sufferings due to all those He saved.[7]

---

7. For a few examples: John Owen demanded the *"idem"* and *"tantundum"* of sufferings (John Owens, *The Works of John Owen* [Edinburgh: Johnson and Hunter, 1853], 12.492); Francis Turretin wrote, "[Christ] satisfied to the uttermost farthing… the debts which man owed…." (Francis Turretin, 1827, 181–182); John Brown of Wamphray taught, "Christ suffered the same in substance that the elect were liable to suffer; the same curse and death, the same punishment in its essential ingredients" (in James Walker, *The Theology and Theologians of Scotland* [Edinburgh: T&T Clark, 1872], 46). In fact, in his overview of Scottish theologians generally, James Walker concluded: "…the old Scotch divines cling to the view that Christ not merely suffered, but bore the same sufferings in kind which were due to His people" (p. 46).

Symington wrote to show that: yes, Jesus' sufferings were supremely equal to so great a salvation; but no, Jesus did not have to suffer on the cross in mechanical equivalence to the penalties due to those He redeemed. Symington explains,

> The value of Christ's atonement, we conceive to arise, not from the nature, or intensity, or continuance of His sufferings. The work of Jesus was not a mere commercial affair of debts and payment. We have no conception that, had the number of those for whom He suffered been greater than it was, or had their sins been more numerous or more aggravated than they were, His sufferings must have been proportionately increased. (p. 162)

Symington used the analogy of the sun to elaborate this point. Whether God had made the world for just one person or for millions, the same sun and same amount of daily sunshine would have been necessary. Similarly, there is no reason to suppose that Jesus' sufferings would have increased or decreased according to the number of people saved. In fact, in terms of *value,* Jesus' death is actually greater than the effect achieved.

Symington would argue that Jesus' sacrifice is of *infinite* value, and is therefore *worthy enough* to have atoned for the whole human race. The gospel can be freely declared to the whole world because Jesus' death *really is valuable enough* to atone for every single human being. Not every human being *is* atoned for by Jesus' death (as will be more closely examined under the "Extent of Christ's Atonement," below). Nonetheless, in terms of its *value,* Jesus' death really was sufficient to save all humanity.

To demonstrate "The Value of Christ's Atonement," Symington provides a biblical exposition of these six points:

- *The Dignity of the Savior's Person*—Jesus is the Son of God, "the brightness of his glory, and the express image of his person" (p. 162; Heb. 1:3). Symington notes that Jesus' worth as a sacrificial Lamb is profoundly adequate to the task because of His *infinite* moral worth as the Son of God. He was not just one man upon the cross, He was the perfect Son of God giving Himself for sinners. (Cf. 2 Sam. 18:3; Heb. 9:12–14; 1 John 4:9–10)

- *His Relationship to His People*—Although Jesus was truly divine, and hence a sacrifice of unspeakable worth, He was also truly man. His humanity is what made Him of value as a substitute *for men.* Bulls, goats, and sheep were never "causes" equal to the effect of removing human sin. The humanity of Christ is an important aspect of His value to atone for human sin. (Cf. Gen. 3:15; Heb. 2:11, 17; 1 Cor. 15:21)

- *His Freedom from Sin*—Because Jesus was without sin Himself, He had no obligation to suffer. This freedom from any penalty *of His own* meant that His suffering was of great value *for others.* Not one iota of all that immense value inherent to His suffering was needed to atone for Himself. All that sacrificial merit was *for others.* (Cf. Num. 19:2; Deut. 21:3; Ps. 16:10; Isa. 53:9; Matt. 27:4; Mark 1:24; Luke 1:35, 23:4; John 8:29, 46; 2 Cor. 5:21; Heb. 4:15, 7:26–27; 1 Peter 2:22; 1 John 3:5)

- *His Voluntary Sacrifice (1)*—Jesus was under no obligation to die for mankind. Jesus Himself said, "I lay down my life... No man taketh it from me, but I lay it down of myself..." (John 10:17–18). In this truth, Symington draws a parallel to the previous point (above). Not only (as seen above) was Jesus under no penal obligation to die, He also was under no preceptive obligation to die. Nothing of His sacrificial merit was necessary for His own obligations. "He...acted voluntarily" (p. 176), and so the value of Jesus' gift is *wholly* attributable to others.

- *His Voluntary Sacrifice (2)*—Closely related to the previous point: Symington sees in the voluntary nature of Christ's sacrifice another factor magnifying its great moral worth. "In all that He did," Symington notes, "to make atonement for sin, Jesus manifested no degree of reluctance" (p. 177). Scripture points to this willingness of Christ as one of the features of His sacrifice: "I gave my back to the smiters, and my cheeks to them that plucked off the hair..." (Isa. 50:6). Symington believes this untarnished willingness itself contributes to the superior moral value of Christ's sacrifice. (Cf. Ps. 40:7–8;

Isa. 50:6; Matt. 16:22–23; Luke 2:49; 9:51; John 10:17–18, 18:11; 1 Tim. 2:6; Eph. 5:25)

- *The Appointment of the Father*—Last of all (and perhaps most importantly), Symington remarks, "In a compensatory arrangement, such as the atonement is, *both* parties must be voluntary. Not only must the one party be willing to make the compensation; the other must be willing to accept of it when made" (p. 180). Of utmost importance is not only the fact that Jesus suffered, but the knowledge that *God the Father accepted this payment as compensation* for the sins of the many. The Father did accept Jesus' sacrifice to satisfy His wrath against so much sin. This fact, in itself, confirms that *Jesus' value as a sacrifice* was great enough to atone for the many, even if His sufferings were not literally the same. "The sufferings borne by Christ," Symington states, "were not the identical punishment required by the law but a proper equivalent, with which the great moral Governor was pleased to be *satisfied* in its place…" (p. 16). (Cf. John 10:18, 14:31; Acts 2:23, 4:27–28; Rom. 3:25; Gal. 1:4; 1 Peter 1:19–20; Rev. 13:8)

It is not necessary to suppose that there was a mathematical equivalence between the pain of Jesus and the pain of a billion eternities, or a "drop-for-drop" equivalence between His blood shed and the blood of all the redeemed. It is rather because of the unique worth of this Lamb that Jesus' atonement was completely sufficient for a myriad of sinners.

Jesus' words, as He hung on the cross, can be trusted. "It is finished," He declared (John 19:30). Everything has been paid. The atonement is fully accomplished, and there is nothing more for those trusting in Him to pay. His single sacrifice, of infinite moral value, was more than equal to the effect secured.

The Extent of Christ's Atonement: All God's Elect

The next question Symington addresses is the *who* question: for whom did Jesus' die? Did He die to atone *for all humanity*, or was His suffering and death *for a subset of humanity* only? In theology, the terms "unlimited" atonement and "limited" (or, "particular") atonement are used for these views. When we speak of the "extent" of the atonement, we are asking whether Jesus atoned for all mankind ("unlimited atonement") or for some of the human race ("particular atonement").

This question has been one of the most controversial topics in the church since the Reformation. It was the teaching of the late sixteenth-century Dutch theologian, James Arminius, that brought it to the forefront of Protestant debate. Arminius taught the "unlimitedness" of Jesus' atonement. (Those holding this view have, therefore, become known as "Arminians.") In contrast, the "particular" position is generally ascribed to John Calvin. (Thus, those holding to "particular atonement" are often called "Calvinists.") It is not really fair to either Arminius or Calvin to place such weight on this single doctrine as "the" proof of agreement with one or the other's teachings. Nonetheless, the question of extent has become so controversial in Protestant churches as to be often used as "the" distinctive identifier of a "Calvinist" or an "Arminian."

Because of the heightened controversy surrounding this topic, Symington devoted special attention to clarifying the question before answering it. Unfortunately, many of the teachings put forward on the "extent" of atonement fail to distinguish *what aspect of Jesus' atonement* is being measured as "unlimited" or "limited" in the first place. Symington began by clarifying more precisely what the question of extent actually is (and is not) about:

1. First of all, "the point in dispute…does not respect *the intrinsic worth* of Christ's death" (p. 185). The question here at issue is not whether Jesus' death was of limited or unlimited *value*. "As has been shown in the preceding section [The Value of Atonement]," Symington writes, "…the sacrifice of the Lord Jesus Christ possessed an intrinsic value *sufficient* for the salvation of the whole world" (p. 185). Calvinists and Arminians can all agree: In terms of worth, Jesus' atonement was "unlimited." But it is not the value of the atonement that is here being considered.

2. Symington states in his second point, "[neither does] the present controversy turn on the *application* of Christ's atonement" (p. 186). That is, Calvinists and nearly all Arminians agree that not all persons are, ultimately, saved. Only some men and women are saved in the end. Praise God, it is a

large "some" that will be saved (Rev. 7:9). Nonetheless, Scripture makes it clear that there will be those who do not participate in the benefits of the atonement, but rather suffer in hell for eternity (Rev. 20:15). Both sides of the debate can agree: In terms of the results (or application) of the atonement, the extent is "limited." But it is not the final results of atonement that are debated.

(There are those who believe in an "empty hell"—that no one will actually be eternally judged. Such people are called "universalists." Scripture is clear enough, however, that eternal punishment is real [e.g., Dan. 12:2; Matt. 7:13; Mark 9:43; 2 Thess. 1:9; Rev. 20:12–15] that most Arminians are agreed with Calvinists on the "limited" results of the atonement.)

3. "The present question, then," Symington remarks, "hinges solely on the *divine intention* regarding the subjects of atonement" (p. 187). The question at issue is not about the extent of the atonement's *value* (which was unlimited) or its *results* (which are limited), but its *intent*. Did God *intend* for Jesus' death to atone for a limited or unlimited number of humanity? Was it the whole human race, or just particular people, that Jesus had on His heart when He went to the cross? It is the extent of the atonement's *intent* that is here at issue.

By opening with these three points, Symington already contributes significantly toward clarifying the controversy, and helping make way for its resolution. Focusing on the *intent* question, Symington offers several possible answers. There are three conclusions which might be suspected, and they can be outlined as follows:[8]

On the cross, Jesus intended His atonement for—

ⓐ	**some** of the sins	of **all** people;
ⓑ	**all** of the sins	of **all** people;
ⓒ	**all** of the sins	of **some** people.

---

8. Symington actually introduces a fourth possibility as well: that Jesus died for *all* sin generically, but *no persons* specifically. For simplicity's sake, it will be adequate to consider this fourth option as a variation of ⓑ, as the "all people" under point ⓑ might be conceived as either specific or generic.

Symington shows that we can rule out alternative ⓐ right away as a biblical impossibility. To leave men with some sins unpaid for is to leave them condemned. As previously seen (p. 145, above), it is utterly impossible for man to make *any* atonement for himself. Scripture assures us that there are, indeed, *many* who are saved (Rev. 5:9). Furthermore (and most importantly), Scripture is clear that Jesus *completed* the payment for the sins of those for whom He atoned. "By the which will," Hebrews tells us (speaking of the Father's intent which Jesus made His own intent)—"by the which will we are sanctified through the offering of the body of Jesus Christ once *for all*" (Heb. 10:10). It was the will of God that *all* the sins of those atoned for be wiped away in Jesus' sacrifice.

Alternative ⓐ—that Jesus died for *some* of the sins of *all* people—can be ruled out from the start. (Another alternative not stated by Symington, that Jesus might have intended to atone for *some* of the sins of *some* people, can also be ruled out for the same reasons.)

The question really boils down to possibilities ⓑ or ⓒ. These are the positions of "unlimited atonement" (that Jesus had *all people* on His heart when He went to the cross), and "particular atonement" (that Jesus had only *specific people* on His heart when He went to the cross). Between these two alternatives, Symington finds the latter ("particular" atonement, ⓒ) to be supported by Scripture. The supposition that Jesus intended His atonement for all men ("unlimited" atonement, ⓑ) arises from misunderstanding of a few key texts as can be readily shown.

Symington defends particular atonement based on the following teachings of Scripture:

- *The Certainty of the Divine Purpose*—The first fact Symington shows from Scripture is that the purposes of God can never be thwarted. "I know," Job confessed after his encounter with God, "that thou canst do every thing, and that no thought can be withholden from thee" (Job 42:2). It cannot be supposed that God should ever intend to atone for a person and not bring it about. Even the Apostle Paul, who called himself the "chief of sinners" (1 Tim. 1:15), could not resist the pursuit of God. The Lord knew how to bring the full effects of the atonement to bear on that persecutor of the church (Acts 9:3–18). That all God's intentions are always accomplished, is a truth which alone mitigates against supposing His *intent* in the atonement was any different than its final *result*. (Cf. Ps. 33:11, 115:3, 135:6; Eccl. 3:14; Rom. 8:30)

- *The Integrity of Divine Justice*—Scripture also teaches us that God is perfectly just. He judges for sin, but He does not judge men for sins for which they bear no guilt (Deut. 24:16; 2 Kings 14:6; Ezek. 18:17, 20). If Jesus' atonement, therefore, was intended for *all* the sins of *all* mankind, how can any man be condemned to hell? If their sins were all washed away at the cross, then nothing remains against any man's account for which he can be eternally judged. Because of the integrity of divine justice, Symington reasons, it must be that the *intent* of Jesus' payment matches with its final *results*. Those who are eternally condemned were not atoned for at the cross. (Cf. Gen. 18:25; Ps. 11:5–7)

- *Those Included in the Covenant of Grace*—Scripture teaches us that salvation is granted *through a covenant*. In both Old and New Testaments, Scripture speaks of that covenant as established by God with *a specific family* of humanity: the believing seed of Abraham in the Old Testament (Gen. 17:7; Rom. 9:6–8), and the adopted seed of Abraham through Christ in the New Testament (Gal. 3:29). The covenant of grace is consistently represented as between God and a specific circle of humanity. Symington would urge that the intent of the covenanted atonement ought surely to be recognized as embracing the same circle of humanity as addressed by the covenant itself. (Cf. Gen. 3:15; 17:7; Ex. 24:8; Luke 22:20)

- *The Nature of Atonement*—To suppose that the atonement is intended for all men is to contradict the very "Nature of Atonement" demonstrated earlier. Atonement cannot be a complete, full, and final payment in the place of others (i.e., "penal substitution") if only some of those "substituted" for are thereby relieved of guilt. Symington believes that a consistent embrace of biblical teaching on the *nature* of the atonement requires the expectation of its particular intent. (Cf. pp. 136–142, above.)

- *The Evidence of Christ's Resurrection and His Spirit*—Scripture makes a close connection between the death of Christ, His resurrection, and the giving of the Spirit. Those who benefit from any one of these consistently share in the benefits of the others as well. To suppose that all men were provided with benefits from Christ's death (atonement), but do not share in the resurrection-hope and the Spirit, is to contradict Scripture on this point. Symington therefore concludes that the scope of the atonement is the same as the effects of the resurrection and the outpouring of the Spirit. (Cf. John 17:9, 24, 20:20–22; Rom. 4:25, 8:32; 1 Cor. 15:20–23; 1 Thess. 4:14; Gal. 3:13–14, 4:4–6; 1 John 5:6)

- *The Limited Extent of Divine Revelation*—In both Old and New Testaments, the application of salvation has always been connected to the proclamation of the gospel. In the Old Testament, God made a "limited" revelation of the gospel through its announcement to a particular people (not the whole world). In the New Testament, although the gospel now goes out into all lands, the application of salvation is still tied to its proclamation, which necessarily limits its effect. If God's *intent* for the atonement was unlimited, it must be regarded as peculiar that He chose to tie its effect to such a *limited* means of application as preaching. God sends His *Word* where He wants men to be saved, and sometimes He goes to amazing lengths to insure the Word goes forth (e.g., 2 Kings 5:2–4, 17). But God has not been "unlimited" in His spread of Revelation. Symington sees in the "limited" nature of divine revelation a further indication that God's *intent* in atonement is specific, rather than universal. (Cf. Ps. 103:7, 147:20; Acts 16:31; Rom. 10:17)

- *The Unreasonableness of Other Suppositions*—It is from Scripture that Symington draws his conclusions. Nonetheless, even simple logic can sometimes be used to show the inconsistency of one position in contrast to another. Symington accordingly works through the logic for each of the various possible views on the extent of atonement noted earlier (p. 162, above). Even from a strictly logical examination,

Symington shows that only position © is reasonable: that Christ died for *all* the sins of *some* people.

- *The Direct Testimony of Scripture*—At the last, then, Symington produces a compilation of scriptures which expressly state the "limited" (rather than "unlimited") focus of the atonement. In the Old Testament, for example, the prophet Isaiah foresaw the atonement of Christ as aimed at a *particular* people: "for the transgression *of my people* was he stricken" (Isa. 53:8). Furthermore, in Jesus' prayer on His way to the cross, Jesus plainly states that He had a very specific circle of humanity on His heart as He prepared to die: "I pray for them: I pray not for the world, but for them which thou hast given me" (John 17:9; cf., v. 20). In that prayer, Jesus consecrated His body as an atoning sacrifice for particular people, "not the whole world." It was for all the sins of some people that Jesus offered Himself a sacrifice on the cross that night. (Cf. Amos 3:2; Matt. 7:21–23, 11:25; John 10:11, 15, 26–28, 17:19, 24; Rom. 5:8–9; 2 Cor. 5:21; Eph. 5:25; 2 Tim. 2:19; Titus 2:14; 2 Peter 3:9)

Through his elaboration on each of these eight points, Symington wrote to show that the biblical teaching on the atonement is the "particular" (or "limited") view (alternative ©, above). Scripture uses the term "the elect" to describe those whom God has thus appointed to salvation (e.g., Rom. 8:33; 1 Peter 1:2). Symington, and other particular-atonement theologians, often use the biblical terms "elect" and "election," therefore, to speak of those included in the atonement.

Symington was conscious that of all the topics addressed thus far, this is probably the most delicate. Many who embrace the Arminian position ("unlimited atonement") do so because of a sincere effort to be faithful to Scripture and the loving character of God. Even after advancing his defense of "limited" atonement, therefore, Symington devoted an additional twenty-nine pages to handling specific objections on this point. Without reviewing all that Symington has to say in those twenty-nine pages, two kinds of objections commonly raised might be considered.

1. Objections Based on God's Word—One of the most frequent objections (both in Symington's day and our own) is the language of certain scriptures which seem to say that Christ atoned for "the whole world." The following are probably the most frequently mentioned:[9]

> For *God so loved the world,* that he gave his only begotten Son, that whosoever believeth in him should not perish but have everlasting life (John 3:16).

> And he is the propitiation for our sins: and not for ours only, but also *for the sins of the whole world* (1 John 2:2).

How are such "whole world" expressions to be understood? Does Scripture contradict itself when we read these "whole world" expressions on the one hand, and then we find Paul writing, that *"whom he did predestinate...he* also called,... he also justified,... he also glorified" (Rom 8.29–30)? Did Jesus die with the whole world on His heart, or did He die to justify only a predestined group? Symington shows that there is no contradiction here, as long as these "whole world" texts are interpreted *within the New Testament's own context.*

It is a prominent theme throughout the Apostolic writings that the gospel is no longer tied to a particular race (the Jews). After the cross, the gospel is to be taken aggressively beyond Israel into all the world. As Paul writes so extensively in all his epistles, "There is neither Jew nor Greek...if ye be Christ's, then are ye Abraham's seed..." (Gal. 3:28–29). Texts which emphasize the "whole world" nature of the atonement are part of the prominent, New Testament effort to correct the influential, first-century Jewish teaching that salvation is only for Jews (Acts 10:34–36, 45; 11:18; 15:1, 24–29). Though Jesus died according to the laws of the Jewish temple sacrifices, it must not be supposed that His death benefited Jews alone. Saying that He died "for the whole world" was another way of saying that

---

9. Symington individually explains each of the following passages where the "whole world" is connected with the atonement: John 1:29, 3:16–17, 4:42, 6:51; 2 Cor. 5:19; 1 John 2:1–2 (pp. 284–7). He also explains passages where "all men" are said to be connected with atonement: John 12:32; Rom. 5:18; 1 Cor. 15:22; 2 Cor. 5:14–15; 1 Tim. 2:6, 4:10; Heb. 2:9 (pp. 288–92).

people "of all nations, and kindreds, and people, and tongues" are included in the atonement (Rev. 7:9).

In fact, it was the Apostle John who penned those two texts quoted above (John 3:16; 1 John 2:2), that are so often cited to support unlimited atonement. However, John elsewhere offers his own elaboration on what he means by the "whole world" extent of Christ's atonement. In another of his writings, John describes the extent of Christ's atonement in this way:

> And they sang a new song, saying, Thou art worthy...for thou wast slain, and hast redeemed us to God by thy blood out of every kindred, and tongue, and people, and nation (Rev. 5:9).

Although "whole world" passages such as the above are a common basis for unlimited atonement teaching, more careful attention shows that there is no contradiction in Scripture. Scripture consistently teaches particular atonement, but it is a particular atonement that includes a vast circle of humanity from all nations and peoples.

2. Objections Based on God's Character—More often than not, the reason proponents of unlimited atonement gravitate to that view is because they are (rightly) passionate about the love of Christ. As Symington has so beautifully affirmed from the beginning of his book, it is divine love—and lavish love, at that—which motivates the atonement. Christians often embrace the doctrine of unlimited atonement because it seems, at first blush, that unlimited atonement is more loving and thus more consistent with God's character. Symington would urge us, however, to consider the nature of God's love more carefully.

The three views on the extent of atonement might be restated in terms of the love thereby displayed, in the following manner:

Through His work of salvation, Jesus *shows His great love* by—

   ⓐ   **partially** saving   **all** people;

   ⓑ   **totally** saving   **all** people;

   ⓒ   **totally** saving   **some** people.

Viewed this way, line ⓑ would be the position of *universalists*. Universalists completely discount all biblical testimony about

eternal torment, presuming that the love of God means all humanity must be saved in the end. Such a position, however, completely
ignores the authority of Scripture as our textbook on the real nature
of God's *holy* love.

Those who take seriously the reality of eternal torment, but
maintain an unlimited *intent* behind the atonement, would therefore be compelled to adopt position ⓐ. This view expects that God
manifests His love by *intending* to save all people, though for some
reason leaving off from (or proving unable to) totally save them
all. It is thus perceived that God's universal *intention* displays the
glory of His love, even though entrance to heaven will not *actually*
be granted to everyone.

Instead, Symington would lead us to marvel at the love displayed in God's *total salvation* of all those He "set his love upon"
(Deut. 7:7). He leaves nothing undone, and nothing hanging in the
balance. His love is manifest in its thorough and certain application
(position ⓒ, above). There is no limitation on His power to save
(Matt. 19:25–26), and everyone on whom God sets His love He does,
utterly and unfailingly, bring all the way into eternal glory.

> Let saints rejoice that not one of those for whom Christ died
> shall come short of eternal life, for whom God did predesti-
> nate to be conformed to the image of His Son, them He shall
> certainly glorify [Rom. 8:30].... We deny that [the atonement]
> is universal, but we rejoice to think, notwithstanding, that
> it extends to a multitude which no man can number [Rev.
> 7:9]—that "number without number" of redeemed men,
> who, gathered from every nation, and people, and kindred,
> and tongue, shall, with harmonious voices and grateful
> hearts, sing praises to the Lamb that sitteth on the throne, for
> ever and ever. (pp. 233–234)

It is not because God's love is limited that not all mankind are
saved in the end. Rather, it is because God is *holy* that there remains
an eternal punishment for sin. We can praise God that He is also
loving, and that His love is perfectly fulfilled for all the elect. No
one for whom Christ atoned will be left out of heaven—and vast is
the number of those redeemed.

The Results of Christ's Atonement: All God's Promises Fulfilled

All that has gone before has to do with "the way atonement works."
It remains now to consider "what atonement brings about." The
final question to be considered could be stated this way: "What are
the results brought by the atonement?" Symington admits the inad-
equacy of any effort to completely answer that question:

> The results of the great doctrine we have thus endeavoured
> to explain, establish, and defend, are so numerous and diver-
> sified that an attempt fully to discuss, or even to enumerate
> them all cannot be presumed. But...we beg the reader's at-
> tention to the following.... (p. 234)

Symington gives these seven results of Christ's atonement:

- *God's Character is Revealed*—The atonement makes a public
  manifestation of the vast power of God, His manifold wisdom, and also His numerous moral attributes. His holiness,
  justice, grace, compassion, mercy, and love are all given
  public expression at the cross. The cross is, within the whole
  span of Scripture, the supreme demonstration of God's
  wholly just and wholly merciful character to us. (Cf. Rom.
  5:8, 8:32; Eph. 1:8; 1 Peter 1:5; 1 John 4:10)

- *God's Moral Law is Affirmed*—The perfect moral law which
  God has appointed for His creation is vindicated and upheld
  by the cross. Rather than abandoning His creation to sin on
  the one hand, or abandoning His moral holiness for the sake
  of the creation on the other, the atonement establishes both.
  God's moral law is vindicated by the atonement. (Cf. Gen.
  2:17; Matt. 5:17; Rom. 7:12)

- *Sin's Wickedness is Exposed*—The cross makes the true nature
  of sin clear. It is the horror of sin's price at the cross that causes
  us to understand the true extent of its wickedness. Without
  the penalty of sin so vividly before us, we would always tend
  to belittle the seriousness of sin. (In fact, even with the horror
  of the cross before us, we often tend to dismiss the seriousness of sin.) Quoting another, Symington remarks, "The cross
  is 'the mirror which reflects the true features and lineaments
  of moral evil'" (p. 239). The atonement reveals the true character of sin. (Cf. Rom. 1:18; 7:13; Heb. 10:3)

- *Glory is Purchased for the Elect*—By Christ's atonement, "Every legal obstruction to the salvation of man is thus taken away" (p. 241). Sinful men are reconciled to God and restored to His favor. The way has thus been opened for further works of grace, such as the Spirit's ongoing sanctification of the inner man after righteousness and the believer's certainty of final glory. Symington points out that, among all the glories of heaven portrayed in the book of Revelation, it is Jesus—*by His sacrificial title, the Lamb*—who is constantly at its center. All the blessings of eternity, which Symington takes great delight to wade through in his recitations of Scripture, are secured by and because of that cornerstone work of "The Lamb" on the cross. (Cf. Ps. 16:11; Rom. 8:1, 33; Gal. 3:13–14; Eph. 2:18; Col. 1:14; Heb. 4:16, 10:10, 13:12; Rev. 5:6, 9, 13; 6:16; 7:9, 10, 17; 22:1, 3)

- *Divine Mercy is Extended Among Men*—The cross is not just a static event, but it is a dynamic means by which mercy flows out among men. The atonement gives the sinner reason to hope and believe. It gives the believer reason to rejoice and be filled with the fruits of gratitude. The message of the cross, in and of itself, has an ongoing result—softening and applying God's mercy to human hearts. (Cf. Matt. 11:28; Luke 5:32, 23:27–28; Rom. 10:4; 1 Tim. 1:15; Heb. 13:15; 1 Peter 1:8)

- *All God's Works in the World are Advanced*—The cross is the center of God's work in history. Even the creation of the world is presented in Scripture as preparing a stage for the atonement. Symington writes, "'All things were created *by* him, and *for* him.' He is the *final* as well as the *efficient* cause of this world's creation" (p. 248). All God's works among men find some vital link to the cross. (Cf. Ps. 78:38; Rom. 5:1; 1 Cor. 1:23, 2:2; Gal. 6:14; Col. 1:14, 16)

- *A Theme of Eternal Praise is Begun*—Not only will men and women continue to contemplate and rejoice in Christ's atonement for all eternity, but even beings outside of our race—the angels—find their cause for eternal meditation and praise in that one-time event. The atonement is the chorus at the heart of all creation's eternal praise. (Cf. Eph. 3:10; Heb. 2:3; 1 Peter 1:12; Rev. 5:12)

In essence, Symington draws the conclusion that all God's grace toward man stands upon and flows through the cross. The atonement is nothing less than the centerpiece of all God's work. Without the atonement, all humanity would be utterly without hope and already engulfed in the torments of His just judgment. Because of the cross, there is opened up a way of life—and how rich and glorious indeed is that life. This is what Jesus prayed for on behalf of His elect on His way to the cross:

> The glory which thou gavest me I have given them; that they may be one, even as we are one [i.e., atonement].... Father, I will that they also, whom thou hast given me, be with me where I am; that they may behold my glory, which thou hast given me: for thou lovedst me before the foundation of the world.... I have declared unto them thy name, and will declare it: that the love wherewith thou hast loved me may be in them, and I in them" (John 17:22–26).

✦   ✦   ✦

In his characteristic concern to help his readers, Symington summarized the whole teaching of his book on the atonement in a single definition. In four lines, Symington concisely outlined the whole scope of the atonement which his book treats in detail—

The atonement means:

- *That perfect satisfaction given to the law and justice of God,*
- *by the sufferings and death of Jesus Christ,*
- *on behalf of elect sinners of mankind,*
- *on account of which they are delivered from condemnation.* (p. 12)

That definition is a mouthful, but it is one which Symington carefully compiled to reflect the riches of an immense doctrine in a concise phrase. Symington's whole book, in a sense, can be regarded as an explanation of that definition (or, conversely, this definition might be viewed as a summary of his book).

- *The atonement is "that perfect satisfaction...on behalf of...sinners."* "The *Nature* of Atonement" is *penal substitutionary.* Christ, by His payment, perfectly satisfies, and really satisfies, the penalty of the law on someone else's behalf.

- *The atonement is a "satisfaction given to the law and justice of God."*
  "The *Necessity* of Atonement" is *holy love*—that is: God's holiness made it necessary for atonement to happen this way, even though it was only because of His free love that such atonement is provided at all. For divine "law and justice" to be *satisfied,* penal substitution had to be made if there was to be any salvation.

- *The atonement is accomplished in the "death of Jesus Christ."*
  "The *Reality* of Atonement" is seen in *the altar and the cross.* Not only is atonement something to long for, but it is something as historically real as the cold stones of the temple altar and the rough splinters of Christ's cross.

- *The atonement is "by the sufferings and death of Jesus Christ."*
  "The *Substance* of Atonement" is *Christ's sufferings.* The sufferings of Jesus (including all His sufferings and only His sufferings) were necessary to remove the penal obligation of the law against sinners.

- *The atonement is a "perfect satisfaction."*
  "The *Value* of Atonement" is evinced by *the worth of the Lamb.* There is every reason to rest assured that when Jesus uttered those words from the cross, "It is finished," the atonement was truly complete. Enough had been paid to guarantee salvation for men.

- *The atonement was secured "on behalf of elect sinners of mankind."*
  "The *Extent* of Atonement" is *all God's elect.* There is a particular and specific circle of humanity for whom Jesus fully paid the price. Jesus did not die for all mankind or generic humanity, but He died with specific men and women on His heart.

- *It is "on account of" this atonement that we "are delivered from condemnation."*
  "The *Results* of Atonement" involve *the fulfillment of all God's promises.* Because the legal barriers to our standing before

God have been removed, every other promise and blessing of His gracious love flows freely to us. The implications of the atonement are innumerable and eternal.

Symington's definition provides a concise summary of the whole doctrine, and it offers a useful mnemonic for students of the atonement.

Symington's *On the Atonement* is at once both a theologically astute and a pastorally warm text. It is both intricate and complex in its handling of profound matters, and it is at the same time concise and clear in its application of those matters to the hearts of his readers. It is impossible to read Symington's work on atonement attentively without constantly reflecting on one's own standing before so great a doctrine. From the opening sentence of the work ("How then can man be justified with God?" [p. 9, Job 25:4a]) to the last ("How shall we escape, if we neglect so *great salvation?*" [p. 255, Heb. 2:3]) Symington writes for the edification of his readers, not just their education.

Symington's rare capacity to bring out the warmth of refined doctrine led to the widespread use of his writings in his day. These same factors warrant renewed attention to his text today. Most importantly, however, one ought not leave off the important topic Symington sets before us without asking the intensely practical question with which Symington would leave us:

> We cannot part with our readers, without reminding them of the necessity of making a personal application of the glorious truths which have occupied their attention.... Let them not regard them as matters of curious speculation, or content themselves with a mere doctrinal belief.... Let not the reader, then, rise from the perusal of these pages, without seriously and conscientiously asking himself...: Has my soul been sprinkled with His precious blood? (p. 302)

✦   ✦   ✦

Wherefore the rather, brethren, give diligence to make your calling and election sure.... If thou shalt confess with thy mouth the Lord Jesus, and shalt believe in thine heart that God hath raised him from the dead, thou shalt be saved.... For whosoever shall call upon the name of the Lord shall be saved (2 Peter 1:10; Rom. 10:9, 13).

CHAPTER 11

On the Intercession of Jesus Christ

The word *intercede* simply means "to go between." It comes from the Latin words *inter* ("between") and *cedere* ("to go"). An *intercessor* is, quite literally, a "go-between."

In politics, such a go-between is usually called a *diplomat*. A diplomat is one who represents the concerns of one government to another, negotiating between them to bring about an agreement. A diplomat is a political intercessor. In the realm of law, such a go-between is usually called a *lawyer*. (Sometimes, the titles *advocate* or *solicitor* are used.) As an expert in the law, a lawyer knows what laws favor his client's position and how to present his client's concerns in the proper terms. A lawyer is a legal intercessor.

In religion, a go-between is generally called a *priest*. A priest is one who intercedes with a god (or God) on behalf of his people. The priest is an expert in the rituals and sacrifices necessary to satisfy the anger of an offended deity. More than that, a priest is one who maintains himself in holiness in order to be in good standing with heaven. A priest, therefore, is able to approach the deity when sinful men and women cannot do so. In the Scriptures we learn that Jesus is our Priest—and indeed the *only* Priest—who is able to mediate between mankind and the true God (e.g., Heb. 3:1).

It is as our great High Priest that Jesus presented the only acceptable sacrifice for our forgiveness. He interceded with God on our behalf by the sacrifice of His own flesh. We call this sacrifice *the atonement*. In the preceding chapter, we have considered this atonement; but the atonement is not the end of Jesus' intercession for us.

Jesus not only atoned for our sin (and that, once for all), He continues to intercede before God for all our needs, all the time, every day—even right this moment. As the author of Hebrews wrote:

"Jesus...because he continueth ever, hath an unchangeable

priesthood.... He ever liveth to make intercession for them"
(Heb. 7:22–25).

It is this *ongoing* intercession which Jesus makes for us that
Symington wrote the second section of his book on Jesus' priesthood to explain. "There is a [tendency among] many," Symington
wrote, "to regard what Christ *has done,* to the neglect of what He *is
doing*" (p. 299). Christians speak much (and rightly so!) of the cross
and what Jesus *did* for our atonement. Certainly Symington has no
desire to decrease the important attention given to the cross and the
atonement. Nonetheless, he would urge us *also* to give more attention to what Jesus is still doing—even after the cross—to intercede
with the Father for us.

Symington's attention to the doctrine of *intercession* seeks to
address this important, ongoing facet of Christ's priestly work. His
exposition of this doctrine is presented in the following sections:

- The *Reality* of Intercession   *How do I know Jesus is still
                                        interceding for me?*

- The *Nature* of Intercession   *What exactly is Jesus doing to
                                        intercede for me?*

- The *Subjects* of Intercession   *For what does Jesus ask, and
                                        on whose behalf?*

- The *Character* of the Intercessor *What kind of Intercessor is
                                        Jesus?*

- The *Implications* of Intercession *What benefits should I derive
                                        from knowing about Jesus'
                                        intercession?*

The Reality of Christ's Intercession: His Abiding Priesthood

The Book of Genesis (chps. 1–2) tells us that God created all things
in six days, and rested on the seventh. The creation was finished,
but God's involvement with the world did not end there. On the
contrary, Scripture makes it abundantly clear that the same God
who made all things at that one time, now long past, still continues
to govern the operation of everything He made.

This is what the psalmist so beautifully describes in Psalm 104.
The God revealed in Scripture, this psalm confesses, is the God who
made all things in the beginning:

> Who laid the foundations of the earth,
> that it should not be removed for ever.
> Thou coveredst it with the deep as with a garment....
> They go up by the mountains; they go down by the valleys
> unto the place which thou hast founded for them. (vv. 5, 6, 8)

Furthermore, the Psalm continues, He is the same one who provides ongoing care for His creation:

> He watereth the hills from his chambers:
> the earth is satisfied with the fruit of thy works.
> He causeth the grass to grow for the cattle,
> and herb for the service of man....
> These wait all upon thee;
> that thou mayest give them their meat in due season.
> That thou givest them they gather:
> thou openest thine hand,
> they are filled with good. (vv. 13–14, 27–28)

Theologians use the terms *creation* and *providence* to refer to these two aspects of the Creator's care. *Creation* refers to that one-time act, completed at the beginning of time, when all things came into existence. The creation was a one-time act (or series of acts) which ceased when God "rested" from His labors on the seventh day. *Providence* is the ongoing rule of God, by which He insures that plants and animals properly reproduce; sun, moon, and stars continue on their courses; and human history itself unfolds according to His will.

God is no watchmaker who makes a watch and then leaves it to run on its own. He is a Creator who once formed all things (creation) and continues to look after its proper operation (providence).

Symington begins his work on the intercession by noting this important relationship between creation and providence. He sees in creation and providence an analogy to the relationship between Christ's atonement and His intercession.

Atonement, like creation, was a one-time act. It is done. Nothing more can be added to what Christ fully completed on the cross. "[Jesus] needeth not daily...," the author of Hebrews writes, "to offer up sacrifice..., for this he did once, when he offered up himself" (Heb. 7:27; cf. 9:12, 10:10). The atonement was a one-time act, finished at the cross.

That the priestly work *of atonement* is done does not mean, however, that Jesus' priestly work is done. No, He continues to intercede for us as our great High Priest. Just as the Creator (by providence) continues to manage and apply the natural forces begun at creation, so our High Priest (by intercession) continues to draw out and apply the redemptive blessings secured at the atonement.

A number of scriptures are highlighted by Symington to affirm this important truth. In Romans, for instance, the Apostle Paul tells us,

> ...If God be for us, who can be against us?... It is Christ that died, yea rather, that is risen again, who is even at the right hand of God, who also maketh intercession for us. Who shall separate us from the love of Christ?... (Rom. 8:31, 34, 35)

Not only did Jesus die to secure our acceptance with God (and all the blessings flowing from it), but "yea rather," He rose to God's right hand where He "*maketh* [that is, even now] intercession for us." It is because Jesus is continuing to intercede for us, that all the blessings and privileges of our acceptance with God continue to be applied to us in the face of each particular need. Indeed, what an amazing assurance this is for God's people: "Who shall separate us from the love of [this still-interceding] Christ?" (Cf. Lev. 16:12–34; Ps. 110:4; Zech. 6:13; Heb. 7:24–25, 8:1)

It is the reality of this intercession that Symington hopes every Christian will come to comprehend. It is the reality of Jesus' ongoing intercession for us, for whom He has atoned, that gives us great comfort in our many daily needs. Symington writes,

> Numerous and daily are their wants;... their necessities are innumerable and constant. Blessings to supply these necessities, it is true, are procured by the atoning sacrifice of the Redeemer. But who shall apply to God for the bestowment of these purchased benefits? (pp. 259–260)

> While His church has a want, while His people's necessities continue, [Jesus] will count it His delight, His pleasure, His honour, His glory, to present their case to His Father, and to secure for them the bestowment of every needed boon. (p. 262)

The Nature of Christ's Intercession: Applying the Atonement

What is it that Jesus does to intercede for us? What kind of activities are taking place as Jesus represents us before the Father in heaven?

To a certain extent, such questions cannot be answered. Some theologians have tried to speculate concerning the precise nature of Jesus' intercessory activities in heaven. Symington warns against "indulging in foolish conjectures" (p. 268) over matters Scripture does not reveal to us. We cannot describe with precision the intercessory acts of Jesus in heaven. Nevertheless, Scripture does reveal enough to give us an important indication of its nature.

1. Jesus appears before God in our stead—In a letter to one of the New Testament churches, the Apostle John urged Christians to cease from sin. "And if any man sin," he continued, "we have an *advocate* with the Father, Jesus Christ the righteous" (1 John 2:1). Sin has no place in the Christian life, but even Christians fail. John used a legal term, *advocate,* to indicate the nature of Jesus' ongoing intercession for believers who sin. "This is a law term," Symington explains, "which was in common use among the Greeks and Romans, to denote one who appeared in a court of justice...in the room of his client..." (p. 263).

In other words, the intercession of Jesus is more than a "friend" putting in a good word for another. He intercedes as our legal representative. Symington continues, "When our case is called, so to speak..., He *appears* in our room; when we are summoned to appear, He *stands* up in our name" (p. 264). Whenever there is a charge against us for sin, Jesus intercedes as our legal representative to plead the benefits of His atonement for us.

Scripture reveals to us that there is another who speaks before the Father's throne. The Apostle John has also told us that Satan, whom John describes as "the accuser of our brethren" stood and "accused them before our God day and night" (Rev. 12:10). But Jesus is there as our Advocate, our lawyer, speaking for us. When a charge is brought against the believer, Jesus stands in our place. If the charge is a lie from "the accuser of our brethren," Jesus is able to dispel it with the truth. If a true charge concerning real sin in our lives is brought, Jesus is able to plead His own blood for our forgiveness. Jesus intercedes before God *in our stead.* This is why Paul could write,

There is therefore now no condemnation to them which are
in Christ Jesus.... Who shall lay any thing to the charge of
God's elect?... It is Christ that died...[and] is even at the right
hand of God, who also maketh intercession for us (Rom.
8:1–34).

Jesus stands to intercede for us in matters of sin and accusation. He also, as will be seen more fully when we come to consider
the *subjects* of His intercession, "stands up for us" in our other daily
needs. In all our daily needs, for forgiveness and for blessing, Jesus
is able to bring our case before the Father as our legal representative—our Advocate, our Priest.

Jesus also stands to plead our entry into heaven at the end of
life. It is this "plea of entry" which Symington finds beautifully portrayed in the account of Stephen's martyrdom. As Stephen's enemies
prepared to kill him, "he, being full of the Holy Ghost, looked up
stedfastly into heaven, and saw the glory of God, and Jesus *standing*
on the right hand of God" (Acts 7:55). Symington believes that there
is legal significance to the posture of Jesus in Stephen's vision. As
our heavenly *King,* Jesus is consistently described as one *seated* on
His heavenly throne (e.g., Ps. 110:1; Luke 22:69). It is in His role as
our interceding *Priest,* however, that Jesus is portrayed *standing* to
plead in our stead. Thus, when Stephen was called to appear before
the throne of God, Jesus *stood* for him. Symington sees in this a sig-
nification of Christ's priestly intercession for Stephen's acceptance
into the eternal kingdom.

"Behold," Stephen cried out, "I see the heavens opened, and
the Son of man standing on the right hand of God.... Lord Jesus,
receive my spirit" (Acts 7:56, 59).

2. Jesus exhibits His sacrifice—Jesus appears before the Father to plead
the case of His people, but He does not approach the throne empty-
handed. Jesus is able to plead our needs, presenting His own shed
blood "as the ground on which the blessings for which He pleads
are to be conferred on His people" (p. 264). Jesus does not appear in
our stead with mere words and wishes, but with the purchase price
to insure the fulfillment of what He requests.

In the Old Testament law, we are given a foreshadowing of
this presentation made by Christ. In the old tabernacle and temple
order, the High Priest was instructed to make a special offering for

the nation's atonement once a year (the Day of Atonement). The sacrifice itself was offered outside the temple, on the altar located in the courtyard where all the people could see. It was that sacrifice which atoned for the people's sins. However, once the sacrifice was finished, the High Priest carried the blood of the sacrifice (in a bowl) inside the temple. While the people waited outside, the Priest entered alone into the holy place. There, in the heart of the temple before the ark of the covenant ("the testimony" covered by "the mercy seat"),

> "he shall take a censer full of burning coals of fire from off the altar before the LORD..., and he shall put the incense upon the fire before the LORD, that the cloud of the incense may cover the mercy seat that is upon the testimony, that he die not: and he shall take of the blood...and sprinkle it with his finger upon the mercy seat eastward...seven times...." (Lev. 16:12, 13, 14)

It is this need *to present* the blood of the sacrifice before God that the book of Hebrews tells us Jesus fulfilled: "For Christ is not entered into the holy places made with hands, which are the figures of the true; but into heaven itself, now to appear in the presence of God for us" (Heb. 9:24). Furthermore, He took His place there with "the *blood of sprinkling*, that speaketh better things than that of Abel" (Heb. 12:24; cf. 9:11–12, 23). Jesus fulfills this temple ritual in reality: He enters into the heart of heaven itself, the dwelling of God, there *to present the blood* He has shed. He does not appear on our behalf empty-handed.

Now, Symington is quick to add this caution, lest our imaginations get the better of us in our contemplation of this truth:

> By His blood and sacrifice, represented in these passages as carried by Him into heaven..., we are not to understand the material blood which flowed in the garden and on the cross, but the merit of His sufferings and death, the virtue of His atonement, the substance of His sacrifice, the whole essence of His passion. (p. 264–265)

It would be an unnecessary, and perhaps theologically dangerous, speculation to insist on the literalness of the blood rites here ascribed to Jesus in heaven. The point of the Old Testament rites was to represent spiritual realities in tangible elements: the presentation of the sacrificial blood in the holy place indicated the merits of the sacrifice presented before God. This same language of blood-presentation is ascribed to Jesus to assure us that He, after His death, presents His merit on our behalf. It is this spiritual truth, not the literalness of the symbols, that we are to embrace.

Jesus does not appear on our behalf with mere words of petition—He has the purchase price to guarantee our acceptance, and all the blessings which that assures us in our daily needs.

3. Jesus makes His will known—The third aspect of Jesus' intercession indicated in Scripture is His petitioning for us. He not only (1) stands in our place, He not only (2) brings forth the fruits of His sacrifice, but He also (3) *makes specific petitions for us.* Two examples of Jesus' intercessory prayers, recorded in Scripture, illustrate this point.

The first is the intercessory prayer recorded in John 17—a chapter frequently referred to as Jesus' "High Priestly Prayer." Jesus offered that prayer, with His disciples listening in, because He wants us to know how He intercedes for us in heaven. This is what Jesus said as He spoke to the Father in heaven, "And now come I to thee; and these things I speak in the world, that they might have my joy fulfilled in themselves" (John 17:13). This prayer is, therefore, a special witness to the Christian of how Jesus intercedes for us in heaven.

In that prayer, Jesus made a number of specific requests for His disciples. "I pray for them," He declared, "Holy Father, keep through thine own name those whom thou hast given me.... Keep them from the evil.... Sanctify them through thy truth.... Father, I will that they also...be with me where I am" (John 17:9–24). Knowing the sorrows and temptations His disciples face, Jesus wanted us to see how He intercedes for our keeping, our continuing sanctification, and our entrance into heaven ("with me where I am"). These and other petitions incorporated into that prayer show us Christ's concern for our specific needs in the present world.

A second example is the intercession Jesus made for Peter, personally, in Peter's hour of weakness. As Jesus sat with His disciples in the Upper Room, Jesus spoke about the great trials that were about to come upon them all. He knew that Peter was going to be confronted with particularly forceful temptations to abandon Christ. "Simon, Simon, behold, Satan hath desired to have you, that he may sift you as wheat," Jesus explained. On his own, Peter was not strong enough to withstand Satan's sifting. "I tell thee, Peter," Jesus warned, "the cock shall not crow this day, before that thou shalt thrice deny that thou knowest me" (Luke 22:31–34). Peter was about to face a specific trial, one which he was not strong enough to withstand. But Jesus not only knew Peter's vulnerability, He interceded on Peter's behalf. He gave Peter this precious word of assurance: *"but I have prayed for thee, that thy faith fail not"* (Luke 22:32).

Here is a glimpse at how the accuser of the brethren, who accuses all believers before the Father "day and night" (Rev. 12:10), seeks "to sift them like wheat" (cf. Job 1:6–12). Here, moreover, is a witness to Jesus' intercession, and its certain fruits. "I have prayed for thee," He told Peter, "that thy faith fail not. *And when thou art converted, strengthen thy brethren"* (Luke 22:32). Peter may not be strong enough to stand in the face of Satan's temptations, but Jesus' intercession insures that Peter will not fall. On the contrary, Jesus *by intercession* turns the experience to Peter's strengthening, and the strengthening of the whole church through him. Jesus not only intercedes for all believers generally, but He intercedes for each believer precisely, individually, and in the face of specific needs.

Many details about the nature of Jesus' intercession might not be known, but these three important features are clear: Jesus (1) appears in the presence of God for us; (2) He presents His own sacrificial merits to purchase all He requests; and, (3) He makes His petitions for His people.

The Subjects of Christ's Intercession: All God's Blessings for All the Elect

Under the heading, "Matter [or, Subjects] of Christ's Intercession," Symington answers two questions: (1) for whom does Christ intercede? and, (2) what is it that He requests for them?

1. The people for whom he intercedes—Symington identifies the people for whom Christ intercedes by first referring to the extent of the atonement (see pp. 160–169, above). After all, "it is unreasonable to suppose Christ to make atonement for any for whom He does not intercede," and "it [is] preposterous to allege that He intercedes for any but those for whose sins He has atoned" (p. 269). It has already been seen that Jesus atoned for the elect, and Symington further shows that Jesus intercedes for the elect. He examines this point from three angles: Jesus intercedes "for the elect only," He intercedes "for all [the elect]," and He intercedes for "each of the elect" (p. 269).

"That He intercedes for the elect only," Symington states, "is abundantly plain...from the explicit testimony of Scripture" (p. 269). Paul writes that the reason Christians do not stand condemned before God (when unbelievers do) is because Jesus died and "maketh intercession *for us*" (Rom. 8:34). The author of Hebrews also affirms that Jesus "is able also to save them to the uttermost that come unto God by him," because "he ever liveth to make intercession *for them*" (Heb. 7:25). Also, the Apostle John's text about Christ's advocacy states, "My little children [that is, the church],... if any man sin, *we* have an advocate with the Father..." (1 John 2:1). Jesus intercedes "for us," that is, for His own people.

Jesus makes this especially clear in His High Priestly Prayer, where He states for whom He is praying:

> I have manifested thy name unto the men which thou gavest me out of the world.... I pray for them: I pray not for the world, but for them which thou hast given me.... (John 17:6, 9; cf. Ps. 16:4; Jer. 7:16; 11:14; 14:11)

As has already been seen in the previous chapter, Jesus *atones* for the elect alone. Similarly, according to Scripture, Jesus also *intercedes* for the elect alone. In our modern, democratic culture, we are used to people electing their leaders. It is somewhat counter-intuitive for us, therefore, to think of a leader who elects his people. This, however, is indicative of the monarchical nature of Christ's leadership. It is He who elects His people, and in love He atones for and intercedes for them. Why He elects whom He does is beyond our ability to comprehend (Rom. 9:11–18; 11:33–36). All we can do is marvel that He so often sets His love upon the most unlikely sorts (1 Cor. 1:26–29; 1 Tim. 1:15). He is a monarch, but He is a gracious monarch.

Symington further affirms that Jesus intercedes for *all* the elect. That is, Jesus intercedes for all the elect whatever their current spiritual condition (believing or unbelieving), and He intercedes for all the elect whatever their time and place in history (before the cross or after the cross).

It might be expected that Jesus intercedes for *Christians*—for those who already believe in Him. However, Jesus also intercedes for those who do not yet believe but are being drawn to Christ. This is made especially clear in His High Priestly Prayer, where Jesus reveals, "Neither pray I for these alone, [that is, His present disciples], but for them also which *shall* believe on me through their word" (John 17:20). Jesus is interceding for all the elect purchased by His atonement, whether they are already believers or not. (Indeed, if Jesus were not interceding for elect unbelievers, they would never be protected from Satan's devices and brought to faith!)

The second dimension of totality mentioned by Symington is the inclusion of all the elect, before as well as after the cross. "We are apt," Symington remarks, "to conceive of the work of intercession as conducted only since the Saviour's ascension, or at most since His appearance on earth. But He was always *the Angel of God's presence* who saved His people" (pp. 271–272). Symington is referring, in those words, to this Old Testament description of Jesus:

> In all their affliction he was afflicted,
> and *the angel of his presence* saved them:
> in his love and in his pity he redeemed them;
> and he bare them, and carried them all the days of old.
> (Isa. 63:9)

All the days of old God Himself bore the afflictions of His people, because the Angel of His Presence interceded for them. This "Angel of His Presence" can be none other than the Second Person of the Godhead, an Old Testament reference to Jesus.

Symington says that we can further confirm Jesus' pre-incarnate intercession through reference to a specific "act of intercession on record" in the Old Testament (p. 272). The prophet Zechariah records how "the Angel of the Lord" was interceding for the forgiveness of the people in his day:

> Then the angel of the LORD answered and said, O LORD of hosts, how long wilt thou not have mercy on Jerusalem and on the cities of Judah, against which thou hast had indignation these threescore and ten years? And the LORD answered the angel that talked with me with good words and comfortable words. (Zech. 1:12–13)

What a blessing it is for *all* the elect—in all ages, ancient and modern—to have the witness of "good words and comfortable words" from heaven. We have these comforts assured to us because of what Christ has purchased in the atonement, and because He intercedes for the full application of those atonement benefits. Although the atonement took place in time (on earth), the intercession is able to be conducted throughout eternity (in heaven) through its merits. (Cf. also Rev. 8:3)

Jesus intercedes for the elect *alone*. He intercedes for *all* the elect, whether saved or not yet saved, whether before or after the cross in history. Symington further draws attention to the intercession of Jesus for *each* of the elect—personally. "His intercession is not general," Symington writes,

> but particular. With a speciality such as might be supposed if there were only one, does He attend to the interests of each individual in the vast number of those given Him by the Father. (p. 272)

This principle was foreshadowed in the old, high priestly garments. The Lord had instructed Moses, in setting up the priestly orders,

> Thou shalt make the breastplate...and the stones shall be with the names of the children of Israel, twelve...[with] engravings [on them].... And Aaron shall bear the names of the children of Israel...upon his heart, when he goeth in unto the holy place, for a memorial before the LORD continually. (Ex. 28:15, 21, 29)

In the high priest's attire, God presented a symbol of the need for "the names of the children of Israel" to be on the priest's heart when he intercedes. Jesus announced with even greater precision the *individual* focus with which He fulfills this principle. He promises, "I will confess his name before my Father, and before his angels" (Rev. 3:5). The prayer of Jesus for Peter, previously discussed, offers an example of this personal concern: "Simon, Simon, behold, Satan hath desired to have you, that he may sift you as wheat: but I have prayed for thee, that thy faith fail not..." (Luke 22:31–32).

Jesus' intercession is for the elect, for all the elect, and for each one of the elect according to his or her personal needs at each moment.

2. The blessings for which He intercedes—Considering the "subjects" of Christ's intercession, Symington looks not only at the people for whom Jesus intercedes, but also at the particular blessings which He requests on their behalf. Seven such blessings are identified by Symington:

- *He pleads our justification*—The elect are sinners just like all others. Though marked out by God for salvation, the elect are surrounded by all the same sins and influences as the rest of the ungodly. The only distinctive that sets them apart is that Jesus is interceding for their admittance to divine grace on the grounds of His own sacrifice. It is this Intercessor's right to lay claim, by petition, to unbelievers: "Ask of me, and I shall give thee the heathen for thine inheritance" (Ps. 2:8). "The procuring cause of justification," Symington writes, "is the Saviour's merits [by atonement], but the immediate cause of actual justification [for each individual] is the Saviour's intercession" (p. 273). Jesus prays for the conversion of the elect.

- *He pleads our daily forgiveness*—Our need for forgiveness does not end at conversion. Christians still sin (though hopefully less and less). "For in many things we offend all" (James 3:2), and, "if we say that we have no sin, we deceive ourselves" (1 John 1:8). It is by the sinner's initial conversion that he is justified once and for all before God. Nonetheless, it is because Jesus continues to intercede for the believer that the security of his standing remains unshaken by continuing sin. "If any man sin, we have an advocate with the Father, Jesus Christ the righteous" (1 John 2:1). Jesus intercedes for our daily forgiveness in the face of daily sin, thereby keeping our justified standing with God secure.

- *He pleads our protection from Satan*—The devil is an active enemy of the believers. He is an adversary who seeks "to steal and to kill and to destroy" (John 10:10). He, "as a roaring lion, walketh about, seeking whom he may devour" (1 Peter 5:8). He brings accusations against the brethren (Rev. 12:10), and he opposes them with temptations (Luke 8:13). Jesus however intercedes for His own, pleading their preservation in the face of such attacks. When Satan makes accusation, Jesus intercedes with His blood. One of the Old Testament prophets witnessed such intercession, when he saw—

> Joshua the high priest standing before the angel of the LORD, and Satan standing at his right hand to accuse him. And the LORD said to Satan, ...The LORD that hath chosen Jerusalem rebuke thee: is not this a brand plucked out of the fire? Now Joshua was standing before the angel, clothed in filthy garments. And the angel said..., Take away the filthy garments from him.... I have caused thine iniquity to pass from thee (Zech. 3:1–5).

The priest Joshua was guilty—his garments were stained with sin. Nonetheless, Jesus rebuked the accuser and pled His own atonement on Joshua's behalf. Jesus protects His people from the enemy's accusations. He is also the one who protects His people in the midst of Satan's temptations: "Simon, Simon, behold, Satan hath desired to have you, that he may sift you as wheat: but I have prayed for thee, that thy faith fail not" (Luke 22:31–32). Jesus, our atoning and interceding Priest, "is able to keep you from falling, and to present you faultless before the presence of his glory with exceeding joy" (Jude 24; cf. John 17:15; 1 Cor. 10:12–13; 1 Peter 1:4; 2 Peter 2:9).

- *He pleads our sanctification*—Jesus also intercedes for our spiritual growth. "The *progressive sanctification of the saints,*" Symington writes, "*and their general perseverance* stand connected with the intercession of Christ" (p. 278). To quote from Jesus' High Priestly Prayer: "I pray for them.... Sanctify them through thy truth: thy word is truth" (John 17:9, 17). The growth of a Christian in the face of all the onslaught of evil in the world is rather like a delicate flower blossoming in the midst of a raging hurricane. That the Christian is able to grow in spiritual victory is not because of the personal power of the Christian, but because Jesus intercedes for him. "Here lies the secret of the saints' perseverance," Symington observes, "If Christ only persevere[s] to pray for them, they cannot fail to persevere in the enjoyment of what He has procured, and the practice of what He has commanded" (p. 280).

- *He pleads our peace with God*—By His atonement, Jesus purchased our peace with God. By continual interposition of His blood (already shed once for all), Jesus *maintains* our peace with God. Though God's face may be hidden from the believer for a time (Ps. 22:1, 89:49; Isa. 59:2), and sinfulness will steal even the believer's inner peace (Ps. 6:3; 38; 42; 43), such separation cannot be permanent. "For a small moment have I forsaken thee; but with great mercies will I gather thee" (Isa. 54:7; cf. Ps. 51:12; Ezek. 39:24, 29). Jesus intercedes for Christians in dark valleys, that the peace won by His atonement might be restored and continued. (Cf. Eph. 3:12; Heb. 4:14–16; 10:21–22)

- *He pleads the acceptability of our works*—God's law requires perfection, "but the services of the people of God are at best imperfect" (p. 281). Curiously, however, the imperfect works of believers are frequently commended in Scripture as *acceptable* to God (Matt. 10:40–42; Heb. 6:10). This is remarkable since, in themselves, all our good deeds are "as filthy rags" (Isa. 64:6). Symington sees in this remarkable acceptability of Christian service the effects of Christ's intercession. "Our services," he writes, "as well as our persons" are made acceptable by Christ's intercession (p. 282).

  Although Symington does not raise this example, we might discern an indication of this principle in the firstfruit rites of the Old Testament. The *blood* sacrifices of the temple were for atonement, but *grain* offerings represented a consecration of one's labors. When a firstfruit offering was brought, however, it could not be acceptably presented on its own. The consecration of labors required an addition. It had to be covered with frankincense to make it "a sweet savour unto the LORD" (Lev. 2:1–2). This would seem to be a ritual foreshadowing of the truth Symington recognizes in Christ's intercession. It is the sweet incense of Christ's intercession that renders the services of His people acceptable for presentation to the Father. (Cf. Ex. 28:38; Eccl. 3:11; Isa. 56:7; 1 Cor. 3:10–15; Titus 2:14)

- *He pleads our entrance to glory*—Finally, Symington writes, "the intercession of Christ secures *the complete salvation of the chosen of God, their entrance into heaven, and their everlasting continuance in a state of perfect blessedness*" (p. 282). Symington sees an example of this in the martyrdom of Stephen. Stephen lifted his eyes to heaven and saw Jesus standing to plead his entrance into glory (Acts 7:55). Symington also points out that our entrance into heaven is part of Jesus' intercessory prayer in John 17: "Father, I will that they...be with me where I am" (John 17:24). The believer's reception into heaven is an act accomplished by Jesus' intercession.

Symington goes even farther than this, moreover. He further shows that all our perpetual joys and glory in heaven are eternally maintained by Christ's ongoing intercession. The author of Hebrews intimates this when he proclaims of Christ, "he...hath an unchangeable priesthood. Wherefore he is able also to save them to the uttermost...seeing he ever liveth to make intercession for them" (Heb. 7:24–25). Jesus' intercession is an eternal work, insuring our salvation "to the uttermost"—that is, to the uttermost detail of glorification and to the uttermost extent of eternity. Symington eloquently teaches,

> [There is] not a ray of light, not a smile of favour, not a thrill of gladness, not a note of joy, for which the inhabitants of heaven are not indebted to the Angel standing with the golden censer full of incense, before the throne. Remove this illustrious personage from the situation; divest Him of His official character; put out of view this sacerdotal function; and all security for the continuance of celestial benefits is gone,—the crowns fall from the heads of the redeemed, the palms of victory drop from their hands, the harps of gold are unstrung, and the shouts of halleluiah cease for ever; nay, heaven must discharge itself of its human inhabitants.... But no such appalling catastrophe need ever be feared: *Christ ever liveth to make intercession!* (p. 283)

Symington's listing of the contents of Christ's petitions is not meant to be exhaustive. All the many promises of Scripture are the things for which Christ intercedes on the behalf of the elect. Nonetheless, in this broadly comprehensive outline of seven points,

Symington seeks to highlight the absolute (and, indeed, eternal) dependence of the believer on Jesus' perpetual priesthood. Comprehending our ongoing dependence on the active intercession of Christ is a source of great comfort to the believer, for what greater security could we have?

The atonement has already been finished and was proven, by the resurrection, to have been sufficient. The eternal standing of that High Priest, with the infinite value of that sacrifice in His hands, is our rock-solid guarantee that every blessing thereby purchased will be applied "to the uttermost."

The Character of the Intercessor: An Infallible Advocate

The work of Christ is *personal.* Jesus is not a spiritual force one "taps" into. He is not a machine one "plugs" into. Jesus is a person one relates to and gets to know. Any study of Jesus' priestly work, therefore, ought to include careful recognition of the Priest Himself. Under the heading, "The Properties [or, Characteristics] of Christ's Intercession," Symington speaks about eight personal qualities that distinguish Jesus as our personal Intercessor.

- *He is a skillful Intercessor*—Any courtroom advocate, to be effective, must possess insight into the client he represents, the judge before whom he pleads, and the law itself. The wisdom of Christ in each of these points distinguishes His skill as our Advocate. "He knows perfectly all His people, and all their cases," Symington affirms. "Even their inward breathings and secret groanings" are well known to Jesus (p. 284; cf. John 2:25; Rev. 2:23). Jesus also knows intimately the Father before whose bar He represents us (Matt. 11:27). Furthermore, Jesus possesses perfect knowledge of God's law by which men are held to account (Matt. 5–7). In His wise use of the law, however, Jesus' advocacy is markedly different from many human advocates. Symington draws this distinction: "It is not, as is too often the case among men, by...perverting, or explaining away the law, that this advocate exhibits His skill" (p. 285). Jesus rather upholds the law, but He also *satisfies* its demands against us by His atonement. Jesus uses His perfect knowledge—of our needs, of the Father's character, and of the demands of divine law—to insure that His intercession for us is thorough.

"Such, in short, is His skill," Symington concludes, "that...no cause can ever fail in His hands from want of knowledge or wisdom to conduct it." (p. 285)

- *He is a morally pure Intercessor*—The purity of Jesus is presented by the author of Hebrews as especially important. "For such an high priest became us, who is holy, harmless, undefiled, separate from sinners, and made higher than the heavens" (Heb. 7:26). The perfect effectiveness of Jesus as an Intercessor of righteousness is connected to His perfect righteousness as a person. We could have no other such Intercessor than the sinless Christ. (Cf., 1 John 2:1.)

- *He is a compassionate Intercessor*—What good is it to approach the most eminently qualified lawyer in practice if he has no concern for your case? Jesus is not only perfectly skilled and morally unimpeachable, but He is also full of compassion. "For we have not an high priest which cannot be touched with the feeling of our infirmities; but was in all points tempted like as we are, yet without sin" (Heb. 4:15; cf. 2:17). Symington writes on this point,

> He tasted of all the sorrows of human life. Of the severest afflictions, the bitterest temptations, the most pungent sorrows, the most awful privations, He had full and frequent trial. He was not only cast into the same mould as His people with respect to nature, but into the same furnace with respect to affliction....
>
> The pity of Christians for themselves can never equal the pity with which they are regarded by their Saviour; for theirs is the pity of a corrupted nature, His of uncontaminated humanity; theirs the pity of mere human nature, His of human nature indissolubly linked with all the tender mercies of Deity. (p. 287)

That latter point deserves some pondering. Jesus' pity for His people is the pity of *uncorrupted* human nature. It is absolutely selfless, loving, and full. His pity for the believer is fuller than any human pity we, in our corrupted nature, can ever know. Furthermore, being Himself God, "all the tender mercies of Deity" are present in the compassion of Jesus for His people. Not only is His the fullest expression of human compassion, but it is divine compassion. What a great comfort this ought to be for all those who name the name of Christ! It is no wonder the author of Hebrews pointed to Christ's compassion as the cause of great confidence: "For we have not an high priest which cannot be touched with the feeling of our infirmities; but was in all points tempted like as we are, yet without sin.. *Let us therefore come boldly unto the throne of grace...in time of need*" (Heb. 4:15–16).

- *He is a prompt Intercessor*—Symington rejoices to speak further of Christ's "promptitude" as our Intercessor. That is, "He is never absent from His place; [His people] know always where He is to be found; He is ever at the right hand of God, waiting to undertake what they may commit to His charge" (pp. 287–288). Because Jesus is always "on duty," and always accessible, we are able to pray in the moment of need knowing we are heard immediately (Heb. 4:16; 1 John 5:14–15). Scripture shows us an Intercessor who does not delay to provide what we need. Jesus does not indulge every felt need desired by His people (James 4:3; 1 John 5:14). Nonetheless, He always insures that every grace truly necessary to sustain trial is provided without delay, and that every other benefit and holy desire follows in proper time, according to His own infallible wisdom. (Cf. Isa. 46:13; 49:8; Zech. 1:12; John 14:13–14; 1 Cor. 10:13)

- *He is an earnest Intercessor*—In connection with the preceding points, Symington shows us that Christ is a fervent Intercessor. His is not a wooden stance before the throne. He is an earnest Intercessor, whose heart is revealed in His petitions witnessed while here on earth. "The earnestness He displayed," Symington writes, "in laying the foundation of our salvation...[with] strong crying and tears, may be taken as a pledge that He will not be less earnest in carrying out His benevolent undertaking to its completion in heaven" (p. 289). The example of His intercessory prayer in John 17 is certainly full of warmth, devotion, and wholehearted concern, and His tears and bloodied sweat in Gethsemane show us the heart of one wholly devoted to His prayers (Luke 22:44). If the "fervent prayer of a righteous man availeth much" (James 5:16), the believer can take much comfort in this Intercessor.

- *He is an authoritative Intercessor*—In a human courtroom, a lawyer can only be admitted if he is properly licensed. Skill, concern, and uprightness account for little if the advocate does not have proper authorization to practice. Symington uses this observation from the human courtroom to illustrate another feature of Jesus' advocacy: He bears the authority of divine appointment. It is the author of Hebrews who explains the importance of this principle in biblical religion. No priest, we are taught, can operate under self-appointment: "no man taketh this honor unto himself" (Heb. 5:4). Instead, a priest must be appointed by God, as Jesus was: "So also Christ glorified not himself to be made an high priest; but he that said unto him...Thou art a priest for ever after the order of Melchisedec" (Heb. 5:5–6 quoting Ps. 110:4).

- *He is the only Intercessor*—In the Old Testament order, a lesson on the exclusiveness of Christ's intercession was given. "No man," Symington remarks, "not even the king himself, might intrude" into the holy place in the temple (2 Chron. 26:18). Only "the high priest [was] permitted to carry incense... into the holy of holies" (p. 291). By these ritual restrictions, the people were being taught about the exclusivity of the intercessor's office. There can be only one intercessor, and that intercessor is ultimately realized in Jesus Christ, alone. "There is...one mediator between God and men, the man Christ Jesus" (1 Tim. 2:5).

  One of the reasons Symington wanted to stress the uniqueness of Jesus' character as Intercessor, was to guard his readers from the errors of Roman Catholicism (and, implicitly, Eastern Orthodoxy). These religions do preach Christ as the only *atoning* Priest, but they introduce a whole pantheon of other *interceding* priests into their prayers. Mary, various saints, and even angels are held by them to intercede for us. "To represent either angels or men as joint intercessors with Christ," Symington argued, "...is to be guilty of a daring invasion of a high and exclusive prerogative of the one Mediator" (p. 291). It is Jesus *alone* who completed the atonement, and it is He who (like the Old Testament high priest) *enters alone* into the holy place to intercede for us (Lev. 16:17; Heb. 9:24). Therefore, Jesus declares, "I am the way, the truth, and the life: no man cometh unto the Father, but by me" (John 14:6; cf. Ezek. 44:2–4; Eph. 2:18).

- *He is a faithful Intercessor*—The atonement was completed within a short period of time. Jesus' intercession, however, is an ongoing work. "He continueth [His intercession] ever"— that is, all the time, for all time (Heb. 7:24–25). Symington sees in this teaching, not only an amazing fact about Christ's priestly work, but also an inspiring insight into His *character* as an Intercessor. He writes,

  > Human benevolence may become languid, may inter-mit for a time, or may finally die away altogether. But not so the benevolence which prompts the petitions of our Advocate. (p. 295)

  What an amazing, immutable love this Intercessor must possess, that He never wearies in His earnest petitions on our behalf! His constancy is proof of His faithfulness—His undying love for the elect which never cools and grows lax. (Cf. Rom. 7:34–39)

Such, in a sketch, is the character of this Intercessor: Jesus Christ. His intercession is infallibly reliable. It is not, however, the reliability of a well-oiled machine, a scientifically documented phenomenon, or a carefully regulated system. The infallible reliability of Christ's intercession *is directly rooted in His personal character.* It is because Jesus is personally wise, virtuous, compassionate, prompt, and earnest, endowed with full authority (and uniquely so), and because He is motivated by a faithful love for His people, that His saints can take great comfort in the infallibility of His intercession.

The delight which Symington took, personally, in this view of Christ's character is obvious in his doxological summation:

> His love is abiding.... So long as His people sin, He will plead for pardon; so long as they are tempted, He will procure them strength to resist; so long as they continue to perform services, He will continue to give them acceptance; so long as they are in the wilderness, He will procure them guidance and safety; nay, so long as the blessings of Heaven are enjoyed, will He plead His merits as the ground on

which they are bestowed. Through eternity will He continue to plead on behalf of His people. Never shall they cease to be the objects of His care; never shall their names be erased from His breast; never shall their cause be taken from His lips; never shall the odour-breathing censer drop from His hand; nor shall His blessed merits ever cease to rise up in a cloud of fragrant incense before the Lord: *He ever liveth to make intercession for them.* (pp. 295–296)

The Implications of Christ's Intercession:
Availing of our Advocate

Symington was a theologian, but he was first and last a pastor. He wrote on the atonement and intercession of Christ, not to publish a book or to stir academic discourse. He wrote to edify the believer and urge the unbeliever in the real claims of a real Christ. He therefore concludes his study of the intercession with specific responses—practical implications which the reader, having considered the doctrine, ought not fail to implement in his faith and life.

Symington leads us to consider several implications (or "results," as he calls them), in particular: four which relate to the reader's *beliefs*; and four which relate to the reader's *practice*.

1. Implications for what we believe—The Christian faith is expressed both in terms of certain claims and certain practices. "Faith without works is dead," the Apostle James wrote (James 2:26), by which we understand that neither beliefs nor practices can be rightly held without the other. In regard to *faith-claims* (what we believe), Symington cites these four convictions we should draw from the doctrine of Christ's intercession:

- *The conviction that God is love*—Symington urges us to consider what "a bright display of the *love of God*" the doctrine of intercession presents (p. 296). God was under no obligation to save mankind at all. Nevertheless, He not only provided a way of salvation, but what a way of salvation! He provided an atonement, in Christ, sufficient to *completely* save us. He did not give us a 50%, or even a 95%, payment. In Christ we are provided with the whole payment for our atonement.

But even more than that, the love of God is displayed in the perpetual intercession of Christ. We have not been left to "make what we can" of the atonement for ourselves. He who knows exactly all our daily needs, He who knows precisely all the benefits now available to us through the atonement, He intercedes continually to insure their complete application to us. "Herein is love!" Symington exults, "Let us contemplate it with grateful adoration, and dwell upon the theme till our enraptured hearts reciprocate with the emotion, till we can say, 'We love Him because He so loved us!'" (p. 297)

- *The conviction of Christ's deity*—The priestly office of Christ is one which He fulfills primarily by virtue of His *humanity*. Because we are "flesh and blood, he also himself likewise took part of the same.... Wherefore in all things it behoved him to be made like unto his brethren, that he might be a merciful and faithful high priest..." (Heb. 2:14–18). The priesthood of Christ is an office particularly tied to His humanity. But Jesus never ceased to be God in His becoming man (Phil. 2:6–7, 11). Symington shows how, even in His human priesthood, Jesus exhibits the full marks of His divinity:

  > To know minutely all the cases of so many millions of people; to listen to, and understand, such a multitude of simultaneous applications; to represent them all...must require qualifications nothing short of divine. No finite being could ever be fit for such an undertaking.... None but a divine person is qualified to be the intercessor of elect sinners. Such is our advocate with the Father. 'This is the true God, and eternal life.' (pp. 297–298; quoting 1 John 5:20)

- *The conviction that Christ's death was sufficient and effective*—The full power of the atonement is revealed by contemplating the intercession. It was in the sufferings of Christ—His atonement—that God's favor was procured for us who trust in Him. The full application of that divine favor, however, continues to unfold in the loving care of Christ for His people as He daily intercedes for their every need. We might look at the cross and suppose that its effects were meager when we consider the results which took place in its immediate wake. However, the benefits there purchased are still being poured out through the intercession of Christ, saving and caring for His people in every age. The benefits sealed at the cross are those which will continue to be poured out through all eternity in glory. The cross-event, though of short duration, secured an infinite account of divine favor. It is the doctrine of the intercession that causes us to fully appreciate how vast, and effectual, the atonement was.

- *The conviction that our salvation is secure* — There are those in the church who teach that, once a person becomes saved, he can never lose that salvation. "Once saved, always saved," it is said. Symington would affirm that teaching, but would urge us to go further than that. "Once saved, always saved," is only half the story, and the minor half of the story at that. The reason a believer is kept secure in his salvation is *because Jesus continually intercedes for him.* The believer can rest assured that his salvation is secure *because he has a faithful Intercessor at the throne.* "I have prayed for thee," Jesus says, "that thy faith fail not" (Luke 22:32). When the believer does abandon his God and turn to sin, Ezekiel shows us this promise: "According to their transgressions have I done unto them, and hid my face from them.... Neither will I hide my face any more from them: for I have poured out my spirit upon the house of Israel..." (Ezek. 39:24–29).

  The security of the Christian's salvation is not due to some contractual clause that obliges God (cf. 1 Kings 9:9). Rather, the security of the Christian's salvation is because of the character of our High Priest. He unfailingly continues to present His merits for our forgiveness, and He insures that every necessary grace is applied to restore and hold us to the path of spiritual growth (1 John 1:8–2:1; 1 Peter 1:4–5). It is the doctrine of intercession that teaches us that everything purchased at the cross will not fail to be continually applied for our salvation "to the uttermost."

  Symington even goes so far as to say, "the principle of the new life may, in itself, be liable to decay" (p. 299). A Christian would be liable to fall away from Christ if left to his own devices. However, "Christ by His intercession will uphold it;

their sins may deserve condemnation, but He intercedes for pardon" (p. 299). It is because of the intercession of Christ that His atonement always achieves the unfailing salvation of all the elect. Theologians in the Reformation tradition speak of this security of the believer as the "perseverance of the saints." Symington shows how the "perseverance of the saints" derives from the *intercession* of Jesus.

2. Implications for what we do—In addition to these (and other) convictions which we believe, the doctrine of Christ's intercession has implications for *how we live,* as well. Symington identifies at least four practical implications to draw from the doctrine of Christ's intercession:

- *The practice of prayer*—One of the most obvious, and important, implications is the discipline of prayer. It is this lesson which the author of Hebrews urges: "Seeing then that we have a great high priest.... Let us therefore come boldly unto the throne of grace that we may obtain mercy, and find grace to help in time of need" (Heb. 4:14–16). We do not always know what to pray for, or how to pray; nevertheless, we have a perfect Intercessor to carry our petitions for us. Knowing this wonderful truth encourages us to pray (Rom. 8:26–34). Because we have an Advocate, ready to take up our cause on our behalf with great wisdom and perfect merit, we have every reason to seek His help often. Our High Priest's constancy in intercession should lead us to constancy in prayer (1 Thess. 5:17). Jesus stands ready to intercede for us in all our needs; how quick and constant in prayer ought we to be, knowing this truth.

  The doctrine of Christ's intercession leads the believer to frequent, joyful, and expectant prayer (John 14:12–13).

- *A topic for contemplation in difficulty*—The knowledge of Christ's intercession is a source of great encouragement in times of distress. As great an encouragement as it is to know that a friend is praying for you, how much more assuring it is to know that *Christ Himself* is interceding. Reflecting on this doctrine is, in Symington's words, "an antidote" (p. 300) to despair. Christians are apt to face heartache like anyone, but we have many divine truths with which to encourage our hearts (Ps. 42:5, 11). The doctrine of intercession is chief among those truths, and should be consciously brought to mind to bolster the heart in trouble.

This doctrine also reassures Christians, overly indulged in gloom over their sins, of their right (indeed, their need) to rejoice. "There are professing Christians," Symington wrote, "who give themselves up to a morbid melancholy brooding over their sins and shortcomings." To persist in this attitude is, according to Symington, "[to suppose] that there [is] no advocate with the Father, no intercessor within the vail...to plead their cause and secure their salvation" (p. 300).

The doctrine of Christ's intercession should be brought to mind and pondered for encouragement in dark hours.

- *The increase of Christian devotion*—It is the cross of Christ which demonstrates His great love for us, and which inspires our love for Him (1 John 4:10, 19). Symington wrote extensively on the atonement in order to increase our under-standing of that amazing love. Having written further on the intercession, as Christ's continuing application of the atonement, Symington believes the reader to have reason for only greater marvel and love to Christ. "Surely the pre-ceding pages," he wrote, "have been read to little purpose, if they have not left the impression on the mind that the *pres-ent* work of Christ in heaven is of no inferior moment [to His past work on the cross]" (pp. 299–300). The inspired penmen of Scripture have written much to show us our High Priest, having completed the sacrifice and now interceding its mer-its. "Let us then think highly, and think much," Symington urges, "of the intercession as well as the death of Christ" (p. 300). Such conscious meditation on His intercession rightly stirs a heart of gratitude, of greater love for Christ, and honor to Him.

  Recognizing that Jesus is interceding for us each day and every day, ought to be an impetus to stir similar devotion to Christ on our part, each day, every day. The doctrine of the intercession is cause for the discipline of daily worship.

- *The grounds for self-examination*—As the knowledge of Christ's intercession lifts the believer's heart to great heights of joy, the same doctrine ought to fill the *unbeliever's* heart with great fear and trouble. To *not* have Jesus interceding for you is to be excluded from the saving fruits of the atonement. "Oh that men would consider the misery of being without an interest in this part of the Saviour's work!" Symington urges (p. 301). In fact, "Not to have His prayers *for* us is to have them *against us*...," the author continues. "That blood which speaks so powerfully for the salvation of those who believe, cries out loudly for vengeance on such as despise and abuse it" (p. 301; cf. Heb. 2:3). The doctrine of Christ's intercession is not only a cause for the believer's great security and comfort, but this doctrine shows the unbeliever why it is so necessary for him to seek for the intercession of this High Priest!

With urgent pastoral concern, therefore, Symington exhorts—

> Be it then the concern of all who read these pages, earnestly to seek such an interest in what the Saviour has done and is still doing.... Let them not regard [these] as matters of curious speculation, or content themselves with mere doctrinal belief.... They must become the subjects of saving faith....

> Let not the reader, then, rise from the perusal of these pages, without seriously and conscientiously asking himself these questions:—Am I interested in the atonement and intercession of Jesus Christ? Have I faith in the sacrifice of the great High Priest? Has my soul been sprinkled with His precious blood? Does He plead in my behalf with the Father?... Were I called, at this moment, to recline my head on the pillow of death, could I indulge the comforting assurance that the advocate within the vail...would present on my behalf the request, 'Father, I will that they also, whom thou hast given me, be with me where I am' [John 17:24]...? These are solemn questions. Let no one neglect to put them to himself. (pp. 301–303)

Certainly many other lessons—both propositional and practical—are to be derived from this doctrine. Those just outlined illustrate the need Symington recognized for a personal and living response to this doctrine. Christ, as our High Priest, not only thought about His love for us, He practically applied—and applies—it in His atonement and intercession. A truly loving response will be just as practical and active. Symington shows his pastoral earnestness by emphasizing the practical nature of the doctrine of Christ's intercession.

Symington concluded his momentous study *On the Atonement and Intercession of Jesus Christ* with this prayer—a fitting prayer with which to close a study of so important a topic:

> May the Spirit of all grace, whose prerogative it is to take the things of Christ and show them unto men, be pleased to grant, that the perusal of these sheets may thus prove the means of salvation to many; and to the only wise God, our Saviour, be all the glory. Amen! (p. 303)

✦   ✦   ✦

Consider the Apostle and High Priest of our profession, Christ Jesus... For we have not an high priest which cannot be touched with the feeling of our infirmities; but was in all points tempted like as we are, yet without sin. Let us therefore come boldly unto the throne of grace, that we may obtain mercy, and find grace to help in time of need. (Heb. 3:1; 4:15–16)

WRITINGS:

Messiah the Prince, or
On the Mediatorial Dominion
of Jesus Christ
(1839)

———————————

CHAPTER 12

Introduction to
Messiah the Prince (1839)

On December 25, 1066 A.D., William the Conqueror chose West-minster Abbey in London as the place to receive his crown. For a millennium since that time, kings and queens have continued to be crowned in Westminster Abbey. Not only is it interesting that so many crowns have been presented in one place; but it is significant that a *church-building* has been so long deemed the ideal place for such a *political* event.

A clue as to the reason for this longstanding tradition can be found in an inscription above the high altar at Westminster Abbey. There, at the most esteemed point in the cathedral—and over that altar on which the crown is traditionally placed before being taken up and put on the new monarch's head—the altar canopy bears this quotation from Scripture: "The kingdoms of this world are become the kingdoms of our Lord" (Rev. 11:15). As the one whom Scripture calls, "King of kings and Lord of lords," Jesus is the one by whom kings reign and *from whom* they receive their crowns. Recognition of this doctrine has led to such longstanding practices as the crowning of British monarchs at Westminster Abbey. It has also profoundly influenced the nature of governments, of the church, of church-state relationships, and of the very idea of society in those lands where this truth has been embraced.

It must also be acknowledged, however, that *misuse* of this doctrine has led to certain dreadful abuses. It is often the case that irreligious men will use the guise of religion for their ends, seeking to "hijack" powerful truths for self-serving purposes. Certainly, the doctrine of Christ's supremacy over state government has been a particular object of such misuse.

In the medieval years, for example, the Roman Catholic Church used the claim of Christ's sovereignty over all earthly kingdoms as the basis for asserting *church* control over the state. There is, it should be noted, a significant difference between *Jesus* ruling over kings and *the church* ruling over kings. Nevertheless, in the year 800 A.D., Pope Leo III provided the "historical paradigm" of the Roman Catholic Church's supposed right to give (and take) crowns, when Pope Leo placed Charlemagne's imperial crown on his head. Likewise another European emperor, upon offending Pope Gregory, was compelled to stand barefoot in the snow for three days outside Gregory's palace. Henry IV was being "reminded" of his place (as were all other political rulers who would be often reminded of that incident). Henry was finally admitted to bow and do penance for his offenses against the Pope.

According to Rome's interpretation of Christ's title "King of kings," the *church* by right ought to be sovereign over state governments. This, however, is a misappropriation of the doctrine, as Symington was to show in his work. *Christ* indeed is the King of kings, but the church is not.

The medieval monarchs of Scotland and England, on the other hand, came to be associated with the opposite abuse of this doctrine. Because Jesus is King of kings and Lord of lords, the Stuart dynasty (especially) asserted "the divine right of kings." These political kings saw themselves as appointed by Jesus to rule over both church and state on His behalf. Here was the opposite use of this same teaching, placing *the state* over the church. It is this interpretation of the doctrine which continues to be perpetuated in the Anglican Church, where the British monarch is also acknowledged as the head of the Anglican Church.

Many of those who fled to the American colonies in the seventeenth and eighteenth centuries were fleeing from religious persecution by kings asserting such "divine rights" over religion. Kings who believed themselves authorized to govern the church executed criminal prosecution (persecution) against doctrines not conducive to political agendas. Conditions in old Europe became difficult for the likes of the Pilgrim and Puritan forefathers of America.

Although many of the religious founders of the American settlements continued to recognize the right of King Jesus to rule over both church and state, a third misuse of the doctrine was eventually to emerge in America. In response to the other misuses of Christ's kingship, it became common in American theology to completely "spiritualize" His crown. Jesus' reign is so spiritual that state government has no need to establish any literal relationship to Christ. In contrast to the many early constitutions of American States which *did* acknowledge Jesus as a real King to whom their governments owed submission, the Federal Constitution ratified in 1789 was completely silent on the state's relationship to Christ. Only in the First Amendment, soon added to the Constitution, was the intent of this silence explained: "Congress shall make no law respecting an establishment of religion, or prohibiting the free exercise thereof...."

Here was a third way—an alternative to Roman Catholic "church-over-state" ideals, and the British "state-over-church" thinking. Instead, the federal government would remain wholly neutral toward Christ and His church ("separation of church and state"). The French Revolution advanced a similar movement in Europe. Today, this "third way"—the secularization of state government—is the dominant view of the modern world.

The theory of state neutrality toward religion has proven much more sticky than supposed, however. Gradually, not only civil government, but other social institutions like colleges, schools, businesses, and the family itself have been moved from the "religious" sphere to the "secular" sphere. Although the biblical title "King of kings and Lord of lords" is supposed to reflect Christ's *universal* dominion, the complete spiritualization of His crown has led to the view that only the church actually needs to submit to His law.

The Scripture text on the high-altar canopy at Westminster Abbey is now, for many, little more than rhetoric.

William Symington's second book, and the one for which he is best known, is entitled, *Messiah the Prince, or The Mediatorial Dominion of Jesus Christ*. It was written as a Covenanter's response, from Scripture, to the various misunderstandings of Christ's kingship just described. The biblical doctrine of Christ's "Mediatorial Dominion" does not mean: (1) that *the church* rules over the state, as per Rome, nor (2) that *the state* rules over the church, as per Anglicanism. Neither is Christ's kingship (3) so "spiritual" that there is no duty of society toward Christ, nor a valid church-state relationship. Nonetheless, Jesus truly is "King of kings and Lord of lords," and both church and civil government have real obligations to His crown. Symington's *Messiah the Prince* was written to reassert "the crown rights and royal prerogatives of King Jesus" in a period when the practice of the first two errors was still a fresh memory, and the third (secularism) was beginning to spread across the Western world.

Two centuries later, the effects of that "secularization movement"—and the resulting lack of moral absolutes for society—are increasingly being felt. Perhaps now, as much as ever, the time is ripe to revisit Symington's study of this important subject.

Symington's work is presented in three parts: (1) a section setting forth the doctrine of Christ's dominion; (2) a section specifically applying this doctrine to the obligations of the church; and, (3) a section applying this doctrine to the obligations of civil government. The following three chapters will be arranged accordingly.[1]

---

1. Page numbers cited in this and the following chapters, without other source indication, are from Symington's *Messiah the Prince* (American edition 1884; reprint, Edmonton: Still Waters Revival Books, 1990).

CHAPTER 13

On the Mediatorial Dominion of Jesus Christ

On an appointed day every autumn, the British monarch enters the House of Lords to open the next session of Parliament. At that opening ceremony, the king or queen, dressed in royal robes and wearing the Imperial Crown, delivers a speech from the throne. In that speech, the monarch assigns to Parliament the government agenda for the coming session.

For centuries, British kings have set the agenda for the government. In modern times, however, it is actually the *prime minister* who writes the speech which the monarch delivers. Although it is still the crown that presents the government agenda, it is no longer the crown that sets the agenda. British royalty is, today, a ceremonial rather than governmental office.

In an age of democracy, we in the western world have largely forgotten what it means to have a king with real authority. Some modern nations like France and the United States have abandoned monarchy altogether. In those industrialized nations that do still have kings and queens, like Britain and Spain, the royalty are ceremonial figureheads and do not bear actual authority. True authority resides in elected officers while the hereditary monarch fulfills diplomatic or ceremonial functions.

As a result of these circumstances, we in the modern West often think of kings and queens in terms of ceremonies and ritual, while other titles like president, prime minister, and governor are the titles that evoke a sense of true importance. We must be careful, however, not to confuse our modern experience with biblical references to royalty. The Old and New Testament writings were composed in times when kings were still kings wielding real sovereignty and bearing true responsibility for the welfare of the people.

When Scripture calls Jesus a "King," we ought not miss the significance intended by this ascription. This is not simply respectful rhetoric. It has become popular in many Christian circles today to think of Jesus' royal titles as essentially figurative, or as indicating a future reign which He will establish after His Second Coming. Symington, however, desired that Christians would pay closer attention to the Bible's teachings on the subject. He was concerned that the church fully appreciate the real and practical implications of Christ's present reign for faith, the church, and all aspects of human society.

Written with the same carefulness demonstrated in his work on Christ's priestly office (*On the Atonement and Intercession of Jesus Christ*, published in 1834), Symington's book on Jesus' kingly office appeared in 1839. This latter work has undergone various editions and reprints over the nearly two centuries since.

Before examining the main content of Symington's work, one important clarification should be made. It is a matter of clarification which Symington sought to establish in the opening pages of his book. Specifically, we must have clearly fixed in mind a distinction between Jesus' authority *as God*—an authority which He always enjoyed over all things—and His authority *as our Savior*. By His very nature, Jesus always was God. To bring about our salvation, however, Jesus had to become a man. It is in Jesus' *becoming* a man that *He took up* the responsibilities and prerogatives of a Priest, a Prophet, and a King. We should have it clearly in mind that Symington was writing, in this book, about the royal authority Jesus *obtained* as our Incarnate Savior. This is an aspect of His authority distinct from that which He always enjoyed as the Creator God.

This might seem a confusing distinction to make, but it is a biblical distinction that needs to be upheld. Just as it is hard to comprehend how Jesus can be both God *and* man, similarly it is difficult to comprehend how Jesus can be at once both eternally sovereign (as Creator) and yet also to have needed to obtain sovereignty (as Savior). Yet such distinctions are taught to us by Scripture, and are important to have in mind as we approach Symington's book. Perhaps an illustration will help to fix this concept more clearly in our thinking.

For the sake of illustration, we might imagine a lawyer whose son has been charged with a crime—maybe he was caught shoplifting. Informed of the charges against his boy, we will further suppose that this father decides to act personally as his son's lawyer in his trial. Here is an example of one individual (the father) who takes on two roles of authority in relation to the same person (the boy). As a parent, the father always had authority in the boy's life. Now, as his lawyer as well, the father takes *a particular kind* of authority *for a particular purpose:* to represent his son before the court and resolve the charges against him. In a somewhat similar sense, the same Jesus, who as Creator always held sovereignty over us, now takes on mediatorial kingship as well *for the purposes of our salvation.*

In the case of Jesus, we might speak of the first kind of authority—His eternal sovereignty as God—as His *natural dominion.*[1] It was Jesus who made all things, and having made everything, Jesus naturally owns all things. Simply because of who Jesus is (His *nature*), He has sovereign authority over everything. Paul wrote about this kind of authority held by Jesus in his epistle to the Colossians:

> For by him were all things created, that are in heaven, and that are in earth, visible and invisible, whether they be thrones, or dominions, or principalities, or powers: all things were created by him, and for him: and he is before all things, and by him all things consist (Col. 1:16–17; cf. Ps. 24:1–2).

As *the Creator God,* Jesus always had absolute authority over all things. Just as there was never a time when He was not God, there was never a time when Jesus was not King, in this sense. Symington refers to this authority of Jesus the Creator God as His *essential,* or what we here have termed His *natural dominion.*

The second kind of authority Jesus held, however, is something which He had to obtain as part of His work of salvation. It is what Symington calls His *mediatorial dominion.* As a man, Jesus took "the form of a servant" (Phil. 2:7). In respect to His *humanity,* Jesus was not (at first) revealed as a king, but a servant. Nevertheless, from that position of servanthood, Jesus went on *to be exalted* to a throne: "Wherefore God also hath highly exalted him, and given him a name which is above every name" (Phil. 2:9).

---

1. Symington actually used the term *essential* instead of *natural.* However, the meaning of the word *essential* has changed some in modern usage so that the word *natural* might be more clear for present purposes.

Peter also preached about this authority Jesus *received* as our incarnate Savior in Acts 2. Using one of David's Psalms (Ps. 110) as a preaching text, Peter proclaimed,

> Therefore being a prophet, and knowing that God had sworn with an oath to him, that of the fruit of his loins, according to the flesh, he would raise up Christ to sit on his throne... David...saith himself [of Jesus], The Lord said unto my Lord, Sit thou on my right hand, until I make thy foes thy footstool. Therefore let all the house of Israel know assuredly, that God hath made that same Jesus, whom ye have crucified, both Lord and Christ (Acts 2:30–36; cf., Isa. 9:6).

Jesus was exalted to a throne and endowed with titles of sovereignty. Peter is clear to indicate these privileges as being "new" acquisitions—authority ascribed to Jesus at a specific point in time and in specific connection with His work as our Savior. This is a second kind of authority obtained by Jesus in specific connection with His work of salvation. Like the lawyer-father in the earlier illustration, although Jesus already held natural authority over the creation, in His love He went further to obtain for Himself *mediatorial authority* for the specific purpose of guaranteeing the effectiveness of our redemption.

It is this *mediatorial dominion* that is the subject of Symington's book. In a manner similar to his work on Jesus' priesthood *(On the Atonement)*, this work views various facets of Jesus' kingship, one at a time:

• The *Necessity* of Christ's Reign	*That Jesus needed to be a Priest is evident. Why does He need to be a King to save men?*
• The *Reality* of Christ's Reign	*How do we know Jesus is not just a Prophet and Priest, but also a King?*
• The *Qualifications* of Christ's Reign	*What standards qualify Jesus to be King of kings and Lord of lords?*
• The *Source* of Christ's Reign	*Does Jesus obtain authority from the people? By force...? Where does He get His authority?*

- The *Nature* of Christ's Reign   *Is Jesus a political king? A spiritual king...? What kind of King is He?*

- The *Extent* of Christ's Reign   *What are the boundaries of Christ's dominion? What realms are under His rule?*

- The *Duration* of Christ's Reign   *How long will Jesus continue to rule as a mediatorial King?*

The Necessity of Christ's Reign: To Accomplish Redemption

The fact that Jesus *needs* royal authority as part of His redemptive work is plainly stated by the Apostle Paul. "He must reign," Paul wrote to the Corinthians—"he must reign, till he hath put all enemies under his feet" (1 Cor. 15:25). Paul teaches us that royal authority is a necessary part of our Savior's work. Jesus himself also indicated this need for kingly authority. In His interview with Pilate, for example, we read the following:

> Pilate therefore said unto him, Art thou a king then? Jesus answered, Thou sayest that I am a king. To this end was I born, and for this cause came I into the world...." (John 18:37)

It can be clearly seen in such texts that Jesus *did* need authority as part of His saving work. In the first chapter of his book ("The Necessity of Christ's Mediatorial Reign"), Symington seeks to help us appreciate *why* this is so. Symington's survey of reasons for this necessity can be summarized under the following three points.

*1. The Savior needs sovereignty **over the elect**—*In order to guarantee the salvation of His elect, Jesus needed to become not only our Priest and our Prophet, but also our King. "As priest," Symington explains, "He makes atonement for the sins of the chosen.... As Prophet, He makes known to men that all this has been done..." (pp. 7–8). These alone are not sufficient to complete the work of salvation, however. In addition to purchasing and publishing the atonement, it is also necessary that the atonement be *applied* by Jesus if He is to guarantee its effectiveness.

By way of illustration, we might think of the lame man by the pool of Bethesda (John 5:1–17). The Apostle John tells us that this man had been lame for thirty-eight years. John also tells us that, according to some miraculous provision of God, the waters of the pool of Bethesda near the temple were occasionally "stirred" by an angel: "an angel went down at a certain season into the pool and troubled the water: whosoever then first after the troubling of the water stepped in was made whole of whatsoever disease he had" (v. 4). Many of the sick and invalid, like the lame man featured by John, lay waiting beside the pool for its next stirring. There was one problem, however, which made it impossible for the lame man to obtain the desired healing. The *provision* for healing was there whenever the water was divinely stirred; the *knowledge* of that healing was grasped by the lame man; but the *ability* to get to the water was lacking.

> When Jesus saw him lie, and knew that he had been now a long time in that case, he saith unto him, Wilt thou be made whole? The impotent man answered him, Sir, I have no man, when the water is troubled, to put me into the pool...." (vv. 6–7)

Here was one for whom the provision and knowledge of healing were present, but he was hindered from obtaining it. Jesus, seeing the man's need, healed him on the spot. Rather than leaving the man helpless to get to the healing, Jesus brought the healing to him. In a similar way, Symington points out that the work of salvation requires more than the *provision* of atonement (by Jesus the Priest) and the *announcement* of that atonement (by Jesus the Prophet). We need also for Him, as a King with authority, to go throughout the earth and insure that whatever may stand in the way of the effective *application* of that atonement to any of the elect might be overcome. We need a Savior who not only purchases, prays for, and proclaims the atonement, but who also goes out with authority to apply it. (Cf. Ps. 110:4; Matt. 28:18–20; John 17:1; 18:37; Eph. 1:22)

There is another reason why we need a Savior who is sovereign over us. Even the elect, Symington points out, "are all of them, by nature, rebels, enemies to Christ, both in their minds and by wicked works" (pp. 14–15). As the Apostles frequently wrote, we did not choose Christ, but He chose us. We who now believe were, in our own natural bent, opposed to Christ. None of us, of our own accord, would have even desired salvation, unless Jesus had exercised the authority to overrule the reign of our own sinful nature (John 15:16;

Luke 22:32; Rom. 7:24–25; 1 Cor. 15:57–58; 2 Cor. 10:5; Phil. 1:6). Not only must the obstacles that hinder us from obtaining salvation be overcome by Jesus, but, Symington states, the elect "must be *made* willing—their imaginations must be *brought* down" (p. 15).

Numerous illustrations of this need can be noted in Scripture. For example, Naaman was the head of the Syrian army but was afflicted with leprosy (2 Kings 5). Through a Hebrew servant girl, he learned that the God of Israel was merciful to heal. He went to the prophet Elisha. When, however, Elisha instructed Naaman to dip in the River Jordan seven times for healing, Naaman "turned and went away in a rage" (v. 12). He was insulted at the humiliation of the procedure and insisted that bathing in one of the noble rivers of Damascus would be more fitting. Naaman was too proud to receive God's healing, until another servant urged, "My father, if the prophet had bid thee do some great thing, wouldest thou not have done it? how much rather then, when he saith to thee, Wash, and be clean?" (v. 13). Naaman did wash, was cleansed physically, and also submitted himself to the worship of Israel's God. Naaman's own stubborn heart had to be humbled, however, before he would even be willing to undertake the means of his healing.

The Prodigal Son provides a further, New Testament example of the same principle (Luke 15:11–32). In that familiar parable, Jesus spoke of a son who knew what his inheritance was, but he rejected his father in order to spend his inheritance on himself. Through a series of natural catastrophes, however, such as the exhaustion of his funds, the timed emergence of a famine, and the opening up of employment feeding pigs, the hard-hearted young prodigal finally humbled himself. Returning to his father, the son was welcomed in loving arms.

Jesus knows the hardness of our hearts. He also knows how to bring about the required softening to lead each of the elect to salvation. Even the "chief [of sinners]," the Apostle Paul, was brought from "breathing out threatenings and slaughter against the disciples of the Lord" to himself calling Jesus "Lord" (1 Tim. 1:15; Acts 9:1–9). Jesus knows the hardness of every heart, and He must have the authority to employ every necessary external measure, as well as dominion to restrain and soften the prideful reign of our own sinful hearts within us, to bring us to salvation.

It is not possible, such being the case, that [the elect] should embrace of themselves the overtures of reconciliation.... No; they treat them with despite, they spurn them with scorn. They must be reconciled—they must be *made* willing.... And how but by the Saviour's rod of omnipotent strength sent forth out of Zion; by the irresistible scepter of His grace, swayed with authority for this very end; by the sharp arrows of conviction which penetrate the heart.... (p. 15)

We who are elect unto salvation *need* more than the purchase and announcement of salvation. We need a Savior with authority to overcome every obstacle between us and the application of salvation. We need a Savior with authority to overrule the very hard-heartedness of our own selfish hearts to make us willing to submit to His grace. *It is necessary that the Savior of God's elect be one with sovereign, kingly authority over the elect themselves.*

There is, in this first reason, a degree of overlap (or close harmony) with Symington's teaching on the *intercession* of Christ. In an earlier chapter (pp. 128–149, above), it was seen that Jesus' priestly intercession is also necessary for the continual working out of our salvation. The overlap between Jesus' intercession and His dominion, on this point, might be likened to the relationship of a corporate financial officer and the company president. The financial officer is needed to make sure that the funds rightly belonging to the company are available, in the right accounts, and dispersed as needed. The president makes sure that each business deal is actually set up and carried out using those funds. Both offices are necessary for the same ends, though distinct.

Jesus likewise, as our priestly Intercessor, insures that every benefit *from the Father* is brought to bear on our account as we need it. Moreover, as our mediatorial King, He further governs *all the circumstances of life and history* to insure that those benefits have their proper effect. For the elect to be saved and sanctified, they need a Priest who continually intercedes for every benefit and a King who sovereignly insures the effective application of those benefits.

2. *The Savior needs sovereignty **over the enemies of the elect**.*—Salvation is not a work without opposition. There are enemies of the gospel who actively oppose the work of salvation. The *world* is at enmity with God. The *devil* and his hosts resist the advance of the gospel. Furthermore, many *false religions* defy and contradict the

truth. There are many enemies of Christ actively at work in the world, seeking to oppose the spread of the gospel and to cut off the church.

In many places around the world today, such opposition takes the form of physical persecution and even bloodshed. For the gospel to continue to bring fruit in the face of such opposition, the church needs a Savior more powerful than these foes. In those lands where "freedom of religion" prevents physical persecution, opposition to the spread of the gospel is nonetheless real. Even in places like America and Western Europe, legal and cultural influences have often been employed to limit the spread of the Christian faith. When movies are made that mock and discourage faith in Christ, this is a powerful hindrance for those who fall under its spell against their heeding the gospel. When court orders are imposed that censor Christ from public schools and other public places, these are formidable obstacles against the gospel reaching those who are elect but not yet saved. There are enemies actively employing many kinds of obstacles, blatant and subtle, to hinder, limit, constrict, dilute, and oppose the spread of the gospel.

In the face of such opposition to the gospel, the Savior *needs* authority over His enemies. "Are these enemies to meet with no resistance?" Symington asks, "Certainly not.... To the accomplishment of this work, investment with regal power and authority is indispensable" (pp. 13–14).

By authority *over* these opponents, Jesus not only resists their efforts; He is also able to *subject* their intentions to His own purposes. Take, for one example, the persecution begun by Saul against the church in Acts:

> And at that time there was a great persecution against the church which was at Jerusalem; and they [the believers] were all scattered abroad throughout the regions of Judea and Samaria.... As for Saul, he made havoc of the church, entering into every house.... (Acts 8:1–3)

Here is one of the first outbreaks of widespread, physical violence against the church after Christ's ascension. Yet what was appointed by men as an effort to squelch the gospel, ended up proving the very basis of its ongoing growth: "Therefore they that were scattered abroad [i.e., by the persecution] went every where preaching the word..." (Acts 8:4). The subsequent paragraphs of the account describe several examples of how the gospel was brought to new territories by that scattering. The scattering introduced by this persecution was *subordinated* by Christ to serve His purposes. This is an example of Jesus exercising His sovereignty, not only against but *over* His enemies.

Christ does not work every scenario in exactly the same manner, nor is persecution—even with the assurance of Jesus' reign over it—ever to be regarded as an "ideal condition" for the church to grow. On the contrary, the church is to pray constantly for peace, that the gospel might be promoted even more fruitfully through times of security:

> I exhort therefore, that, first of all, supplications...be made... that we may lead a quiet and peaceable life in all godliness and honesty. For this is good and acceptable in the sight of God our Saviour; who will have all men to be saved, and to come unto the knowledge of the truth (1 Tim. 2:1–4).

Persecution and oppression are never to be viewed as "good things." Nevertheless, the fact that constant and formidable opposition to the gospel does exist means that the work of salvation needs a Savior *who is endowed with sovereign dominion over His foes.* "He must reign," Paul wrote, "till he hath put all enemies under his feet" (1 Cor. 15:25. Cf. Gen. 50:20; Isa. 34:5–6; 63:1–4; John 15:19; Rom. 7:21; Eph. 6:12; Heb. 2:15)

*3. The Savior needs sovereignty **over the whole course of history**.*—In the parable of the Prodigal Son rehearsed earlier (p. 215, above), Christ used regional economics, natural phenomena like a famine, available jobs, and other social factors as part of His methods to bring the prodigal to repentance. These illustrate a third point under which we may speak of Christ's need for dominion. Not only as Creator does Jesus exercise authority for the orderly operation of the universe, but as Savior He must have authority to suspend, interrupt, or otherwise guide the order of nature and of human institutions for the purposes of the gospel.

Symington points to the political and military aspirations of the Babylonians, which proved to be God's means for bringing Judah to repentance. After the people of God had been sufficiently humbled by Babylon, the Chaldeans were raised up to overthrow the Babylonians and were used by Him to grant the exiles freedom to return to Judah (p. 14). *In order for the purposes of salvation to be advanced, it is necessary for our Savior to have dominion even over the events of history.*

✦   ✦   ✦

Symington is by no means alone in his articulation of these truths. Other theologians have likewise emphasized the importance of Christ's absolute sovereignty in the working out of salvation. It is, in fact, a prominent feature of Reformation (or, Reformed, or "Calvinistic") doctrine that Christ as Savior is *sovereign*. What Symington is highlighting, however, is that this very sovereignty of Christ for the working out of salvation is a *royal* characteristic, and one which He needed to obtain as part of his mediatorial work. It is *as a King* that Jesus reigns sovereign for the purposes of redemption—*and it is necessary that He do so*. Without this ongoing authority, all that Jesus purchased as a Priest, and all that He announced as a Prophet, would go unapplied. Just as, in a human government, the existence of a Constitution is of little effect without an executive officer empowered to implement and maintain that Constitutional order, so it is necessary for Jesus to reign, and to continue to reign, in order perfectly to execute the design of redemption in all its points. Symington writes:

> Without Christ's kingly work, the gracious purposes of God could not be executed; the mediatorial character itself would not be complete; the work of salvation must continue unrewarded; the enemies of truth and holiness should finally triumph, and the necessities of the children of God remain for ever unsupplied. Such things cannot—shall not be. 'The Lord is our king, he will save us' (Isa. 33:22). The exalted Redeemer is at once 'a Prince and a Saviour' (Acts 5:31). (p. 16)

The Reality of Christ's Reign: The Testimony of Witnesses

That we *need* a King with universal authority is a cause for concern. That we *have* such a King is a cause for joy.

In the second chapter of *Messiah the Prince*, Symington compiles evidence to demonstrate "The Reality of Christ's Mediatorial Dominion." Some of the historical accounts cited in the previous section are, in themselves, a kind of proof that Jesus' reign is real. The turning of various oppositions against the church, and the subjection of historical events, to the ends of redemption are in themselves evidence of His reign at work. Nevertheless, lest these be considered coincidences, Symington gives particular attention to biblical *testimonies* of Christ's kingship.

The claim of dominion is not heard from the lips of Jesus alone. *"Others* [also]," Symington notes, "recognise the validity of His claim. It is acknowledged by intelligent and moral beings of every class and rank" (p. 22). In his book, Symington summons the witnesses of God the Father (e.g., Phil. 2:9–10), of angels (e.g., Luke 1:31–33), of "the star-led wizards" (i.e., the Magi; Matt. 2:2), of Nathanael (John 1:49), and of Paul (1 Tim. 1:17), all of whom, in their various capacities, recognize the fact of Jesus' royalty. Furthermore, not only these friends of Christ have testified to His royalty, but certain of Jesus' enemies also have confessed His crown. For example, the Jewish multitude (who later crucified Him) at first welcomed Him into Jerusalem *as a King* (e.g., John 12:13). Pontius Pilate also gave affirmation of Jesus' kingship with the title affixed to the cross, despite the opposition of Jewish leaders (John 18:19). The above New Testament accounts give us a varied collection of period eyewitnesses to the royal rights of Christ.

To accompany these eyewitnesses of Christ's life and work, Symington also produces the testimonies of Old Testament prophets (e.g., Num. 24:17; Isa. 9:6–7) and the witness of ancient prefigurations of His rule (such as Melchizedek, Moses, David, and Solomon). Symington also identifies numerous ascriptions of royal titles to Jesus by various inspired authors throughout both Old and New Testaments (e.g., Mic. 5:2; Acts 2:36). And he compiles an inventory of royal accoutrements—like a throne, crown, scepter, ambassadors, and so forth—seen in Christ's possession by those granted such revelations.

Symington's evidence reads like a lawyer's catalog of witnesses and material implements which he would have ready for summons to the trial. In a modern court of law, a knife with the murderer's fingerprints and a handful of eyewitnesses offer adequate proof of the suspect's identity. In Scripture, Symington points out, the abundance of royal appliances ascribed to His hand and the countless witnesses of His royal activities, offer abundant proof that His dominion, as taught by Scripture, is something real and not just figurative.

> Of the reality of Christ's mediatorial dominion there can thus be no doubt.... To [deny it] is to nullify types; to contradict prophecy; to blot out the Saviour's titles; to give the faithful and true Witness Himself the lie; to convert His regalia into empty baubles; and to reduce His prerogatives to mere mockery and show. (p. 27)

Scripture attests to us a Savior who bears real kingship. He is more than a Prophet and a Priest, He is also truly a sovereign King. To suppose otherwise is, in Symington's words, to be guilty of the crime of the Roman soldiers. The soldiers at Jesus' trial scorned His claim to be a true King. They "placed on His head a crown of thorns, put on Him a purple robe; and as they shouted, 'Hail, King!' smote Him with their hands" (p. 27). We who know Christ as our Priestly Intercessor must not make this error of esteeming His royalty an empty symbol. The Scriptures present us with extensive evidence that the kingship possessed by our Lord is real.

The Qualifications of Christ's Reign: His Dignity and Power

That we *need* a Savior with sovereign authority has been seen. That we *have* a Savior with such power has now also been seen. Symington would next have us consider the *qualifications* of Jesus to reign. The importance of this matter can be illustrated by comparing two kings from medieval history: Edward II and his son, Edward III.

Edward III, the son, was one of the greatest kings to ascend the throne of England. He reigned prosperously and effectively from 1327 to 1377. Edward's greatness was due, in part, to his reclaiming for England much of what his father had lost. His father, Edward II, had been one of the weakest kings of the period. The elder Edward had shown himself more concerned with entertainment and sports than government, and he proved to be pliable under the manipulations of various courtiers throughout his twenty-year reign. For all his ineptitudes and failures, Edward II was eventually compelled to abdicate in 1327, and his son, Edward III, was crowned in his place.

Such histories remind us that not all kings are equal to the task. A weak king, upon ascending to his throne, can bring great damage to his people. The weak rule of Edward II brought trouble upon his whole kingdom. It is when a king arises whose qualifications are equal to his task that a nation rejoices. The book of Ecclesiastes summarizes this principle, thus:

> Woe to thee, O land, when thy king is a child,
> and thy princes eat in the morning!

> Blessed art thou, O land, when thy king is the son of nobles,
> and thy princes eat in due season,
> for strength, and not for drunkenness! (Eccl. 10:16–17)

For those who place their trust in Christ as the King of their salvation, it is crucial that we know whether He is indeed equal to the task. That we *need* a kingly Savior has been shown. That we *have* such a King in Jesus has been shown. That Jesus is indeed *competent* is the next subject of Symington's exposition on the reign of Christ: "Christ's Qualifications for the Kingly Office." Symington deduces from Scripture seven categories of qualification that suit Jesus as the King of our redemption:

1. *Personal Dignity*—That Symington chose "personal dignity" as the opening feature in his list indicates something of the difference between his time and ours. Rather than beginning with pragmatic qualities, such as wisdom to make decisions or power to act (as will appear later in the list), Symington has chosen to begin by highlighting Christ's noble disposition. Although modern, democratic politics have taught us to prize pragmatic qualities with only secondary concern for a candidate's personal decorum, Symington wrote out of a social heritage that recognized court etiquette and personal majesty as also essential for effective government. "That the reigns of government," Symington wrote, "should be placed in the hands of one entirely destitute of [natural majesty] is repugnant to all our feelings of propriety" (p. 28). Such a concern for personal dignity was not just a historically European trait, however, but something reflected in Scripture as well, such as the Ecclesiastes text concerned with the "noble birth" of a king quoted above (Eccl. 10:16–17; cf. also Judg. 8:18).

Jesus, Symington notes, supremely meets this quality of a king. Jesus is not just "a son of nobles," He is "the Son of God." By this title, in addition to all its other implications, we are assured that our Mediatorial King is a King with great personal majesty—indeed, "such dignity as belongs only to God" (p. 29). Jesus, the Son of God, demonstrates in His person a demeanor that suits Him for royalty. (Cf. Luke 1:32; John 5:18)

2. *Near Relationship*—Since the earliest days of Israel, it was an express requirement that a king be of close relationship to the people he would govern. In the laws of the king, Moses instructed Israel, "One from among thy brethren shalt thou set king over thee: thou mayest not set a stranger over thee, which is not thy brother" (Deut. 17:15).

"The height of His personal dignity as the Son of God," Symington writes of Jesus, "seems to preclude the possibility of natural relationship to His subjects" (p. 31). As a divine being of supreme majesty, Jesus was far above being "our brother." "By the mystery of the incarnation, however," Symington continues, "this difficulty is overcome" (p. 31). Jesus has indeed become a man like us, and one of "near relation" to capably know and administer our needs. Jesus, by the incarnation, has been qualified as a King of near relation to us. (Cf. 2 Sam. 19:42; Luke 1:31)

3. *Knowledge and Wisdom*—In addition to the personal attributes noted above, certain practical qualities are of obvious importance for one who would effectively implement the agenda of a kingdom. A king fit for his office must have knowledge, and he must have wisdom.

By *knowledge,* Symington remarks, "we speak...not so much of knowledge in general," (such as the knowledge gained by a regular school education), "[but] of that which qualifies for rule" (p. 32). In particular, Symington notes four kinds of knowledge uniquely required for one who rules. First, a king must know "the principles of the government which he is delegated to administer." As head of state, a king must know how the state operates (or is supposed to operate). Ronald Reagan, for example, is respected as having been an effective American president; but this does not mean he could have made an effective president or prime minister for Pakistan. Pakistani government operates under a different system and with different principles than American government. To be an effective leader one has to have not only general leadership qualities, but one also has to understand the principles of that particular government he is charged to organize and uphold. Jesus, Symington affirms, "knows well the principles of the government which He is delegated to administer; for they are founded on the nature of God and man, and on the relation subsisting between them" (p. 32). By His name, Immanuel, Jesus is announced as that one who manifests the reign of God Himself among men (Isa. 7:14). Jesus holds perfect knowledge of the principles of divine rule which He, as Mediatorial King, applies to His people. (Cf. 2 Sam. 7:14; Ps. 2:7; Acts 13:33)

A second kind of knowledge which a king must have is "knowledge...of the laws of the kingdom." It was a basic requirement of the kings of Israel that they possess a copy of the Mosaic laws, and that they read in them daily (Deut. 17:18–20). Jesus not only demonstrated such knowledge of the law, even in His youth, as to astound the Temple teachers (Luke 2:46–47), but in His own life He perfectly upheld the holy decrees of God (Mark 14:55; 2 Cor. 5:21). Jesus "knows well the laws of His kingdom..." (p. 32).

A third kind of knowledge which qualifies a king is his knowledge of the people he will rule: "knowledge...of the character, state, and necessities of the subjects" (p. 32). A king must understand the circumstances and needs of his people. It is necessary to understand their character and disposition. It is for this reason that kings often have counselors about them. In ancient times, it was common for kings who conquered a foreign land to appoint someone from that foreign land to serve in his court and help him know how to relate to the newly subjugated people. Jesus, however, needs no such counselors to teach Him the nature of the people He rules. As the Apostle John informs us: "Jesus...needed not that any should testify of man: for he knew what was in man" (John 2:24–25; cf. John 21:17; Rev. 2:23). As that one who created us, Jesus perfectly knows us and is ideally suited to rule over us.

The preceding three kinds of knowledge encompass the basic features of the kingdom itself: its order, its laws, and its people. An effective king must furthermore possess knowledge of those *outside* his kingdom. The importance of such knowledge, especially in a state of war, can be illustrated by General George S. Patton of World War II fame. One of the factors contributing to Patton's success in North Africa was his study of Erwin Rommel's book on tank warfare tactics. Rommel was the commander of the Panzer tank division Paton was fighting against. When Rommel was finally driven from North Africa in March, 1943, Patton legendarily shouted across the field of battle, "Rommel..., I read your book!" An effective general (or king) knows his enemy. In the case of Jesus, we have a King who "is thoroughly acquainted with the rival king-dom of this world, from whom He has to reclaim His subjects, and against whose assaults He must defend them" (p. 33. Cf. Matt. 9:4; Luke 10:18–19; 11:17)

A king must be knowledgeable. He must also possess *wisdom:* "wisdom to foresee, judgment to contrive, [and] prudence to exe-cute" (p. 33). It is one thing to *know* what the situation now is and what the situation needs to be; it is another to possess *the wisdom* to manage events to bring about the movement from one condition to the other. Such a King is Christ whom the Apostle Paul called "the King eternal...the only wise God" (1 Tim. 1:17).

"In short," Symington concludes of Jesus' knowledge and wisdom,

> nothing can fail either from ignorance or from indiscretion. There is no lack of information or of prudence. No event can occur unforeseen by Him. He is prepared for every occurrence. Nay, such is His wisdom, that what His enemies design for injury, He, by skilful management, can cause to operate powerfully for good. (p. 33)

4. *Power*—"But all these qualities will be of no avail," Symington states as he opens the next feature on his list, "without *power*" (p. 33). By power, Symington intends to indicate the force of a ruler's own will, his strength of moral energy to execute it, and the resources at his disposal. A king who embarks upon a task, but whose inten-tions waver in the face of opposition, cannot succeed. There is an old military adage that expresses this principle: "It is more fearful to meet an army of lambs led by a lion than an army of lions led by a lamb."

In His office as our sacrifice, Jesus is the Lamb of God; how-ever, in His office as our King, He is the Lion of Judah (Rev. 5:5). The power of Christ's own purpose is as unflinching as flint, as when "he stedfastly set his face to go to Jerusalem" and let noth-ing hinder His mission (Luke 9:51). Such is the power of a great king's volition. In Jesus, this power of purpose is also matched by the power of indefatigable moral energy. Though often afflicted by physical exhaustion during His earthly ministry, Christ's purposes were never derailed from His course. He perfectly *finished* His work in His human weariness (John 17:4), He certainly lacks no energy for His tasks in His now glorified estate.

Jesus also has the power of inexhaustible resources at His command:

> He can call to His aid all the perfections of the Godhead, and all the fulness of the new covenant. The elements of heaven, apostate spirits, and angels of light, are under His control, advancing His cause and opposing His enemies. At His command, the stars in their courses fought against Sisera; a messenger of Satan was sent to buffet an apostle, in fulfilment of His gracious designs; and it was no empty boast, that He could have commanded more than twelve legions of angels. (p. 34; citing, Col. 2:9; Heb. 8:10; Mark 4:41; Mark 1:27; Acts 12:11; Judg. 4:15; 5:20; 2 Cor. 12:7; Matt. 26:53, respectively)

"With such vast might," Symington concludes, "with such immense resources, no purpose can fail from inability to carry it into execution" (p. 34). Jesus is a King of unmatched power.

5. Moral Excellence—"He that ruleth over men must be just, ruling in the fear of God" (2 Sam. 23:3). Those are the words of David, composed at the end of his own reign over Israel. Even when a king is endowed with personal dignity—that is, majestic deportment and honorable demeanor—such may simply be a guise for advancing selfish and corrupt ends. Many a ruler in history has worn the crown nobly and published admirable laws in the throne room, only to engage in immoral alliances and dubious business from his private apartments. A righteous king must himself embody the purity and perfections of moral excellence.

Such, Scripture assures us, is the character of our King. "The sceptre of thy kingdom," writes the psalmist, "is a right sceptre" (Ps. 45:6). The saints in eternity also sing of Him, "Just and true are thy ways, thou King of saints!" (Rev. 15:3). So pure is the character of Jesus that, when confronted by those who had meticulously searched for charges against Him, Jesus could ask, "Which of you convinceth me of sin?" with no evidence produced (John 8:46; cf. 1 Sam. 12:2–3).

"His conduct was unimpeachable," writes Symington, "His behaviour was unaffected with the slightest moral obliquity.... Perfect moral excellence adorns His character" (pp. 36–37).

6. *Compassion, Mercy, and Generosity*—Since ancient times, the most celebrated kings have been those who held immense power, yet employed it to defend the helpless and destitute. Hammurabi, for example, was one of the most honored rulers in ancient Mesopotamian history. He ruled from 1792–1750 B.C. (roughly contemporary with the Hebrew patriarchs, Isaac and Jacob). For over a thousand years after his reign, Hammurabi continued to be remembered as "the pious prince, who...prevent[ed] the strong from oppressing the weak.... [who] provide[d] just ways for the waif and the widow."[2] Greatly feared is the king who can conquer his enemies; greatly loved is the king who defends the needy of his land.

Throughout history, many cultures have shared such admiration for rulers who employed vast power with mercy and compassion. Though many kings have aspired to this end, none can be compared to the compassion and tender mercy of Christ. Though He is mighty, He is "mighty to save" (Isa. 63:1). His reign is that described by Psalm 72 in these words:

> He shall judge the poor of the people,
> he shall save the children of the needy,
> and shall break in pieces the oppressor...
>
> For he shall deliver the needy when he crieth;
> the poor also, and him that hath no helper.
> He shall spare the poor and needy,
> and shall save the souls of the needy.
> He shall redeem their soul from deceit and violence:
> and precious shall their blood be [i.e., their life] in his sight.
> (Ps. 72:4, 12–14)

Such is His mercy that He even bears patiently with the wrongdoer, observes Symington: "To the most worthless criminal He extends the golden sceptre of His love" (p. 38). He will not bear

---

2. Statements from the prolog and epilog to Hammurabi's stele found by archaeologists in Susa in 1901. Translations from M. Roth, *Law Collections from Mesopotamia and Asia Minor* (1997), 76–77, 133.

forever with wickedness, but will certainly redeem the suffering and the poor from those who wrong them. Yet in love and patience, He beckons even His enemies deserving His wrath, granting room for repentance. He is full of mercy to forgive and to save the sinner; and He is full of compassion to defend and relieve the victims of sin. Our King, the Scriptures assure us, is a King of great love. (Cf. Ps. 45:7–8; 85:10; Prov. 20:28; Zech. 9:9)

7. *Authority*—Alexander the Great established one of the greatest empires in history. He began his reign as the King of Macedonia—a modest kingdom in Europe then allied with Greece. After just thirteen years, however, Alexander had extended his reign to include all of Asia Minor, Syria, Palestine, Egypt, Babylonia, and Persia. Under Alexander, the Greco-Macedonian world invaded the ancient kingdoms of the Near East, imposing alien rule and a foreign culture upon them.

Though Jesus is also a conquering King, the nature of His conquest is starkly different from that of one like Alexander. The most obvious distinction is that the conquests of Christ are won by truth rather than the sword (John 18:36; Eph. 6:17). A further distinction which must not be overlooked, however, is the fact that Jesus does not conquer *foreign* territory. Jesus' conquests are to retake a world *which already belongs to Him by right.* This is Symington's seventh qualification for kingship: a king must have *valid authority* over the domain he claims.

"*Authority* is necessary to the valid exercise of power," writes Symington. "Other qualifications cannot confer this; nor can the abundance in which they may be enjoyed make up for the want of it" (p. 38). However noble and however just may be the intentions of a king, if he has no legitimate right to govern a domain, he cannot rule with true authority. His conquest would be that of a foreign invader and an oppressor.

According to the Scriptures, God created the world *as His own,* and He placed Adam in regency over it (Gen. 1–2; cf. Ps. 24:1–2). The rebellion of this first king of humanity brought the whole world into rebellion. Nevertheless, God has appointed Jesus as His chosen King, appointed to reconquer and bring the world to its creation purpose (Gen. 3:15; Ps. 2; Dan. 2:35, 44–45; Matt. 21:33–44). Jesus' reign, therefore, ought never be regarded as a foreign power imposing itself illegitimately. His dominion is appointed from heaven: "The Father loveth the Son," Jesus claimed for Himself, "and hath given all things into his hand" (John 3:35). More than any other king, Jesus reigns with *valid authority* because of His divine appointment.

Because of the importance of the appointment of Christ for the validity of His reign, Symington devoted a further chapter to this subject. The next section will review Symington's further treatment of the "Appointment of Christ," and the divine establishment of His mediatorial reign.

Not all kings are equal to their office. Some kings, like Edward II of medieval England, have valid authority but lack personal dignity and moral excellence. Some kings in history wield great power, display august majesty, and act with wisdom, nevertheless their ends are unjust or their conquests violate the bounds of their authority. Even some who have sought to pursue moral ends, and have set on this course with knowledge and sagacity, nonetheless have lacked the power of will or the resources to succeed. A king must be competent and qualified. The Scriptures offer this great encouragement to the people of Christ's kingdom: We not only *need* a king to save us, and we not only *have* such a king in Jesus, but *He is eminently qualified.*

The Source of Christ's Reign: His Divine Appointment

In the next chapter of his book, Symington gives attention to "a topic of great importance" (p. 40): the *source* of Christ's kingship. In speaking about the source of Jesus' reign, our interest is in identifying two things: *where* did Jesus' right to reign come from, and *when* did His reign begin?

The answer to the first question is straightforward and has already been noted under Jesus' *qualifications* to reign: Jesus received His appointment from God the Father. Psalm 2 declares that God Himself authorized His chosen King: "He that sitteth in the heavens...[will] speak.... Yet have I set my king upon my holy hill of Zion" (Ps. 2:4–6).

Jesus also, on several occasions, identified His reign as something received from God. "...a kingdom, as my Father hath appointed unto me," Jesus told His disciples in one place (Luke 22:29). In another place, Jesus spoke of Himself saying, "the Father... hath given him authority to execute judgment also, because he is the Son of man" (John 5:26–27). In His trial before Pilate, Jesus said, "My kingdom is not of this world" (John 18:36). That is, Jesus has a kingdom, but its source is from heaven. The Apostles also wrote of Christ's reign as an appointment from God. For example, Paul wrote to the Philippians, "Wherefore God also hath highly exalted him, and given him a name which is above every name" (Phil. 2:9).

The source of Jesus' appointment, in terms of *where* He derives His authority, leads us back to God the Father. The source of Jesus' appointment, in terms of the *when* He began to reign, is more complex and is the particular focus of Symington's attention in this section.

Symington identifies three points in time which can properly be spoken of as the source (or, beginning) of Jesus' reign: (1) His *appointment* to reign from eternity past; (2) His *ordination* to reign at the start of His earthly ministry; and, (3) His *installation* on His throne at His ascension.

1. His Eternal Appointment—Under the first point, Symington states: "Christ was formally appointed to the kingly office by His Father from all eternity in the covenant of grace" (p. 40). Theologians use that term "covenant of grace," to speak of God's plan of redemption which He determined even before the creation of the world. Scripture teaches us that the unfolding work of God's grace is something which He had planned out before creation itself (e.g., Eph. 1:4). Thus, even though Jesus' *historical* inauguration to the throne took place later in human history, His reign can also be said to have originated from the very beginning of time (when it was determined). This is what the prophet Micah alludes to in his prophecy about the coming Messiah:

> But thou, Bethlehem Ephratah, though thou be little among the thousands of Judah, yet out of thee shall he come forth unto me that is to be ruler in Israel; whose goings forth have been from of old, from everlasting" (Mic. 5:2).

Although the hoped for King was yet to come for Micah, the prophet understood that His reign originated from long before, even from eternity past (cf. Gen. 3:15; 49:10; Ps. 89:3–4). In terms of His appointment, Jesus' reign had its source in eternity past.

2. His Ordination at Anointing—In the ancient world, anointing was an important designation of kingship. In fact, the Hebrew word *messiah* literally means, "anointed one," and it was one of the titles for the Old Testament kings of Judah. In 2 Samuel 22:51, for example, David and his successors are called God's *anointed ones:* "[He] showeth mercy to his anointed (literally, *messiah*), unto David, and to his seed for evermore" (cf. 2 Sam. 23:1; Ps. 2:2; 89:20). After Babylon conquered Judah and there were no more kings in Jerusalem, the promise of God to restore a future Son of David to the throne who would complete salvation for His people led to the use of the term *Messiah* to designate *that specific King* for whom the Jews waited.

In the New Testament, Jesus is called by the word *Christ* because *christos* is the Greek equivalent for *messiah,* also meaning, "anointed one." The Apostles used this title to announce the wonderful news that the long-awaited King of Salvation had come: "And daily in the temple, and in every house, they ceased not to teach and preach Jesus Christ" (Acts 5:42). Many of the Jews rejected Jesus' claim to be the Christ because they did not want a *suffering* king (e.g., Acts 17:3). Nevertheless, the apostolic insistence that Jesus *is* the promised King is a particular emphasis made by their ascription of Him as the Christ, or the Messiah (the "anointed one").

What is here of significance to note is that *anointing* was so central a feature of a king's identification as to be one of the most important royal titles in the Scriptures. While it is certainly true that other biblical offices also involved anointing (such as the prophet and the priest) so that Jesus' title *Christ* can be regarded as encompassing all these offices, Symington points out that it is in connection with the *royal* office that the title "anointed one" *(messiah/christos)* was usually used: "To anoint, was the ancient way of denoting regal designation" (p. 41; cf. Judg. 9:8, 15; 1 Sam. 15:1; 16:3; 2 Sam. 2:7; 1 Kings 19:15).

The meaning of this anointing can be noted in the example of David's anointing. God had told His prophet Samuel to go to the sons of Jesse and anoint one of them to be king of Israel in place of Saul. Upon his arrival, it was revealed to Samuel that David was the one to anoint:

> Then Samuel took the horn of oil, and anointed him in the midst of his brethren: and the spirit of the LORD came upon David from that day forward. So Samuel rose up, and went

to Ramah. But the spirit of the LORD departed from Saul....
(1 Sam. 16:13–14)

The anointing of the king was a sacramental act, designat-
ing the outpouring of God's Spirit upon the one so ordained to
rule. Although Saul had been empowered by the Spirit to rule over
Israel at the point of his anointing to reign (1 Sam. 10:1, 6, 12), once
David was anointed to replace him, the Spirit was no longer with
Saul as king (1 Sam. 16:14; 28:6). The anointing was a *visible* symbol
for an *invisible* reality—the presence of the Spirit to teach and lead
Israel's king.

This background on the anointing of the king is important in
order to fully appreciate the significance of the descent of the Spirit
upon Jesus at the beginning of His earthly ministry:

> In those days came John the Baptist, preaching in the
> wilderness of Judaea, and saying, Repent ye: for the kingdom
> of heaven is at hand.... Then cometh Jesus from Galilee...to
> be baptized of him.... And Jesus, when he was baptized, went
> up straightway out of the water: and, lo, the heavens were
> opened unto him, and he saw the Spirit of God descending
> like a dove, and lighting upon him (Matt. 3:1–17).

It was at that point that Jesus was publicly identified as the
Lamb of God (by His undergoing a baptism of repentance for
His people). He also was identified, by the descent of the Spirit
upon Him, as the one bringing in "the kingdom of heaven" which
John preached. So superior was Jesus' anointing as King to that
of any former king, however, that no symbolic oil was necessary.
The Spirit Himself, in visible reality, descended upon Him. Jesus'
anointing was profoundly greater than that of any previous king.
Symington writes,

> There can be no doubt, that regal appointment is designed
> by the unction [i.e., anointing] which consisted not, as in the
> case of kings among men, of literal oil and aromatic perfumes
> applied to the body by the hand of a prophet, but of the
> Spirit of grace poured out upon Him in rich abundance by
> the Father. (p. 42)

Though not yet actually enthroned at the time of his initial
anointing (cf. 1 Sam. 16:13 and 2 Sam. 2:4), David had already
begun to serve in the Spirit's power as Israel's champion and deliv-

erer (e.g., 1 Sam. 18:7). Similarly, Jesus' anointing at the beginning of His earthly ministry marked an entrance into His royal activity. (Cf. Ps. 2:6; 45:7–8; 89:20; 132:17; Acts 4:27; 10:38) Nevertheless, His historical enthronement was yet to occur.

Jesus' kingship originates in eternity in reference to His *appointment*. Jesus' kingship originated at the beginning of His earthly ministry in reference to His *anointing*. A third point of importance in His regal career, next to be considered, occurred after His *resurrection*.

3. *His Installation after the Cross*—"Christ's appointment [to reign] was still farther intimated," Symington states, "by His actual investiture with regal power at and after His resurrection" (p. 43). In the same way as the atoning power of Jesus' sacrifice was already at work among Old Testament believers based on its promise even before its historical accomplishment, in the same way Jesus' mediatorial reign was already at work among the people of faith even before its historical occurrence. Nevertheless, enthronement had to occur in real time for Jesus to become our mediatorial King.

Symington shows that it was as a reward for His perfect obedience, even to the point of death, that Jesus received His enthronement:

> And being found in fashion as a man, he humbled himself, and became obedient unto death, even the death of the cross. Wherefore God hath highly exalted him, and given him a name which is above every name: that at the name of Jesus every knee should bow, of things in heaven, and things in earth, and things under the earth; and that every tongue should confess that Jesus Christ is Lord, to the glory of God the Father (Phil. 2:8–11).

Just as the first Adam had fallen from his dominion over the creation because of his disobedience, Jesus the "Second Adam" received universal dominion because of His perfect obedience (1 Cor. 15:20–28). It was after the cross therefore, at the resurrection and most specifically in His ascension to "the right hand" of the Father that Jesus took up His throne. Thus the Apostles attest in Scriptures such as the following: "...[God] raised him from the dead, and set him at his own right hand in the heavenly places, far above all principality, and power, and might, and dominion, and every name that is named.... And hath put all things under his feet, and gave him to be the head over all things" (Eph. 1:20–22; cf. Acts 2:33, 36; Heb. 1:3; Rev. 5:13). This, Symington further notes, is the significance of Jesus' remark to His disciples at that very point of His ascending to that heavenly throne, when He said, "All power is given unto me in heaven and in earth. Go ye therefore..." (Matt. 28:18–19).

Just as a royal child in a nation with an empty throne is king from birth, then formally enters the duties of the king at the point of his maturity, and finally is publicly inaugurated to the throne in an open coronation, so Jesus can be said to have been King from birth—even from eternity. Nevertheless, key points at the beginning of His earthly ministry and at His ascension are also important aspects in the process of His taking up His mediatorial reign.

The source of Jesus' reign is, first of all, the appointment of the Father. His reign derives its authority from heaven itself. Furthermore, Jesus' mediatorial reign began with His appointment in eternity past, with His anointing at the start of His earthly ministry, and in its fulness after His resurrection, when He ascended to "the right hand of the Majesty on high" (Heb. 1:3). It is there, on His throne, that Jesus now rules for the purposes of redemption (Eph. 1:20–22).

✦   ✦   ✦

As a final note under this section, it might here be recalled how Symington, in his book *On the Atonement,* pointed to the *sufferings* of Jesus—and *only* His sufferings—as properly belonging to the atonement (see pp. 150–156, above). In that place, Symington had carefully insisted that the suffering of Jesus, and *not* His obedience, should be ascribed to His work of atonement. Symington's reasoning for that insistence can now be more clearly appreciated.

Symington was writing with a discerning eye toward biblical categories of Jesus' royal and sacerdotal works. In Scripture, the *perfect obedience* of Jesus throughout His earthly life is connected to His becoming our King. His *suffering* on our behalf is, Symington noted, connected to Jesus' serving as our Priest. Both are equally essential for our salvation and both characterized the whole of Jesus' earthly life. Nevertheless, there is a conceptual distinction between the royal and sacerdotal works of Jesus which helps us to appreciate the fulness of His labors for our salvation.

By His sufferings in our place, our High Priest has won our atonement. By His obedience in our behalf, Jesus became our King and accords to us all the rights and benefits of citizens in God's kingdom (cf. Ps. 72; 1 Cor. 15:25–26).

The Nature of Christ's Reign: Its Spirituality

If Jesus came to establish a kingdom, His methods for doing so were quite unusual. He was born in obscurity in a cattle stall, not into the wealth normal for an heir to a throne. His education was that of a carpenter, rather than an emperor. His army was a band of disciples and His courtiers fishermen and peasants, whose only use of the sword He reproved (John 18:11). His relation to His subjects was to serve them, rather than being served by them. His authority was exercised by teaching, rather than coercion. In the end, He was lifted up before all on a cross, bruised and beaten like a common criminal, His only crown being twisted thorns and His robe that which was mockingly cast across His shoulders only to be torn away again. What kind of a king—and what kind of a kingdom—is this?

The fifth chapter of Symington's book addresses the nature of Jesus' reign, and in that chapter Symington would have us understand that Jesus' rule is a *spiritual* rule. By this it is not meant that His rule is ethereal and unreal (as this term *spiritual* is often misunderstood). His is a real kingship, and at times He employs very *tangible* instruments. Nevertheless, because the nature of His rule is different from that of all earthly kings, and because His methods and principles are heavenly rather than this-worldly, His reign can be distinctly identified as *spiritual*.

In His trial before Pilate, Christ testified that it was because His kingdom is "not of this world" that His disciples served Him with distinct (in this case, non-military) methods:

> Jesus answered, My kingdom is not of this world: if my kingdom were of this world, then would my servants fight, that I should not be delivered to the Jews: but now is my kingdom not from hence (John 18:36).

Symington offers a number of ways in which the spiritual rather than worldly nature of Christ's kingdom can be seen. For the sake of summarization, Symington's distinctions will be presented below in the form of a table. In this table, four common features of a "this-worldly" kingdom (in the left column) are contrasted with the distinctive features of Jesus' *spiritual* kingdom (in the right column).

	Earthly Rulers...	Jesus the Christ...
ORIGIN	**Receive authority from this world** *Earthly government may be inherited (from parentage), elected (by the people), or taken by force.*	**Received authority from heaven** *Jesus' government is appointed by God.*
PURPOSES	**Rule to better human society** *Earthly government (ideally) offers its citizens peace, prosperity, public justice, social order, etc.*	**Rules to better the human soul** *Jesus' rule provides His subjects with release from sinful passions, new love of righteousness, freedom from death, etc.*
METHODS	**Uphold order by force** *Earthly governments enforce their rule by police, courts, economic and social controls, etc.*	**Upholds order by discipleship** *Jesus' government is enforced by preaching, teaching, and the dispensing or withholding of sacraments.*
PRINCIPLES	**Govern by national ideals** *Earthly governments operate within nationally developed traditions, rights, customs, etc.*	**Governs by divine righteousness** *Jesus' government observes a divine standard of right.*

Jesus' kingdom is spiritual, not because it is "ethereal and unreal." No, spirituality simply means that Jesus obtains His rule by divine appointment (origin), exercises His rule for divine aims (purposes), utilizes divine means (methods), and operates according to divine laws (principles).

The spirituality of Jesus' reign does not mean that His kingdom has no earthly relevance. On the contrary, Jesus' reign is over human men and women living in the present world. His reign is very much concerned with the people and things of this world. However, unlike human kingdoms which seek to order this-worldly society according to this-worldly concerns, Jesus reigns to execute *divine* purposes among mankind. Because of this different plane of operation, Jesus' reign is conducted according to different methods than this-worldly governments.

The American government, for example, exists for the preservation and improvement of American society. When operating ideally, the various branches of American government insure that families, businesses, schools, charities, sports teams, arts clubs, and other aspects of society are protected and free to prosper. As a this-worldly government, American officials oversee the orderly functioning of American society. One day, however, America will no longer exist. In fact, Scripture tells us that, one day, there will be no more nations at all. America, France, Germany, and all other human nations (past, present, or future) will cease. God has appointed a day when the whole creation—the "new heavens and the new earth"—will become the realm of *one* people: His eternal kingdom (Rev. 5:9–10). It is that eternal kingdom that Jesus is already building, and it is for the purposes of drawing men and women into that kingdom and fitting them for that community that Jesus exercises His reign. Jesus' reign is operating on a different plane and for different ends than the governments of the present world. This is why we characterize His kingdom and His reign as *spiritual* in nature.

Symington makes this point, and draws an important implication from it:

> The ends contemplated by the kingdoms of this world terminate in time, but those contemplated by the dominion of the Mediator point forward to...an eternal state of being.... [Nevertheless,] earthly dominion may be so conducted as to subserve the interests of the soul and eternity, just as the dominion of the Mediator cannot but produce the temporal interests and social advantages of mankind. (p. 53)

Here is a very important clarification Symington draws to our attention. Although Jesus' reign is different from earthly governments in its nature and purposes, *the two are not unrelated*. When, for example, Jesus changes the heart of a sinner, cleansing him of sinful passions and replacing them with a growing love for righteousness, that same person will consequently become a better neighbor and citizen in the present world. Similarly, when a human government employs its police force to stop an illegal pornography or drug ring, human government is thereby supporting the labors of Christ's government to free the elect from the sway of sinful passions. This-worldly and spiritual government, though distinct in their nature, are not unconnected in actual experience. These two kinds of government—worldly and spiritual—are not contradictory, but in fact complementary.

As a matter of fact, Symington points out that even human governments and their this-worldly concerns are ultimately subsumed under the spiritual reign of Christ. As the Apostle Paul wrote in his letter to the Ephesians: "[God] raised him from the dead, and set him...above all principality, and power, and might, and dominion.... And hath put all things under his feet, and gave him to be the head over all things to the church" (Eph. 1:20–22). Ultimately, Jesus holds authority even over the governments of men in order that He might insure that every divine purpose and every divine principle finds its fulfillment in the eternal community ("the church") that He is assembling.

The nature of Jesus' government is different from the governments of men: He rules to accomplish divine purposes for the building of an eternal kingdom. His reign therefore can be characterized as *spiritual* in contrast with the strictly this-worldly order which human governments pursue. (But it is not so spiritual as to be intangible and of no this-worldly relevance.)

The Extent of Christ's Reign: Its Universality

Thus far, in our review of Symington's exposition of the Mediatorial Dominion, we have seen the following:

- that we *need* for our Savior to be more than a Priest and Prophet—we need a Savior with kingly authority, as well (necessity);

- that we do indeed *have* a Savior with such authority (reality);

- that our Savior is *fully competent* to reign effectively (qualifications);

- that His reign derives from the *divine appointment* made in eternity past and fully realized with His resurrection and ascension (source); and,

- that His reign is *spiritual* in its aims and methods (nature).

Two points have yet to be considered: the *extent* of His reign, and the *duration* of His reign. The former is what will now be taken up. How much does Jesus reign over? It is often assumed that He is King over the church, and not over the rest of the world. In his treatment of the extent of Christ's reign, Symington exposes the error of such misunderstandings. Jesus' reign is *universal* in its extent. Everything everywhere has been placed under His dominion.

This is what Jesus professed at the point of His ascension: "And Jesus came and spake unto them, saying, All power is given unto me in heaven and in earth" (Matt. 28:18). As if to insure that the totality of this universality might not be missed, the author of Hebrews makes this remark: "For in that he put all in subjection under him, he left nothing that is not put under him" (Heb. 2:8; cf. Matt. 11:27; Acts 10:36; 1 Cor. 15:27; Eph. 1:22; Col. 2:10; Phil. 2:8–10). From the lowest beasts of the earth (Ps. 8:6–8) to the angels in heaven (1 Peter 3:22) and demonic powers (Luke 10:17–18), from elect men and women (Col. 1:18) to those counted as enemies of Christ (Ps. 110:2), Symington summons an extensive collection of historical and theological texts, from Old and New Testaments, to demonstrate the consistency with which Scripture affirms the absolute universality of Jesus' reign (John 17:2; Rom. 14:9; Rev. 4:12).

It is nonetheless true however, as both Scripture and common experience make clear, that not all the world necessarily *reflects* the submission owed to Christ. "But now," writes one biblical author, "we see not yet all things put under him" (Heb. 2:8). "In a kingdom of a rightful sovereign," Symington remarks, "there may be many rebels" (p. 106). Jesus Himself used a number of different parables to describe this present fact of history, and to warn of His coming judgment against all who neglect His rule over them. For example:

> A certain nobleman went into a far country to receive for himself a kingdom, and to return.... But his citizens hated him, and sent a message after him, saying, We will not have this man to reign over us.... When he was returned...[he said,] But those mine enemies, which would not that I should reign over them, bring hither, and slay them before me" (Luke 19:12–27; cf. Matt. 25:14–30, 31–46; Luke 20:9–18).

Although there are, indeed, those who continue to resist His rule, Christ assures His disciples that they can take confidence in His universal sovereignty. "All power is given unto me in heaven and in earth. Go ye therefore, and teach all nations.... And, lo, I am with you..." (Matt. 28:18–20). Symington is hardly able to contain his own enthusiasm as he concludes his contemplations on the magnificence of this glorious truth:

> How delightful the principle thus established and vindicated! It reflects the glory of Christ, on whose head are many crowns. He appears, wearing not only the crown of dominion over the church, but that of dominion over the kingdoms of nature, providence, and grace—over things physical and moral, rational and irrational, animate and inanimate. Things in heaven, in earth, and under the earth, are thus seen to be put under His feet. His kingdom ruleth over all. Ye saints of the Most High! Ascribe to Him the glory that is due. (p. 106)

The Duration of Christ's Reign: Its Perpetuity

Under the question of duration, Symington demonstrates the *perpetuity* of Christ's mediatorial reign. Jesus will continue to be our King through all eternity. Some influential theologians of Symington's day had taught that the reign of Christ would conclude at the end of time, and would not continue into eternity. Symington denied such teachings, showing that Scripture presents Christ as our King (and, indeed, our Priest as well) for all eternity.

For example, Symington quotes the English Puritan minister, John Owen, who taught that, "at the end of this dispensation, [Jesus] shall give up the kingdom to God, even the Father, or cease from the administration of His mediatorial office and power" (pp. 319–320).[3] Owen, and others like him, drew this conclusion from their reading of the Apostle Paul in 1 Corinthians 15: "Then cometh the end, when he shall have delivered up the kingdom to God, even the Father" (v. 24), as though this indicated an end to Jesus' own position as the King of that kingdom. "When this work is perfectly fulfilled and ended," Owens further wrote, "then shall all the mediatorial actings of Christ cease for ever" (p. 320).[4] Symington opposed

---

3. John Owen, *The Works of John Owen* (Edinburgh: Johnson and Hunter, 1853), 1.236.

4. John Owen, *The Works of John Owen* (Edinburgh: Johnson and Hunter, 1853), 1.237. Owen actually seems to have changed his mind (or to have been inconsistent) on this point. Symington notes a place later in Owen's writings where Owen asserts: "The person of Christ, in and by His human nature, shall be for ever the immediate Head of the whole glorified creation..." (Symington, p. 320, quoting Owen, 1.271).

such theories of an end to Christ's mediatorial reign. On the contrary, Scripture speaks frequently of Christ *for ever* continuing to be our King—throughout eternity. It is not only He who brings us to God now, but for all eternity it will be *in Him* that we are united to God in glory.

Symington asserts this doctrine through an extensive survey of biblical texts. (He includes in this survey a careful exegesis of the aforenoted 1 Corinthians text—14 pages, in fact [pp. 319–333]—to expose the mistake of imagining an end of Christ's reign as there being in view.)

The Old Testament prophets foresaw Christ with an eternal reign. Isaiah writes, for example, "Of the increase of his government and peace *there shall be no end*...to establish [his kingdom], *to order it,* and to establish it with judgment and with justice from henceforth even *for ever*" (Isa. 9:7; cf. Dan. 2:44). It is not only Jesus who advances the peace of His kingdom from now to the end of time, but it is Christ who will uphold and maintain the perfection of that kingdom in all eternity. The psalmist also speaks often of the eternality of Messiah's reign. For example, "Thy throne, O God, is *for ever and ever*...therefore God, thy God, hath anointed thee..." (Ps. 45:6–7; cf. 72:17; 89:4; 110:4; 145:13). The royal anointing of this Messiah is that of an eternal throne.

New Testament authors likewise indicate the perpetuity of Christ's reign. Perhaps most striking are John's apocalyptic visions of Christ on His throne for all eternity: "And there shall be no more curse, but the throne of God and of the Lamb shall be in it; and his servants shall serve him" (Rev. 22:3; cf. Luke 1:33; 2 Peter 1:11; Jude 25). Certainly, *as Creator God,* we can expect Jesus to reign over His people for all eternity. However, it is Jesus reigning *as our Mediatorial Sacrifice* that John shows us over and over in his Revelation (cf. Rev. 5:13; 6:16; 7:9, 10, 17; 22:1). It is not only as our Creator God, but also as our Incarnate Mediator that Jesus will forever govern over and care for us for all eternity. "For the Lamb which is in the midst of the throne shall feed them, and shall lead them unto living fountains of water: and God shall wipe away all tears from their eyes" (Rev. 7:17).

Because there will be no more sin or adversity in heaven, it will no longer be necessary for Christ "to subdue rebellious passions, to ward off enemies," and so forth (p. 341). Certain of His royal activities will no longer be necessary. "But are there no other things that may call for the exercise of the mediatorial functions?" Symington continues, "We submit that there are" (p. 341).

Our own eternal existence will not be one of inactivity and boredom. Though the exact character of our duties in heaven cannot be precisely explained, Scripture does make clear that it will be a life of activity and purpose—and it will be activity for which we continue to depend upon the direction of our King. "It is a faithful saying," Paul wrote, "For if we be dead with him, we shall also live with him...[and] we shall also *reign with him*" (2 Tim. 2:11–12). Far from setting aside His royal activity in eternity, Christ will exalt His people to tasks of purpose and authority, reigning with and under Him.

"Our Redeemer will never lay aside His mediatorial authority," Symington concludes.

> Our Redeemer will...never cease to act in the capacity of King of glory. Indeed all the mediatorial offices, would seem to be exercised in heaven;—the prophetical, in diffusing spiritual illumination; the sacerdotal, in securing the blessing and giving acceptance to the service of the saints; and the regal, in bearing rule, receiving homage, and administering reward to the children of the kingdom....
>
> What a prospect! How should it excite us to prepare for its being realised! Happy they who, having submitted themselves to Him in time as King of saints, shall be eternally under His sway as King of glory! (pp. 347–348)

✦   ✦   ✦

On the preceding pages, Symington's articulation of Christ's mediatorial reign has been reviewed. Taken together, his two works—*On the Atonement* and *Messiah the Prince*—provide an exposition of both Christ's priestly and kingly offices.

Both of these offices can be traced historically to the work of Jesus on the cross. It was on the cross that Jesus, by His sufferings unto death, completed His priestly sacrifice. It was on the cross that Jesus, by His obedience unto death, secured His royal dominion. The cross is central to everything Jesus does as our Mediator. However, the cross was by no means the beginning, and it certainly was not the end, of His work. As our Priest, Jesus continues to intercede for His people. Furthermore, as our King, Jesus continues to assemble His eternal kingdom. "The kingdom of God has come" is a common theme among the inspired biographers of Jesus' life (e.g., Matt. 12:28; Mark 1:15; Luke 9:27; John 3:3). Under Christ's now-established reign, His kingdom is being further assembled, prepared, and advanced unto its perfect consummation (e.g., Dan. 2:44; 1 Cor. 15:24; Rev. 12:10).

Symington's documentation of the doctrine of the mediatorial dominion—its necessity, reality, qualifications, source, nature, extent, and duration—is one of the gems of Scottish Covenanter theology. Though it has here been discussed in terms of its dominant principles, this doctrine is not ultimately concerned with abstract concepts, but with Jesus' redemptive activities among real-world people in real-world circumstances through real-world activity. This doctrine might be likened, in this regard, to mathematics. Mathematics is best studied in terms of its basic principles: how to add, how to divide, how to "solve for x." Its great value, however, particularly emerges as it is *applied,* such as in keeping one's checkbook. Ones understanding of Christ's dominion is, likewise, not complete if one stops with a mere articulation of ideas. The reign of Christ is a real-world actuality. It is a truth, therefore, both to be understood (as the previous pages have endeavored to facilitate)—but also to be applied.

In keeping with his characteristic concern for the *practical* implications of theology, Symington the pastor devoted more than half of his 400-page book on dominion to matters of application. In particular, he focused attention on how this doctrine applies to one's life *within the church,* and in regard to *civil government.* Other aspects of life (such as family, business, art, entertainment, agriculture, and so forth) can and should likewise be viewed under the light of Christ's dominion: "His authority extends to associations of every description," affirms Symington (p. 97). Nevertheless, Symington focused special attention in his book on "two associations, which, both from their importance in themselves, and their particular relation to the subject in hand, deserve a separate and more full consideration"—namely, the church and the state and their mutual relations (p. 110).

It is the latter of these—Symington's teaching on civil government—that has undoubtedly received the most attention over the
years. This is understandable, but perhaps unfortunate. To suppose
that the civil government is the most important realm of implication for this doctrine is to completely miss the point. Jesus has been
placed "over all things *to the church*" (Eph. 1:22). It is the church, not
the state, that is at the heart of Christ's reign and, indeed, is the present expression of the kingdom He is building. While the state ought
to be brought into concert with Christ's dominion, it is the church
that most essentially requires constant reverence for His reign, even
when other institutions do not so revere Him. It is in the church that
we ought to find the reign of Christ most clearly comprehended
and observed.

In the next chapter, we will consider some of the practical
implications which Symington draws for the church as understood
in light of Christ's mediatorial reign. In a subsequent chapter after
that, then, Symington's application of this doctrine to the state will
be considered.

✦   ✦   ✦

*...Therefore let all the house of Israel know assuredly, that God
hath made that same Jesus, whom ye have crucified, both Lord and
Christ.... The kingdoms of this world are become the kingdoms of
our Lord, and of his Christ; and he shall reign for ever and ever....
Kiss [i.e., give homage to] the Son, lest he be angry, and ye perish
from the way.... Blessed are all they that put their trust in him
(Acts 2:36; Rev. 11:15; Ps. 2:12).*

CHAPTER 14

Christ's Mediatorial Dominion Applied to the Church

"The church," Symington writes, "[is] without doubt the most important society in existence" (p. 110). Jesus rules over all other aspects of the world for the sake of the church. If there is any area where the comprehension of Christ's kingship should be clearly acknowledged and cooperated with, it is among Christians (i.e., within the church).

Symington's insights on the practical implications of Christ's reign *for the church* will be highlighted in this chapter. Prior to engaging with Symington on these points, however, there is a matter woven throughout Symington's chapter on the church which it might be helpful to note. Although he does not explicitly say as much, it is evident that Symington has made a distinction in his thinking between the *kingdom* of Christ (which is the church) and the *dominion* of Christ (which encompasses all things).

Symington approvingly cites the Westminster Confession of Faith, for example, where it states, "The visible Church...consists of all those throughout the world that profess the true religion... *and is the kingdom of the Lord Jesus Christ...*" (p. 122; WCF 25.2). This is, of course, in keeping with the language of Scripture itself which specifically identifies the church as being the "New Israel" and the "Kingdom of God" in the world (e.g., Isa. 9:7; Eph. 2:12; Heb. 12:23, 28; 1 Peter 2:9). The church is the present manifestation of the kingdom Jesus is building, and it (in contrast with the rest of the world) is uniquely called "his kingdom." In Symington's words,

> The church...is spoken of in Scripture as 'a body,' the members of which exhibit admirable symmetry,... as a 'city,'... whose municipal regulations are calculated to secure the

peace and order of the inhabitants;—as a 'kingdom,' and as a 'nation'.... (p. 120)

This does not mean, however, that Jesus' reign is restricted to the church. It is still *the whole world* that is under the dominion of Jesus. His enemies as well as His own people, the kingdoms of men as well as His own citizens, the lost world as well as the redeemed, all reside under Christ's rule. A distinction should therefore be made between the *dominion* of Christ and the *kingdom* of Christ. The whole creation and all mankind are under the *dominion* of the Mediatorial King, although it is peculiarly the church that comprises the present manifestation of His *kingdom*.

Two early Reformation-era theologians who also made this distinction were Martin Bücer and John Calvin. In a 1550 book entitled *De Regno Christi* ("The Kingdom of Christ"), Martin Bücer spoke about the church as being, what we might term, a "conservation center" or a "staging ground" for heaven. As Jesus is here and now assembling His kingdom for eternity, Bücer taught, the church is the "staging ground" where Christ gathers men and women into His eternal kingdom. "Who hath delivered us from the power of darkness," Paul wrote to the Colossians, "and hath translated us into the kingdom of his dear Son" (Col. 1:13). As Bücer emphasized in *De Regno Christi,* Jesus rules over the *whole* world for the purpose of bringing from its fruits into the eternal kingdom He is building. The church is, in this sense, the "conservation center" for the fruits of this world being prepared and preserved for their enrollment in the next.

John Calvin's writings tended to emphasize another aspect of the church's role as Christ's kingdom in the world. Not only is the church the "conservation center" for those *being brought into* Christ's eternal kingdom, but the church is also the "embassy" or "outpost" of Christ's kingdom *reaching out into* the world. As one scholar summarized Calvin, the heavenly kingdom "presses through the Church, in its obedience to the command of the risen Christ, to bring all mankind under its sway in the gospel."[1] The church is, in this sense, the "outpost" of an eternal kingdom reaching out into the present world.

---

1. T. F. Torrence, *Kingdom and Church* (Edinburgh: Oliver and Boyd, 1956), 161.

These two emphases are, of course, just that: distinct *emphases* but not contradictions. The church is both the family of the redeemed being gathered together and prepared for eternity (Bücer's emphasis), and it is the embassy of Christ's kingdom pressing its influence into the rest of the world (Calvin's emphasis). Taken together, these help to illustrate the reasons why the church can be regarded as "Christ's kingdom" in a special way, even though Christ's dominion is already exercised over the whole creation.

The church is not the only realm under Christ's authority. Nevertheless, the church is uniquely His kingdom in the sense of being the this-worldly "assembly point" and "outpost" of that eternal community being assembled in and from the world of humanity.

Perhaps comparison with another well-known kingdom-building enterprise from history will help to pull these ideas together: the kingdom of Alexander the Great. Alexander's stunning success as a military conqueror in the fourth century B.C. was due to a combination of his own genius and his having struck at the right time. The Persian Empire was vulnerable, and Alexander recognized it. After consolidating his rule at home, he carved his way through the Mediterranean and Near Eastern world with amazing rapidity. Within a decade, Alexander ruled nearly all the known world.

Alexander understood, nevertheless, that *dominating* the world and *forging a united kingdom* out of it are two distinct tasks. Although a vast number of humanity, from the Aegean Sea to the Indian Ocean, paid tribute into Alexander's coffers, these peoples were still diverse in their ways and many of them were unwilling subjects. Alexander, therefore, built "model cities" at strategic locations throughout his empire. Most of these cities were called after his own name: "Alexandria." Exactly how many of these "model cities" Alexander personally founded is not known, although numbers between nine and eighteen (or more) are not uncommon in the records. These Alexander-foundations were organized with Greek-style governments, Greek-style schools, Greek-style sports facilities and theaters, and so forth. They were designed to provide, on the one hand, cities for his own Greek soldiers that they might have a home like Greece in the foreign lands where he settled them. They were also designed, moreover, to influence the native culture of the surrounding regions—"civilizing the barbarians" in Alexander's view.

Alexander's conquests, as noted before in an earlier chapter, certainly cannot be regarded as analogous to Christ's reign. In particular, the violence and even arrogance often associated with the Greek conquests is of a completely different character than the humble, self-sacrificial nature of Christ's victory. "Although blood be connected with the establishment of [Christ's] reign," writes Symington, "it is not the blood of His subjects or enemies, but His own blood" (p. 52). Nevertheless, Alexander's practice of establishing Greek cities after his own name is helpful for illustration purposes. Alexander's establishment of "Alexandrias," which enjoyed special political rights as satellites of Greece itself, might be cited as illustrative of the church's role within Christ's worldwide dominion.

Although Jesus' reign has already been secured over the whole creation, not all the subjects of His dominion are willing subjects. Not all peoples accept or desire His ways. In Christ's program to forge a unified, eternal kingdom drawing its population from the kingdoms of this world, the church plays a central role. The church is, like Alexander's "Alexandrias," a place where Christ's own can enjoy the privileges of His rule and citizenship in the home-kingdom while yet "abroad." Furthermore, in the church, Christians are charged, taught, and being sanctified "to model" in this world the social order, worship, joy, love, and blessings characteristic of life in heaven itself. The church is not a perfect model, as indeed those belonging to Alexander's "Alexandrias" were prone to adopt "barbarian" ways from the societies around them while also expressing "civilized" ways before them. In the case of Christ's church, such adaptations to worldly corruptions are especially tragic. Nevertheless, Christ is patiently and unfailingly using the church both as an "assembly/conservation center" for the construction of His eternal kingdom, and as an "ambassadorial outpost" for modeling and impressing His kingdom-principles out into the dark reaches of His domain.

Thus, although in one sense the whole universe is Christ's kingdom—because He has won it all by a single conquest sealed in His own blood—it is ultimately the church that is uniquely His kingdom within the whole domain. For the sake of clarity, it is probably best to use the term "kingdom of Christ" in reference to the church, and the term "dominion of Christ" in reference to His reign over the whole world (including but not limited to the church). Though not always strictly maintained, Symington generally reflects this terminological distinction in his book, and he certainly operates with this conceptual distinction.

With these fundamental issues of the church's identity as a kingdom within Jesus' universal dominion clarified, we can now proceed to examine some of the practical implications Symington draws for "citizens" and "ambassadors" of this kingdom. It will not be attempted, in this place, to review Symington's entire treatment of the church. A careful reading of his chapter on the subject is certainly encouraged and will prove fruitful for those who would take it up (pp. 110–191). It will be worthwhile to note here, however, a few pertinent themes from Symington on the church.

The Church is a Kingdom

Basic to all that Symington has to say about the church is the fact that the church is—*literally*—a kingdom. Christians, of all people, must recognize it as such and deal both within the church and as agents of the church with recognition that *it is a kingdom.*

1. The Church is a Society—This means, first of all, that the church is a society. "The church possesses a character of a visible organization," Symington writes. "It is spoken of in Scripture as 'a body,'... a 'house,'... a 'city,'... a 'kingdom,' and as a 'nation'..." (p. 120). This is a very basic yet crucial point for Christians to fix in their minds and in their practice. Jesus is not just our Prophet, revealing to us the will of God; He is not just our Priest, restoring us to divine favor. Jesus is also our King, organizing us into a new community. The church is a society *with laws:* "these are contained in the Scriptures" (p. 147). It is, furthermore, a society *with a government.* The importance of proper church government is, Symington seeks to show, an important aspect of the church's operating *as a society* in reverence for her King.

"In every social body," Symington observes, "order is essential to edification, and government is essential to order.... Christ has given to the church a regular form of government." This is true, he insists, despite "the opinion of those who contend that the matter has been left to be regulated by the wisdom of men" (p. 149–150). Some have contended that churches are free to organize themselves however seems most suitable in their varied circumstances. Symington, however, insists that Jesus *as our King* has appointed a particular manner of government for the church which is essential for our operating as His kingdom. Symington builds this argument on such texts as Ephesians 4.

In that place, Paul speaks about church government as appointed by Jesus, and the fruitfulness of its proper operation:

> And he gave some, apostles; and some, prophets; and some, evangelists; and some, pastors and teachers; for the perfecting of the saints, for the work of the ministry, for the edifying of the body of Christ...into him...which is the head, even Christ: from whom the whole body fitly joined together and compacted by that which every joint supplieth, according to the effectual working in the measure of every part, maketh increase of the body unto the edifying of itself in love (Eph. 4:11–16; cf. p. 120).

Paul uses the illustration of a human body to emphasize the importance of Christ-appointed government. In his illustration, Paul identifies the body's "head" as being Christ. He uses "by that which every joint supplieth" as an allusion to church officers. These are placed by Christ to give cohesion and to facilitate the head's care and direction throughout the body. Thirdly, Paul identifies "every part" within the body as representing all the members of the church. It is when the members of the body function under the direction of the head, through the proper functioning of the joints, that the body, as a whole, grows so that it builds itself up in love. This is Paul's illustration of the church as a society, and the importance of Christ's appointed government for its proper growth.

Symington's book stops short of insisting what the exact form of biblical church government is. He does not shy from building a case, nevertheless, for "the presbyterial model, or that form in which different individual churches are regarded as parts of a grand whole, and the office-bearers...forming a gradation of church courts" as being biblical (p. 151; cf. pp. 134–135; 164–179). What is most important to Symington in *Messiah the Prince* is to establish that church government is not at the whim of the congregation, but must be derived from the scriptural pattern. *Jesus* is the one who builds His church (Matt. 16:18). Submitting to biblical church government is one important way in which we practically acknowledge Christ's royal prerogatives. The church is a literal kingdom, and thus a governed society ordered under the constitutional direction of Scripture.

2. *The Church is Monarchical* — A second, related issue further emerges at this point: As we come to recognize the church as a literal society with a prescribed order, we must bear in mind that it is a *monarchical* society.

> It is not a self-existent, self-constituted association merely, formed by voluntary agreement or mutual compact among its members, with reference even to the work of the Son of God. It is expressly founded by the voluntary and authoritative appointment of the Redeemer Himself. (p. 115)

HAMM radio operators often band together into voluntary clubs to encourage and help one another in their radio skills. Political lobby groups, such as pro-life groups or anti-pornography associations, form as citizens voluntarily address shared concerns in society together. Even theological reading groups, or home Bible studies, are often formed as voluntary gatherings of people desirous to pursue a common interest together. Such voluntary associations are completely appropriate and wholesome. However, the church is not a society formed for our own support. It is a society *under a King,* and must always be recognized and treated as such by her citizenry.

This has implications both for church officers and for the laity. In regard to church officers, it is important to note that Jesus alone is the King of His people—no church officers are to usurp that place. Church officers are not appointed to lord over the flock (cf. 1 Peter 5:3), but to bring the whole community into proper subjection to "him…which is the head…Christ" (Eph. 4:15). As Symington writes, "The ministers of religion, neither individually nor collectively, possess any legislative power. Their authority is wholly ministerial" (p. 128). Church officers practically acknowledge Christ's sole kingship over the church by implementing His decrees without asserting their own.

In regard to all Christians (ordained and laity), Christ's sole kingship over the church means that we live and labor according to *Christ's* dictates rather than our own. We teach *His* teachings. We observe *His* laws. We worship according to *His* direction, rather than our own tastes or opinions. This principle is especially significant for Christians in the modern, democratic world to consider very carefully and thoroughly. Throughout the ages, Christians have often (mistakenly) expected the church to function like the societies of the world around them. (Roman Catholic hierarchy, for instance, is remarkably like the governmental structure of the Roman Empire in which it was organized.) This tendency is certainly evident in America today, where churches frequently assume that their pastor serves in a "presidential" capacity, that their elders and deacons "do all the work" like the welfare-state mentality, or that "we the people" in the pews can democratically vote (or revolt!) on unpopular issues in the church. The church is, indeed, a society. It is not, however, a society to be modeled after the current political trends of the age. The church is specifically a monarchical society—under King Jesus.

This means that we do not look to the collective wisdom of the people to instruct the activities of the whole. Rather, we look to our King as our First-Evangelist, our First-Preacher, our First-Caregiver, our First-Discipler, our Admired Head in all respects. Wisdom flows down from the throne to the people, not vice versa. The church is not only a society, but it is a monarchical society. Once embraced, this acknowledgement has profound, practical ramifications on how we live, serve, worship, and function as a Christian community.

3. Christianity is Kingdom-Citizenship—Within this monarchical society, furthermore, every Christian is a *citizen*. To be a Christian is not merely an adoption of certain beliefs, it is enrollment in a certain society—a kingdom which Christ is assembling here and now. "It is anything but honourable to the Head of the church," Symington writes, "to suppose that He has left its members to exist as a confused mass of detached individuals, living separately, without any bond of connexion or plan of co-operation" (p. 120).

On the contrary, Christ has not saved us to leave us alone. He has made us citizens in a kingdom. When we acknowledge Jesus as our King and the church as His kingdom, this doctrine has practical implications for how we practice our citizenship as individual Christians.

In Romans 12, for example, Paul gives this exhortation about our citizenship duties:

> Having then gifts differing according to the grace that
> is given to us, whether prophecy [e.g., preaching], let us

prophesy according to the proportion of faith; or ministry, let us wait on our ministering: or he that teacheth, on teaching; or he that exhorteth [e.g., counseling], on exhortation: he that giveth, let him do it with simplicity; he that ruleth [e.g., administration], with diligence; he that sheweth mercy, with cheerfulness (Rom. 12:6–7; cf. 1 Cor. 12).

Not every Christian fits a cookie-cutter pattern. We have been divinely endowed with unique gifts and capabilities. Some are gifted to preach. Some are gifted to give counsel. Some are gifted in organization. Some are gifted for medical care, poverty aid, or in other ways. Paul's list is not necessarily exhaustive, but rather indicative of the fact that Christ gives His people many different kinds of gifts. What is important, however, is that we take seriously our citizenship responsibility to identify, develop, and practice our gifts.

Elsewhere, speaking about the same topic, Paul tells us that Christ not only gives us such gifts, but He also sovereignly "set [or, placed] the members every one of them in the body, as it hath pleased him" (1 Cor. 12:18). In other words, our practice of our gifts is not only an individual matter, but a social matter—as strategically placed members of His kingdom.

It might be helpful to recall Bücer's and Calvin's emphases on the kingdom's function, in order to point out that the role of the church as a whole is neither wholly internal nor wholly external. The church as a whole exists both to "assemble and prepare" Christians for heaven; it also exists as a "model" or "platform" for impressing the redemptive purposes of heaven out into the world. Our enrollment as citizens of that kingdom not only privileges us *to receive* the nurture of that "preparation" for heaven. Our gifting and placement within Christ's kingdom also obliges us *to contribute* to the internal nurture of the church and to her external witness. "Ye are the salt of the earth: but if the salt have lost his savour, wherewith shall it be salted?" (Matt. 5:13).

When we come to appreciate the doctrine of Christ's mediatorial dominion, we cannot avoid drawing practical and personal applications. The fact that the church is a literal society means that we must submit to the order Jesus has appointed for our organization and growth. The fact that the church is a *monarchical* society means that we must all (ordained and laity alike) reverence *Christ's* laws and ways. Furthermore, that we are *citizens* in this kingdom means that we have privileges to receive and obligations to fulfill.

The Church is a Spiritual Kingdom

Just as Jesus' *reign* is of a spiritual nature (see pp. 235–238, above), His *kingdom* has been endowed with a spiritual commission. Although the church is as real a kingdom as the Kingdom of Denmark or the Kingdom of Tonga, it is a kingdom of a wholly distinct character. "It is a *spiritual* society...," Symington reminds us, "Its head is spiritual: its ordinances and institutions bear a spiritual character: and the purposes for which it exists are altogether of this nature" (p. 126).

It is the spirituality of Christ's kingdom that has led many to assume (mistakenly) that the church is only a kingdom in a figurative or symbolic sense. We often tend to think the word *spiritual* means "intangible" or at least "invisible." That is not necessarily the case. As Symington points out, Jesus not only said His *kingdom* was "not of this world" (i.e., spiritual), but Jesus also told His *disciples,* "ye are not of the world" (John 18:36; 15:19). The latter expression, Symington notes, obviously does not mean that Christians lack physical bodies, are forbidden from worldly property, business, and so forth. Likewise, it must not be supposed that the church "is so absolutely spiritual as to have no connexion whatever with what is secular or earthly" (p. 63). Whether a thing is *spiritual* or *worldly* simply indicates where its point of reference is: from whence it receives its identity, its values, and its purpose (pp. 59–64). The church, as a spiritual kingdom, is not this-worldly in its purposes, but is nonetheless a real kingdom operating in the real world.

The reason for belaboring this point is to pave the way for considering the practical implications of the church's *spirituality* on the life of the believer. By becoming a citizen of Christ's kingdom, the believer does not thereby resign his membership in this-worldly societies. He is still very much a member of his nation, his family, his business, and his other associations. Membership in Christ's kingdom does not negate a person's rightful interest in these other realms. What kingdom-enrollment does is oblige the believer to bring spiritual (i.e., Christ's) concerns to his participation in them. He no longer participates in his civic duties for the sake of improving national infrastructure, schools, and so forth (alone); he now brings divine and redemptive concerns to his civic activity (as well).

The Christian is no longer just an employee seeking to earn a living in his workplace, he is now also an employee who brings redemptive concerns to computer programming, manufacturing, or the other profession to which he belongs.

The church's *spirituality* does not mean that Christian's abandon all worldly property and retreat to monastic cells, nor does it mean that worship on Sundays is the whole of our spiritual service for Christ. Rather, to be spiritual is to bring Christ's purposes to bear on all one's worldly involvements. A diagram may help to present this concept visually:

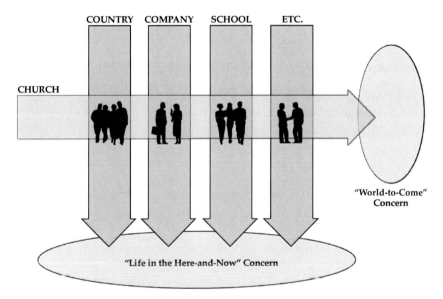

In this diagram, the *vertical bars* represent various "kingdoms" of this world: a country, a company, a school, a club, and so forth. These organizations have an interest in the "life-here-and-now" concerns of their members. The *horizontal bar* represents the church, a kingdom operating *in the same world* and *among the same people* as the other kingdoms in the world, but on a different plane. This kingdom brings spiritual or heavenly concerns to bear on the present world. To become a member of Christ's kingdom is not so much an "add-on" to other involvements, as it is a transformation of one's sense of purpose within them.

The Apostle Paul wrote, "And whatsoever ye do, do it heartily, *as to the Lord*, and not unto men; knowing that of the Lord ye shall receive the reward of the inheritance: *for ye serve the Lord Christ"* (Col. 3:23–24). This is not merely an exhortation to be diligent workers; this is a statement about bringing one's regular work under the light of a new King: "For ye serve the Lord Christ."

Once we come to appreciate the doctrine of Christ's mediatorial kingship and the *spiritual* nature of His kingdom, the way is opened for Christians to make practical applications of Christ's purposes to all areas of our lives as His subjects.

The Church is One Kingdom

Although the church meets in different places of worship under different ministers in different locations around the globe, the doctrine of Christ's dominion assures us that His kingdom is one.

> There may be many members in the body, but the body itself is one; there may be different individuals in the household, but the household itself is one; there may be many provinces and subjects in the kingdom, but the kingdom itself is one. Hence, says the apostle, 'There is one body, and one Spirit.... We being many are one bread and one body.' (pp. 129–130; quoting Eph. 4:4; 1 Cor. 10:17)

The unity of the church does not mean sameness in all respects, as though every state in a country were identical. We might further recall that, even in the Old Testament manifestation of Christ's kingdom (Israel), there were twelve distinct tribes. There may be, as there are today, many different branches within the same, single church of Christ. The doctrine of Christ's reign forces us to look for the unity of the kingdom He is ruling.

Symington's emphasis on this point—both in his book and in his own interdenominational activities (see pp. 59–61, 100–110, above)—are a refreshing corrective to the pessimism over denominationalism that we often confront today. Beginning from the doctrine of one King at the top, and tracing the unity of His reign down throughout His church, gives a more accurate view of the church's condition than simply looking at the many denominational titles at the bottom. Looking at *our* titles for various denominations gives a false impression of widespread division. We should rather look for the marks of Christ exercising His rule throughout the church: "doctrinal orthodoxy, a regular ministry, and the due administration of ordinances of God's worship" (p. 130).

For example, it ought to be recognized that there are many denominations which share common confessional standards. The Westminster Standards and the (Dutch) Three Forms of Unity, for instance, are widely subscribed by many denominations. Symington sees in such common confessions and governmental standards *visible* indication of one King ruling among the many bodies of His one church. Even though there are important differences between different "tribes" of the church, where there is shared doctrine, the same sacraments, common (even interdenominationally recognized) church officers, and the same (even mutually consulting) form of church government, there is unity (pp. 131–135). Here, in Symington's view, is real and visible evidence of Christ building one kingdom. He urges Christians to learn to look at the church from the perspective of this one King administering His one church.

> It is important that all those individual churches which possess the marks formerly enumerated—doctrinal orthodoxy, a regular ministry, and the due administration of ordinances of God's worship—be regarded as so many integral parts of a great whole. (p. 130)

Symington is optimistic, believing that there is already great unity within the church—more than denominational titles might show. It is, nonetheless, a unity which Christians are not always very faithful at recognizing. Failing to recognize it, we often do not do very well at expressing unity in fellowship with other branches of Christ's kingdom. Symington believes that churches, after recognizing the reality of their unity under Christ, should,

> so far as they have opportunities of meeting together, [hold] free and delightful fellowship with one another. Instead of indulging towards each other the jealousies of rivals, and each claiming for itself the exclusive name and privileges of *the church*, it becomes them to keep the unity of the Spirit in the bond of peace. (pp. 130–131)

One can readily see how Symington implemented these words in his own ministry. Symington was a minister in one of the "dissenting" churches in Scotland, and indeed one of the more "strict" bodies of the "dissenting church." He never abandoned the vital importance of the doctrinal distinctives which required his own denomination's independence from other bodies. In fact, he was one of the leading proponents of the Covenanter claims—even to the point of publishing this book, *Messiah the Prince!* Nevertheless, his devotion to Covenanter principles in no way hindered his concern for the unity of the church.

Symington was often found preaching in pulpits of other denominations. He was a leading advocate in his day for improving interchurch relations, especially through interchurch *doctrinal* study. (That is, doctrinal study aimed, not at finding common ground, but at searching the Scriptures together for the right ground.) Because there is one King reigning in His church, Symington regarded such interdenominational labors as not in vain. Christ will bring His people to even greater unity of faith (with *union* as one of the possible fruits, though not itself an urgent necessity).

"The spouse," Symington writes, "the undefiled of Christ, is but one" (p. 129). Rather than implicitly (and, indeed, blasphemously) charging Christ with polygamy, it is incumbent on the church to recognize her unity; unity to be embraced in uncompromising charity to one another *and* in uncompromising faithfulness to her King.

The Church is Authorized by Christ

A particular problem in Symington's day (and in the history of the Scottish Covenanters) was the problem of church and state relations. Roman Catholicism had asserted the right of *the church* to dominate the state; Anglicanism had asserted the right of *the state* to head the church; and most recently in Symington's day, the novel philosophy of complete *separation of church from state* was taking root on the European continent and in America.

Symington's writing on the place of civil government under Christ will be taken up in the next chapter. In this section, Symington emphasizes the church's *direct* subjection to Christ as indicating her rightful *independence* from the state. The state does not stand between the church and Christ. Symington explains,

> The church of Christ is strictly *independent;* meaning...the state may extend to it protection, and...cooperation; but has no right to dictate its creed, to institute its laws, to appoint its ministers, or to interfere in any one way with either its constitution or its administration. (p. 127)

The church operates by virtue of the same divine appointment that gives the state its authority (Matt. 16:18; 28:18–20; Rom. 13:1). It is not the state, therefore, that grants the church its right to function. She is directly accountable to Christ.

This places the church in a category completely distinct from charities, businesses, schools, and other organizations. These other organizations are appointed by men and derive their identity and operational rights from the government. The church does not derive its rights from the state, but from Christ directly.

This does not mean that the church should never accept "incorporation papers" from the state, or otherwise willingly cooperate with state policies for the ordering of social institutions. On the contrary, Symington urges that the church should expect "protection, countenance, pecuniary support, and friendly cooperation" from the state (as is extended through tax-exempt status papers, etc.). It is "the duty of the state to give the church all the advantages of a civil establishment," Symington writes (p. 127), and as Paul himself urged, the church should always seek cordial relations with the state (1 Tim. 2:1–2). However, the royal commission of the church means that

> The highest and warmest patronage of the state is procured at too dear a price, if, in order to secure it, the church has to barter away the least portion of her [biblically appointed] liberties. Every attempt, then, to interfere with its independence, on the part of the civil power, must be regarded as an unhallowed invasion of the rights of the people, and a monstrous usurpation of the inalienable rights and prerogatives of the church's glorious Head. (p. 128)

In societies where the state restricts preaching or bans evangelism, the church is not only at liberty to continue preaching and evangelizing, but is obliged under Christ's royal decree to do so (Acts 5:29). In communities, as was the experience of the Covenanters in Scotland, where the government controlled the creed of the established church and forbad "unauthorized" religious assemblies, the Covenanters were not only free, but obliged under Christ, to continue to meet for worship—even in caves and fields, and under threat of the sword.

In parts of the world where Christianity is explicitly outlawed, this truth is of immediate and obvious relevance. In societies with the "freedom of religion," its application is just as relevant though often more delicate. Even when the church is not explicitly banned from her biblical rights, pressure to conform in church practice to unbiblical state expectations exists. Those pressures which are indeed tampering with the church's royally appointed order must be resisted. Such is not merely the church's right, but it is her obligation because she is bound to the law of her King.

The church has an obligation, under the doctrine of Christ's mediatorial reign, to relate respectfully and cooperatively with the state, but never to subject her rights and duties to state interference.

The Sovereignty of the Church's King

The above implications of Christ's mediatorial reign for the practices of the church are a few of those brought out by Symington. Other implications which he has identified are worthy of reflection for those who would obtain *Messiah the Prince* for further study.

The last, and probably most refreshing, of the implications Symington draws is the certainty of the church's success. Because our King is sovereign "over all things to the church" (Eph. 1:22), the grand objects appointed to the church will not fail to be fully accomplished in every detail. Symington exhorts,

> Christians are apt to feel discouraged when they reflect on the extensive prevalence of error compared with the limited success of the true religion, and despondingly to inquire, 'By whom shall Jacob arise? for he is small.' But if they can only have faith in the mediatorial dominion, they may dismiss their fears, and confidently rely in, not merely the preservation, but the triumphant success and universal establishment, of the church. The Lord reigns: and the children of Zion may well be joyful in their King. (p. 187; quoting Amos 7:2, 5; Ps. 149:2)

The doctrine of Christ's mediatorial reign should be a source of great encouragement to Christians in their service for Him. The church has not been left to her own resources to complete the charge given to it by Christ. In His authority over *all things,* Jesus has promised to continue *with the church* to the end of time to insure her success: "All power is given unto me in heaven and in earth," Jesus said, "Go ye therefore, and teach all nations...and, lo, I am with you alway, even unto the end of the world" (Matt. 28:18–20). The doctrine of Christ's mediatorial dominion is essential for the Christian's encouragement in the face of the overwhelming evil of the world.

> By spiritual conversion [i.e., through the church, now] or judicial destruction [i.e., in the final judgment, at the end], He shall effect the entire subjugation of the globe. And, at the last, there shall not be a spot on the face of the habitable earth where the true church of Christ shall not have effected a footing, nor a single tribe of the vast family of man which shall not have felt the meliorating and blissful influence of Christian laws and institutions. Europe, Asia, Africa, and America, shall then be united in one vast brotherhood, — ranged under one standard: the bond of their union, the holy cement of the gospel, the emblem of their banner, the Cross. (p. 186)

Even Alexander the Great could never have hoped for so absolute a unification of his dominion into one kingdom. Nevertheless, Jesus exercises His dominion over the entire globe toward that end. The church, today, serves an important role—indeed, the central role—in His government. The church is the "outpost" of His gracious outreach into the world today, and the "conservation center" for gathering and preparing the fruits of His harvest unto eternity.

The doctrine of Christ's mediatorial dominion has profound implications for members of His church in many respects. A few of these have been outlined above, and others not here cited can also be gleaned from Symington's chapter on the church. Nevertheless, none is so important to the believer's faith and practical faithfulness as this confidence: Jesus' mediatorial dominion over all things guarantees the successful consummation of His kingdom in all its details.

One day, the kingdom will be finished. What a great joy that will be, when all citizens of His church from all lands and all ages take up our habitation before His throne, in "new heavens and a new earth, wherein dwelleth righteousness," there to dwell with Him for all eternity (2 Peter 3:13).

✦ ✦ ✦

And Simon Peter answered and said, Thou art the Christ.... And Jesus answered and said unto him...I say also unto thee, That thou art Peter, and upon this rock I will build my church; and the gates of hell shall not prevail against it. And I will give unto thee the keys of the kingdom of heaven...." (Matt. 16:16–19)

CHAPTER 15

Christ's Mediatorial Dominion Applied to the State

In the Pledge of Allegiance, Americans profess national submission to the reign of heaven. America confesses itself to be "one nation *under God*." America's coins and bank notes also bear the inscription, "In God We Trust." Every November, the American President issues a proclamation leading the nation in a day of Thanksgiving to God. These are various ways in which America, as a nation, professes faith in the reign of God and national dependence on His favor. America is peculiar among the modern, industrialized world for her many official professions of faith in heaven's rule.

In recent years, however, there has been much furor over the appropriateness of such religious expressions in public life. Prayer was banned from public schools in 1963. More recently, a widely publicized 2002 case provisionally banned the Pledge of Allegiance in public schools due to its oath of submission to God (although this ban was overturned by the Supreme Court on technicalities). In another highly publicized case, Judge Roy Moore's 2.6-ton Ten Commandments monument was removed from the Alabama Statehouse in the autumn of 2003 due to a separation-of-religion-and-government suit, with additional Ten Commandment cases brought before the Supreme Court in 2005. Citing the First Amendment, such professions of faith have been challenged as an unconstitutional "establishment" of the Christian religion.

The church's response to such developments has been divided. Some insist that these religious professions are an important part of America's heritage and ought to be retained. Other Christians insist that faith professions belong in the church but not the state. Such Christians accept that civil government should be secular. In his book, Symington boldly urges a third alternative.

Symington affirms the importance of publicly professing Christ. But he would urge more than religious rhetoric. The state ought to submit to this gracious King in its actual governance.

A nation should acknowledge the heavenly King in her pledge, but she should also submit to His laws in her constitution. A nation should acknowledge the historical significance of the Ten Commandments (as by monuments), but the Scriptures should also receive official sanction as a present source of national justice. It is fitting for national coinage to be inscribed "In God We Trust," but such inscriptions ought to be matched by a real program to shape national economic policy around the financial priorities of Christ. A nation should *profess* the rule of this heavenly King, but the state also can and ought to *govern* in real cooperation with His rule.

This teaching will obviously be controversial. The political theories that are currently dominant in our culture assume that "mixing religion and politics" is always bad. Politics is a powerful force over society. Religion is a powerful force over the heart. "Mixing" the two puts a lot of power together. History is replete with the stories of rulers who abused this powerful combination with great detriment. It is therefore presumed that complete separation of religion from politics is the healthiest way forward.

Symington understands this reasoning—and broadly accepts it. But he offers this bold refinement: the church must not rule the state; the state must not rule the church; *but both can (and ought) to serve the same Christ.* Historical abuses have arisen when a single human authority—a pope or a king—assumed rule over both church and state. These two institutions should be, and biblically must be, kept independent from one another. Symington accepts separation, in this sense, as biblical and proper. What he does not accept is the supposition that only the church can therefore be Christian, and that the independent state is by default secular. Scripture teaches that the same Jesus who ordained the church is also the one who ordained the state (Matt. 16:18; Rom. 13:1).

An independent church and an independent state, in their most natural and proper operation, ought to be harmonious sisters serving the same heavenly King. Their duties are different; their spheres of authority are different; their powers are different; but their King is the same.

It was this vision of "two kingdoms" amicably serving the same King which inspired the old Covenanter call for a reformation of church and state in seventeenth-century Scotland. It is this vision, and its practical implications, which Symington outlined in his book. *Messiah the Prince* was published as an exposition on Christ's universal rule, that all governments—ecclesial, familial, academic, corporate, and civil as well—might consider their proper response.

Christ's Mediatorial Dominion Includes the State

It is nearly unheard of today for a nation to rule under Christ's crown. That the *church* is obliged to Christ is accepted. That *families* ought to serve Christ is also appreciated by many. Some will even agree that businesses, clubs, schools, and other institutions can operate in a way that honors Christ as Lord. But has civil government been left outside Jesus' reign?

Scripture teaches, in principle, that Christ's reign is universal (see pp. 238–240, above). There is nothing outside His reign in all the cosmos. That this, in practice, does include the state is the first point of Symington's chapters on civil government. Before considering *how* the state can serve Christ, Symington wants to make it clear that Scripture does expect civil governments to serve Christ. He writes,

> In looking into the Word of God, we find subjection to Jesus Christ as Mediator directly enjoined upon civil rulers. 'Be wise now therefore, O ye kings; be instructed, ye judges of the earth. Serve the Lord with fear, and rejoice with trembling. Kiss the Son, lest he be angry, and ye perish from the way.' (p. 194)

Symington is here quoting from Psalm 2. Psalm 2 proclaims the divine appointment of Christ (the Son of David) to universal rule and enjoins all other kings to "kiss the Son." This expression, "kiss the Son," is a symbolic reference to kings offering "loyal subjection to a reigning prince" (p. 196; cf. 1 Sam. 10:1). Symington showcases Psalm 2 as a demonstration that civil governors, *as civil governments,* are expected to submit to Christ.

Symington further shows how the New Testament Apostles specifically applied this psalm to Jesus. In Acts 4, Peter, John and the Jerusalem church quote Psalm 2 as indicating the subjection of King Herod, the Roman Governor Pilate, and the Jewish rulers (whether they realized it or not) to Christ's sovereign reign. This text is important for Symington. It shows that the subjugation of civil rulers to Christ's reign in Psalm 2 is a continuing expectation in the New Testament church. It is not "just" an "Old Testament" command. Symington writes,

> Here, then, we have a most decided, unequivocal proof of the right of dominion over the nations of the earth which is possessed by the Mediator...whether belonging to Old or New Testament times. We have here a command of universal and permanent obligation. (pp. 196–197)

Symington was conscious that many Christians tended to disregard much of the Old Testament regal language as belonging exclusively to pre-cross Israel. Symington, however, diligently drew together both Old and New Testament texts in order to demonstrate that there is no change between testaments in the regnal rights of the Messiah. Jesus' rule includes the oversight of nations, both in the Old Testament announcement and the New Testament realization. Just as the Old Testament prophets called the coming Son of David the "governor among the nations" (Ps. 22:28), the King "higher than the kings of the earth" (Ps. 89:27), and the "king of nations" (Jer. 10:6–7), so the New Testament identifies Jesus as being the Son of David who fulfills all those prophecies (e.g., Matt. 21:9; 22:42), "the prince of the kings of the earth" (Rev. 1:5), and "King of kings and Lord of lords" (Rev. 17:14; 19:16). Symington draws on texts from throughout the Scriptures to show that kings and states are included in the mediatorial dominion of Jesus (cf. also Ps. 47:2–3, 8–9; 72; Isa. 49:22–23; 60:11–12, 16; Ezek. 45:17; Dan. 7:13; Rev. 11:15; 21:24, 26). He concludes,

> The proof of the mediatorial dominion over the nations, derived from these sources...is so abundant, varied, direct, complete, that we cannot but express our surprise the doctrine in question should ever have been denied or overlooked. (p. 209)

Of course, many Christians readily agree that Jesus *exercises* sovereignty over human governments. It is no unusual thing to find Christians praying for Christ to intervene when government legislates some moral atrocity, like legalizing abortion or restricting evangelism. By such prayers, Christians demonstrate their conviction that Jesus holds sovereign sway over states and can be appealed to when governments act in contradiction to His purposes.

What Symington found surprising, however, is that so few Christians expect human governments *to recognize and cooperate with* Christ's reign. We might draw the comparison to the crew of a sailing vessel. The winds that blow the ship are what make it go. It is only natural, therefore, that the crew will endeavor to understand the winds that propel them, in order to operate more thoughtfully and productively in response to them. Likewise, Christians should expect their civil governments to acknowledge the Christ who rules over them that they might govern in willing harmony with His purposes. It is this hope of an amicable and open relationship between the reigning Christ and the governing state that Symington expounds in his chapters on dominion as applied to the state.

Having established the principle (that states *ought* to submit to Christ), it remains next to consider the practice (*how* the Christ–state relationship should work out). Symington discusses the practicalities of the Christ–state relationship in two directions: (1) the relationship from Christ to the state, and (2) the relationship from the state to Christ. (It should be kept clear that the matter of *church–state* relations is a different issue, and will be considered later.)

How Christ Exercises His Rule over the State

Jesus reigns over the nations, whether they recognize Him or not. Jesus is there, exercising His rule, just as gravity was always governing the orbits of the planets long before Sir Isaac Newton's famous discovery of this phenomenon. Much scientific progress has followed from Newton's discoveries concerning the nature of gravity, and Symington believes that a nation can expect significant political progress once the reign of Christ is understood and embraced. Nonetheless, Symington first shows *that* Jesus exercises His rule over the state, regardless of the state's awareness. There are eight ways which Symington identifies, by which Jesus exercises His reign over the nations.

1. King Jesus appoints civil governments—From where does a government receive its authority to rule? What makes a government legitimate? Such questions have vexed political theorists for ages. Symington's view, derived from the Scriptures, is that government obtains its right to rule from the consent of the people (immediately), and from the appointment of Christ (ultimately). It is the Son of David, the psalmist declares, who will "make princes in all the earth" (Ps. 45:16). Furthermore, Christians are exhorted to respect "governors, as...*sent by him*" (1 Peter 2:14). The first way in which Jesus, as King of kings and Lord of lords, exercises His rule over states, is by appointing government in general and by sovereignly establishing specific governors. (Cf. Rom. 13:1–2; Ps. 75:6–7)

2. King Jesus guides the affairs of civil governments—It is also Jesus who ultimately controls the operations of human governments. Symington finds this truth particularly well illustrated by John's Apocalypse:

> The events unfolded in this book...[are guided] by the Lion of the tribe of Judah, the root of David, the divine Mediator, who opens the sealed book of God's purposes respecting the nations, blows the trumpets of divine warning, and pours forth the vials of Jehovah's wrath;—thus carrying forward the scheme of predetermined decrees. (p. 217)

This recognition is not to ignore the many acts of governments which oppose Christ (see point 4, below). Nevertheless, it is ultimately Jesus who rules over all the acts of all human governments. (Cf. Isa. 45:1; Ezra 6:22; Prov. 21:1)

3. King Jesus issues commands to civil governments—The commands contained in Scripture are not exclusively addressed to individuals and churches. Many commands in Scripture are specifically addressed to governments. For example: "Ye shall not respect persons in judgment; but ye shall hear the small as well as the great..." (Deut. 1:17); "Judges and officers shalt thou make thee in all thy gates.... Thou shalt not wrest judgment...neither take a gift [bribe]..." (Deut. 16:18, 19); "Deliver the poor and needy: rid them out of the hand of the wicked" (Ps. 82:4; cf. 2 Sam. 23:3; Ps. 2:10–11; Rom. 13:3–4). These and other commands like them in Scripture are acts from the heavenly King issued to civil rulers.

4. King Jesus overrules errant acts of civil governments—It is good when civil governments obey Christ. This is not always the case, however. Civil governments often refuse to establish Christ's justice, preferring to pursue political agendas contrary to Scripture and sometimes even oppressive of the church. Christ exercises His sovereignty by turning even unjust decrees to His own purposes. For example, Pharaoh's opposition to God's people, leading up to the Exodus, was ultimately submitted to Christ's purposes (Rom. 9:17). So also the immoral decrees of Jeroboam (1 Kings 14:16), Pilate (Acts 4:27), and others opposed to Christ were ultimately subjected to His own purposes.

"He makes the wrath of man to praise Him," Symington writes, "The nations and their rulers may refuse to serve Him, but they cannot prevent Him from serving Himself by them" (p. 220; quoting Ps. 76:10). Jesus exercises His sovereign reign to insure that even immoral acts of civil government ultimately serve His own agenda. (Cf. Ps. 46:1–7; 110:2)

5. King Jesus holds civil governments accountable—Jesus explained to His disciples, "For the Father judgeth no man, but hath committed all judgment unto the Son" (John 5:22). Not only in the final judgment, but throughout history, Jesus holds men *and nations* accountable for their deeds. It is He who brings blessings to the righteous land; and it is He who brings warnings, chastisement, and ruinous devastation on wicked kingdoms. (Cf. Ps. 2:5; 110:5–6; Isa. 60:12; 63:1–4; Dan. 2:44; Luke 10:12–16; Acts 12:1, 23; Rev. 2:26–27; 6:15–16; 8:5; 19:15)

6. King Jesus restrains civil governments from hindering the gospel—Jesus directly tied the Great Commission to His universal reign. It is only because "all power is given unto me [Jesus] in heaven and in earth" that His disciples are enabled to "go...and teach all nations" (Matt. 28:18–19). Although human governments may impose barriers to evangelism, Jesus exercises His sovereignty to insure that His intended progress is never derailed. Jesus exercises His sovereignty over states to keep the Great Commission moving forward. (Cf. 1 Cor. 16:9; Rev. 3:7–8)

7. King Jesus uses civil governments to protect His church—Civil government preserves the peace and order of society. Ideally, this includes the protection of Christians, enabling them freely to serve Christ (1 Tim. 2:1–4). On numerous occasions, the Apostle Paul was protected in his ministry by pagan Roman governments (e.g., Acts 16:35–39; 22:25–29; 23:27; 25:16). Jesus uses civil governments to maintain social peace conducive to the labors of the church. Sometimes, sadly, the church is directly opposed by the state. The church is powerless against the forces which are at the state's disposal. She would be extinguished quickly under the heel of state opposition, unless Christ held sovereignty over governments. Christ exercises His rule for the preservation of the church, sometimes in protection *from* the state, and often through the protection *of* the state (cf. Mark 13:20).

8. *King Jesus sanctifies civil governments*—It is Christ's purpose that governments once opposed to Him would become a source of nurture for the church. Isaiah prophesied that, in the time of Messiah, "kings shall be thy nursing fathers, and their queens thy nursing mothers" (Isa. 49:23; cf. 60:16). Symington understands this prophecy as an indication of Christ's intent to sanctify human governments. Daniel also prophesied similarly. Daniel prophesied the fall of the Roman (or, "Latin") Empire, and its gradual subjugation before a new sovereign: the Messiah (Dan. 2:31–45). Based on Daniel's prophecy, Symington wrote,

> The secular tyrannies of the Latin Earth shall be broken to pieces...; and the kingdoms that shall succeed [them] will be actuated with the spirit of that kingdom [of Christ] which is represented by the stone cut out without hands, which is to become a great mountain and fill the whole earth. Thus to purify, sanctify, revolutionise, nay, Christianise, the nations of the world, is what none but He could perform. (pp. 229–230)

Jesus exercises His authority over governments to purify them. It is inappropriate to say that Christ's work aims only at the sanctification of individuals, families, and churches. He is also sanctifying human associations of other kinds, including human government. It is His purpose that "kings and queens" would be nurturing allies of the church. He exercises His authority toward that end.

These are eight ways Symington perceives the reign of Christ being applied to civil governments. Sir Isaac Newton discovered that gravity governs both individual apples (like the one that famously fell on his head) *and* whole planets in their orbits around the sun. Similarly, Jesus exercises dominion over individuals *and* whole nations in their courses. "He is," indeed, "Lord of all" (Acts 10:36).

How a State Can Submit to Christ

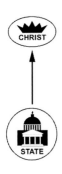

William Ewart Gladstone once remarked, "The Orb is under the Cross whether it knows it or not." Gladstone was Britain's prime minister in the late nineteenth century. His statement was in reference to one of the symbols of the British monarchy. The Orb is a round sphere representative of the earth, and the cross which stands prominently atop the Orb represents Christ's universal reign. Whether the kingdoms of the earth know it or not, Gladstone stated, "the Orb is under the Cross."

It certainly ought to be hoped, however, that "the Orb" would have the privilege of knowing her King. He is, after all, a gracious sovereign. The reign of Christ is not that of a cruel tyrant, but of one who frees men from the cruel tyranny of sin and the curse. His rule is full of righteousness, mercy, and love, and the purpose of His reign is blessing. Jesus declares the purposes of His reign in these words:

> ...the LORD hath anointed me to preach good tidings unto the meek;... to bind up the broken-hearted, to proclaim liberty to the captives,... to comfort all that mourn;... to give...the oil of joy for mourning, the garment of praise for the spirit of heaviness.... [to] build the old wastes;... [to] repair the waste cities, the desolations of many generations (Isa. 61:1–4; cf. Luke 4:17–21).

This King reigns for the ends of redemption, ends which are advantageous for human society and which it benefits civil government to support. There is no reason why civil governments "have" to be antichristian or, as is currently popular, "non-religious." If Jesus is indeed the King of nations, nations ought to be able to acknowledge His reign and serve His purposes cheerfully.

Such submission does not make the state into a branch of the church. Symington would be the first to defend the strict independence of church and state. "The Church of Christ," Symington repeatedly emphasized, "is strictly independent of the state" and *vice versa* (p. 285). Neither the church nor the state have power over each other. Furthermore, each have defined boundaries, the one over concerns of the human soul and the other over concerns of social equity. The church and state are distinct institutions.

Nevertheless, the church and state do have an important relationship to each other as allies serving the same King. As players on a ball team have their distinct positions to play, but do so in harmony under their captain, so church and state are independent in their roles yet allied under their King. Symington insists that independence of church and state does not mean lack of relationship between them:

> This is...a subject on which public sentiment is greatly divided.... That civil government has anything to do with religion is by many pointedly denied.... Nevertheless, believing as we do that it is the duty of nations to concern themselves about religion,... a union between Church and State, of an unexceptionable kind, is capable of being formed, and, moreover,... the formation of such a union is not only lawful in itself, but dutiful and obligatory. (pp. 262–263)

It will be helpful to approach the question of state support of religion in two parts. First, we will take up Symington's teaching on the nature of the state's obligation *to Christ* (the Christ–state relationship). Thereafter, we will take up the nature of the state's alliance with *the church* under Christ (the church–state relationship). The latter, after all, is really only possible where the former is first embraced.

Duties of the State to Christ

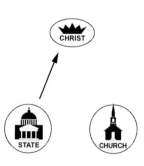

"It is the duty of nations," Symington affirms, "...to have respect to religion" (p. 262). The idea of a non-religious government is unbiblical. It is also unrealistic. "The fact that almost all nations," Symington observes from history, "ancient as well as modern, barbarous as well as civilised, have incorporated with their constitutions laws respecting religion, shews that these extraordinary impulses were in accordance with the dictates of nature" (p. 278). The theory of the religiously neutral state was an Enlightenment innovation which has not necessarily proven workable. In Symington's view, the state will always be supportive of some religion(s) and antagonistic to others, even if it tries to be "pluralistic."

Whether or not Symington is correct about the impossibility of neutral government, Jesus requires kings to submit to *His* reign. This has already been seen. Thus a state profession of allegiance to Christ becomes non-optional—if Jesus' Word truly has royal authority. If Jesus really is King of kings, and if the Christian religion really is the true religion, then civil governments are obliged to take an interest in this Christ and this religion. "It is the duty of nations...to have respect to religion" (p. 262).

Following are six obligations, identified by Symington, which fall upon a civil government in allegiance to Christ.

1. To seek the glory of Christ—Symington upholds the glory of Christ as the first obligation of states and their citizens. To fully appreciate this first point, it will be helpful to compare the idea of "glory" with the idea of "patriotism."

In America, a number of basic convictions are held as fundamental to national greatness. The right to vote is, for example, perceived as a great guarantee of freedom: America is a nation "of the people, by the people, for the people." American patriotism is therefore expressed by exercising, and jealously guarding, the right to vote. "Life, liberty, and the pursuit of happiness," are also ideals regarded as pillars of American greatness. Patriotism is expressed by devotion to, and jealously guarding, these basic freedoms. Citizens in a democracy like America exercise patriotism by protecting and exalting those pillars which make the nation great.

In a monarchy, however, the source of national benefit (or detriment) is not centered on ideals alone, but on *a person.* In an absolute monarchy, the king personally owns all the wealth under his dominion, and he is the master of all the peoples and all their commerce. When such an absolute sovereign is a tyrant, there is no glory. The people agonize under the weight of absolute tyranny. When, however, such a sovereign proves himself gracious, wise, and capable, and he exercises his dominance with compassion for the needy and aptitude for national prosperity, then there is every reason to glory in him. It is not merely the principles of government which the king implements, but the grace and capability of the king himself, which is the center of national glory. Subjects of such a king both celebrate, and jealously protect, the principles and person of this king.

Symington certainly believed in democratic principles of civil government. He contends that Scripture itself endorses the popular voice in civil government (pp. 213–216; 241–42). No single ruler should own and master a nation. There is one exception to this, however. *Jesus* does hold absolute authority over all lands and peoples. Thus, whatever the political system of a particular nation, it is always under a Monarch. Even America, for example, is actually a democratic republic *within a monarchy.*

Once a nation acknowledges Christ as the ultimate source of national blessing, His glory becomes fundamental to patriotic feelings and service. No activity of government should violate the glory of King Jesus. His glory should guide the nation, according to Symington,

> in the formation of their constitution; in the establishment of their various institutions; in the shaping of their policy, whether domestic or foreign; in the selection and appointment of their functionaries, whether supreme or subordinate; in their legislative enactments; and in all their separate acts of administration. (p. 232)

In short, "It is the duty of nations and their rulers, to have respect to the glory of Christ in all their institutions and transactions" (p. 231; cf. Dan. 4:30–32; 5:23; 1 Cor. 10:31).

2. To Observe Christ's law—It was earlier seen that Scripture contains many commands from Christ specifically to governments (#3 on p. 268, above). Scripture is not only binding upon individuals, families (e.g., Eph. 5:22–6:4), and business (e.g., Prov. 1:3; Eph. 6:5–9); states also are obliged to obey Christ's Word. "We contend, then," Symington writes, "that the Bible is to be our rule, not only in matters of a purely religious nature, in matters connected with conscience and the worship of God, but [also] in matters of a civil or political nature" (p. 235). Not only the sixth Commandment ("Thou shalt not kill"), but the fourth Commandment ("Remember the sabbath day, to keep it holy") also, is relevant for civil government. Because there

are matters of state jurisdiction involved in all the Ten Commandments, Symington regards all ten as requiring civil obedience.

Symington is aware that there will be practical questions about
how certain Mosaic laws (outside the Ten Commandments) would
apply to modern governments. He recognizes that New Testament
revelation qualifies certain aspects of what was required under Old
Testament law. Nevertheless, it is Symington's purpose in *Messiah
the Prince* to establish the principle that Scripture does provide the
highest norm for Christian government:

> Neither do we wait to inquire what parts of the judicial law
> given to the Jews, are binding upon Christian states. We build
> at present upon the broad and undeniable *fact* that nations
> as such, and civil magistrates in their official capacity,...
> are under obligation, at all times, to shape and model their
> political conduct by the dictates of this infallible standard.
> (pp. 237–238)

Christians in Symington's time were prone to regard the political concerns of the Bible to the "Old Testament era." Symington
sees this conclusion as no more acceptable than to suppose the Old
Testament concern for the family was repealed in the New. On the
contrary, Symington asserts that "[even in] the New Testament, we
find...many things respecting the nature, origin, and ends of civil
government; the qualifications, duties, and claims of civil rulers;
and the obligations of subjects towards magistrates" (p. 238). Such,
for example, is Romans 13 which expects government officials to be
"ministers of God." Civil governments are obliged to embrace Scripture as the highest law from their King. (Cf. Deut. 4:5–8; 17:18–20;
Josh. 1:8; 1 Kings 2:1–3)

3. To appoint qualified officials—A further way for nations to serve
Christ is by choosing officials according to His qualifications. This is
applicable for those officials chosen by the public through election,
as well as those placed through political appointment. Symington
identifies three kinds of qualifications which Scripture expects.

First of all, government officials require *natural* qualifications.
Quoting from Ecclesiastes, Exodus, and Deuteronomy, Symington
writes, "Wo to thee, O land, when thy king is a *child!* Thou shalt
provide out of all the people *able* men. Take you *wise* men, and *understanding*...and I will make them rulers over you" (p. 243; quoting

Eccl. 10:16; Ex. 18:21; Deut. 1:13). Scripture expects that individuals of intellectual and emotional competence be installed in government offices.

Secondly, government officials require *moral* qualifications. "High and incorruptible integrity," Symington summarizes, "well regulated mercy, strict veracity, and exemplary temperance, are all specified with approbation in the Word of God" (p. 243; cf. Ex. 18:21; 2 Sam. 23:3; Prov. 20:28; 31:4–5). Symington took particular issue with the popular maxim, "measures not men," whereby current political theorists supposed that good laws (i.e., "measures") would be sufficient to restrain bad officers abusing their posts. While Symington agreed that good laws are necessary for good government, nonetheless it is the individual in office who actually conducts government affairs. There is therefore "a much greater likelihood of good men correcting the evils of bad measures, than of good measures restraining the evils of bad men" (p. 247). Biblically, moral uprightness is as necessary a qualification for public office as is intellectual competence.

Thirdly, government officials require *religious* qualifications. It is in this point that Symington expected some readers to raise their eyebrows. Nevertheless, he maintains that "*religious* qualifications are required in the Scriptures" (p. 244). The same text in Exodus that illustrates natural and moral qualifications, also enjoins a right respect for the true God: "Moreover thou shalt provide out of all the people able men, such as fear God, men of truth, hating covetousness; and place such over them..." (Ex. 18:21). Likewise, King David affirmed at the end of his life, "The Rock of Israel spake to me, He that ruleth over men must be just, *ruling in the fear of God*" (2 Sam. 23:3). Citing yet another biblical example, Symington wrote,

> It is a too common maxim with many in our day, that magistrates...have nothing to do with religion,—nothing to do with it, it would seem, not only as an object of legislation, but even as a qualification for office.... How differently did the patriotic Nehemiah feel and act in this matter. "I gave," says he, "...Hananiah the ruler of the palace, charge over Jerusalem: *for he was a faithful man, and feared God above many.*" (pp. 245–247; quoting Neh. 7:2)

These three qualifications for public office are established by Scripture: intellectual capability, moral uprightness, and religious devotion. By observing these qualifications for the election or appointment of government officials, a nation responds to Christ's reign over them.

4. *To obey civil government as from Christ*—Symington's fourth duty of the state (and its citizens) is to obey the laws and order of its government as being from Christ. Not only does the state submit to Christ, but it also receives a measure of heavenly authority as it does so. Government under Christ is to be respected and obeyed, not merely out of fear of legal penalty (i.e., when the police might find out), but out of reverence for Christ. Christ is the monarch over the state and He, from His throne in heaven, sees all.

Symington develops this fourth point with an extended exposition of Romans 13:

> Let every soul be subject unto the higher powers. For there is no power but of God: the powers that be are ordained of God. Whosoever therefore resisteth the power, resisteth the ordinance of God.... (Rom. 13:1–7)

Two sides of Symington's treatment of this passage should be noted. First, Symington observes what this text *does* teach. This text does teach that citizens are accountable to Christ for their submission to legitimate civil authorities. Citizens are enjoined to obey the law, to pay taxes, and to deal with respect and honor for those in office (Rom. 13:5–7). "These duties are to be performed from a principle of conscience...," concludes Symington, "The resistance of lawful authority is thus stigmatised as rebellion against God, and... offensive to the Messiah" (p. 251). Romans 13 enjoins citizens to submit to *state* government *as unto Christ*.

The second aspect of Symington's treatment, however, is to make clear what Romans 13 is *not* saying. Although the universalistic language of Paul (i.e., "there is no power but of God"; Rom. 13:1) rightly affirms that *all* civil authority derives from heaven, Symington is wary of those who go so far as to suppose that *all* human governors without distinction are therefore "the minister of God to thee for good" (Rom. 13:4). Paul, according to Symington, is describing the ideal government in order to present a *universal principle*; he is not, however, intending to state a *universal fact*. The universal principle is this: Every government derives its authority from Christ and is therefore obliged to be "the minister of God to thee for good." Christians should expect governments to become increasingly "Christianized" under the power of the gospel, and should be devoted to the support of such governments. Nonetheless, Paul is not ignoring the fact that Christians will, at times, be required to disobey human governments. Human governments do, at times, rebel against Christ and fail to be His servants for good. Romans 13's statement of the universal principle does not contradict the Apostolic example in Acts: "We ought to obey God rather than men" (Acts 5:29).

Romans 13 is not teaching blind obedience. It is, however, teaching a universal principle. Citizens are to expect Christ to use governments for the promotion of good and punishment of evil. As Christ does this, citizens are to submit loyally and thoroughly to such governments *because of their reverence for Christ.*

5. To covenant with Christ in times of national distress—Symington's own work on the doctrine of Christ's reign stands on the shoulders of the seventeenth-century Scottish Covenanters. This fact becomes particularly clear in this fifth point.

It was during a time of national distress in 1638 that a group of Scottish church and civic leaders met in Edinburgh, Scotland. They discussed the scriptural pattern of covenanting as a way *nations* can corporately respond to public troubles. In 2 Kings 23:1–3, for example, King Josiah led the government, the priests, and all the people "small and great" in a covenant of repentance and reformation before the Lord. This covenant did not involve the drawing up of a "new" agreement with God. Rather, it was a response to the rediscovery of "the Book of the Covenant" (the Scriptures) which had been found in the Temple. The nation *as a nation* entered into a public renewal of covenant allegiance to the Lord. In another biblical example, in Nehemiah 9:1–13, the actual text of a written covenant is recorded, with the names of leading signatories included. Under Nehemiah, the people and their leaders (political and religious) responded to a time of distress by professing their allegiance to the Lord in a signed document. (Cf. Deut. 29:10–15; Josh. 24:25; 2 Kings 11:17–20; 2 Chron. 15:9–15; Ps. 76:11; Isa. 44:3–5) This biblical principle of national covenanting led that 1638 gathering in Edinburgh to draw up a (renewed) National Covenant for Scotland. Throughout the nation, from the royal court down to the commoner, thousands upon thousands of names were signed to copies of the Covenant. (See pp. 7–11, above.)

Writing in the heritage of these Covenanters, Symington included national covenanting in his list of biblical duties of the state:

> It is not supposed that the formal act of swearing allegiance is to be gone into lightly, or on all occasions. But, certainly, in times of deep distress, as a means of animation and comfort; in times of backsliding and danger, for the purpose of promoting stability; as calculated to promote and maintain steps of reformation; and also as a fit mode of expressing gratitude for public blessings, a nation may warrantably and dutifully engage in such an exercise. (pp. 256–257)

Symington was aware that many would suppose the examples of Josiah, Nehemiah, and others were only for Old Testament Israel. Symington shows from the Prophet Isaiah, however, that such covenanting was not exclusive to Israel. Speaking of the future adoption of the Gentiles into the biblical faith, Isaiah writes, "In that day shall five cities in the land of Egypt...swear to the LORD of hosts.... They shall vow a vow unto the LORD, and perform it" (Isa. 19:18–21). Symington observes from this text, "Here it is distinctly made known that, in the days of the gospel, Gentile countries should copy the example of ancient Canaan, in the matter of vowing allegiance to the Lord" (p. 258).

Although this idea of national covenanting is not much discussed in the present day, it is a practice with a long history including nations other than Scotland. "The principle has been exemplified in more modern times," Symington observed, "in France, Germany, Switzerland, and the Netherlands, as well as in our own country [Scotland]" (p. 258). As subjects of Christ, in times of national joy or national distress, the state has the duty of leading the people in a social compact of thanksgiving or reformation under Christ.

6. *To coordinate with Christ's church*—Symington flatly rejected the Roman Catholic idea that state governments should be subject to the church. He also rejected as unbiblical the Anglican idea that the church should be subject to the state. Church and state are inde-

pendent institutions with distinct roles in society. Their jurisdictions must never be usurped.

It is the church that Christ has ordained with oversight of the human soul. The church has the charge to preach the Word for the reproof of the conscience and the forgiveness of sins. The church has the authority to administer the sacraments and lead worship. Such are duties of the church which the state does not have the right to presume upon.

It is to the state, on the other hand, that Christ has granted authority over social intercourse. The state has the power to apply physical punishment and confinement, not for matters of conscience, but for matters of social justice. The state has no authority to imprison a man for what is in his heart, but has every duty to punish (or reward) men for what they do with their hands. The government of the state is in a different sphere of jurisdiction than that of the church.

Despite these distinctions, it is the same community of people for which church and state are alike charged to give care. There is an obvious (indeed, unavoidable) complementary nature between these two institutions which ought to lead us to value their cooperation.

Independence does not mean that close association between church and state is illegitimate. "*Distinction*," Symington writes, "does not necessarily imply *hostility*"—or inability to cooperate (p. 307). On the contrary, because both the church and the state serve the same King, it should be expected that a warm and cooperative alliance would exist between them. If a state government comes to acknowledge its submission to Christ, one of the implications of that confession would be a specific alliance with Christ's church.

It is this sixth duty which opens the matter of the state's relationship to the church. In addition to the state's responsibilities *in allegiance to Christ* (described above), the state also has responsibilities *in alliance with the church* (to be described next).

Duties of the State to Christ's Church

The state owes no *allegiance* to the church. She does, however, owe *alliance* to the church. When a state comes to appreciate its duty to Christ, it must also embrace its mutual interest in Christ's church even if not itself subordinate to the church.

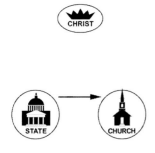

Without contradicting the alliance nature of this relationship, it will also be noted that this alliance is not one of equals. It is the church which is the more important in the relationship. Paul explains that the Father "put all things under [Christ's] feet, and gave him to be the head over all things *to the church*" (Eph. 1:22). Jesus rules even over the state *for the sake of the church.* Although the church and state are *independent* allies, the state does have a particular duty to support the concerns of the church.

At first blush, this might sound unfair to the state. However, it is actually consistent even with modern democratic ideals. Consider, for example, the state's expected relation to business in the modern, Western world. Business, it is held, does not exist to serve government. On the contrary, government is expected to maintain laws for the benefit of business. A democratic government is expected to pass and maintain legislation which will enable legitimate business to prosper. Similarly, democratic government is expected to protect families and encourage the arts, rather than interfering with families or subverting the arts to "toe the government line." In company–state, family–state, arts–state relationships, it is the interest of legitimate business, families, and arts that are preeminent. If this is true of the state's relationship to these institutions, how much more ought the state to seek the prosperity of true religion! Once a nation understands its obligation to Christ, it is only natural for her to desire the success of Christ's church as well.

In accord with this expectation, Symington gives the following definition of the state's duty to the church:

> IT IS THE DUTY OF A NATION, AS SUCH, ENJOYING THE LIGHT OF REVELATION, IN VIRTUE OF ITS MORAL SUBJECTION TO THE MESSIAH, LEGALLY TO RECOGNISE, FAVOUR, AND SUPPORT, THE TRUE RELIGION. (pp. 264–265)

This definition highlights an important feature of Symington's teaching. The state's alliance with the church is, according to Symington, a direct result of her being in proper relation to Christ. To the degree that the state is in right relation to Christ, the church can expect the state to be in right relation toward her. This is an important principle. It means that the church should not take up political issues simply to preserve a moral society. The church's primary prayer in things political must be for the state's submission to Christ: that kings would "kiss the Son" (Ps. 2:12). Certainly the church ought to be "salt and light" in all kinds of moral issues. Her central concern, however, should be that government would know the joy of calling Jesus "Lord." It is the proper Christ–state relationship which is of primary concern; the right church–state relationship is secondary.

Between the two poles of a nation that blatantly resists Christ and the nation that openly submits to Christ, there may be differing degrees of church–state harmony. Actual alliance, however, is not possible except through common allegiance to Christ. Symington makes clear that his argument "is not [for]...the Church of Christ to seek alliance with a *heathen, anti-christian,* and *immoral State*..." (pp. 263–264). Church–state unity is not necessary for the church's success. The church has a task to do for her King whether the state is supporting or opposing her. The amity of the state is much to be desired, but it is not necessary for the church's work. A church–state alliance is not an end in itself to be sought. It is a proper church–*Christ* relationship on the one hand, and a proper state–*Christ* relationship on the other, that are to be the objects of Christian witness. The desired church–state alliance emerges as a result of these.

To the degree that a state is submissive to its heavenly duties, there can be harmony with the church. Symington indicates a number of ways in which, according to Scripture, the church can be expected to benefit the state, and the state benefit the church.

Practical Ways the Church can Benefit the State

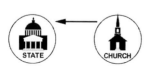

Symington first indicates ways in which the church can benefit the state.

1. *Religion restrains abuse of power*—"Religion alone can restrain the nobles of a land," Symington writes, "from seeking the supposed welfare of their own order, at the expense of that of the humbler classes of society" (p. 279). Human laws can only regulate tangible activity. Only true reli-

gion can change the heart. When a nation establishes the Scripture as the source of government policy, Christ's Word sanctifies government officers not only as private persons but as public rulers as well. Established religion in government introduces a restraint on the hearts of government officers.

2. *Religion restrains abuse of liberty*—"Nor can anything but true religion," Symington continues, "ever prevent the claims of popular liberty from degenerating into licentiousness..." (pp. 279–280). Civil law can only draw boundaries around what is punishable; it can never foster a love for what is good. Religion alone has the capacity to make a populace desirous to use their liberty for good, rather than turning liberty into an opportunity for indulgence (cf. 1 Peter 2:12–16).

3. *Religion promotes increased liberty*—"By checking selfishness," Symington states, "inspiring benevolence, and teaching a strict moral equality, [religion] proves itself decidedly friendly to the rights of the people..." (p. 279). It is widely recognized that government can only be sparing when a population is self-restrained; when a populace lacks self-restraint, social controls must be increased to maintain order and fairness. Biblical Christianity nurtures such self-government among a people, making civic freedoms possible (cf. John 8:36).

4. *Religion stimulates prosperity*—In 1905, Max Weber produced an influential study on the "Protestant work ethic." Weber showed that the spread of the Christian faith in Europe during the Protestant Reformation—with its emphasis on dedication to one's vocation and abstinence from (expensive) indulgences—brought about the rise of capitalism. Nearly a century before Weber, Symington offered a similar insight. "It might even be shewn," he wrote, "that religion is fitted to operate favourably in regard to national wealth, by securing industry." The Christian religion prospers national wealth "by restraining indulgences injurious to health; by hindering all profuse and foolish expenditure of public money; and by...ameliorating the evils of pauperism which spreads like leprosy over an immoral population" (pp. 280–281). National religion, according to Symington, promotes national wealth (cf. 1 Tim. 4:8).

5. *Religion preserves peace*—"It requires little penetration," Syming-ton begins his next point, "to see how religion is subservient to the peace of a nation" (p. 281). Symington was particularly reprov-ing the imperial ideals then current in Great Britain. The British Empire was to reach its height under Queen Victoria in the decades after Symington's book appeared. Ironically, because the Anglican Church operates under the control of the state, many of these *politi-cal* conquests of Britain were given *religious* sanction by the church. Symington opposed such misuse of religion as an instrument of political expansion. "Martial music," Symington reproved, "glitter-ing arms, mustering troops, and far-spreading conquest have about them a glare by which men are apt to be deceived. It should never be forgotten, however, that war is at the best a necessary evil.... Reli-gion directly tends to promote the blessings of peace" (pp. 281–282; cf. Isa. 2:4).

6. *Religion produces morality*—"[Religious] sanctions," the author continues, "are powerfully calculated to restrain those outbreak-ings of injustice and violence which the laws of civil society are designed to repress..." (p. 282). Civil law can only regulate social activity. Religion, however, can confront and transform the heart. National religion will promote the morality of the people in a way legislation cannot.

7. *Religion averts divine punishment*—"In short," Symington con-cludes his list, "without religion no nation can feel itself secure. Ungodliness provokes the anger of the Lord, and, like Israel of old, the nation that neglects religion and gives itself up to iniquity, will not be able to stand before its enemies" (p. 282). Not only does the church strengthen the morality, peace, and prosperity of a nation, but it leads the people into a right standing before God. The favor of God on a land, or His wrath in the case of wickedness, is no light matter. "Warriors and statesmen may affect to despise all this," Symington admits, "while they put their trust in human wisdom and prowess, but God can soon teach them...that the prayers of the godly are more to be trusted than swords of steel,—the sighs of true penitence a surer safeguard than all the thunders of artillery" (pp. 282–283). National religion, embraced in truth and sincerity, secures the favor of God upon a land (cf. Prov. 14:34).

Symington lists such points as these to illustrate the kinds of benefits which the church brings to civil society. It is widely recognized in the present day that a strong economy promotes the welfare of a nation, that "family values" are good for a country, and that quality education contributes to the betterment of society. What Symington desires to show is that true religion is no less integral to the prosperity of a nation. In fact, biblical religion is even more important than any of these. "It will be difficult to shew," he concludes, "that there is any one thing which can contribute more directly or extensively to the true prosperity of a kingdom than religion; and yet," he marvels, "we are asked to believe that this one thing a kingdom must do nothing to introduce, to support, or to diffuse!" (p. 285)

Although independent, church and state are not unrelated. There is much that the church can do—and under Christ is obliged to do—for the prosperity and success of the state.

Practical Ways the State can Benefit the Church

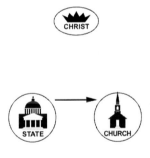

There is also much that the state can and should do for the church. It is, of course, state promotion of religion that is particularly controversial in modern political thought. Nevertheless, Symington offers a number of ways in which the state can actively support the church without violating the church's independence or transgressing its own lack of authority over the consciences of its citizens.

1. *Government can protect the church*—Symington notes that it is the state which has been granted the power of protection. The church has the charge to worship and witness, but has "no power of defence from external attack" (p. 286). The state has a responsibility to protect the church from physical damage or hindrance.

2. *Government can legally adopt the church's creed*—There is no violation of the church's or the state's independence when the state officially adopts the creed of the church. By doing so, the state professes its submission to Christ, establishes the formal authority of Scripture in matters of state, and identifies what religion it is which depart-

ments of the state will countenance in their various dealings. Just as it is necessary for the government to come to an understanding of what constitutes a marriage in order to guide the state's dealings with matters of marriage; and as it is necessary for the government to define what constitutes income for the purposes of taxation; so it is fitting for a state to legally establish the creed which defines true religion as countenanced by the government. "It will be admitted," Symington states, "that the civil magistrate may warrantably legislate on subjects connected with the advancement of the arts and sciences.... Why, we ask, should he be precluded from legislating in behalf of religion...?" (p. 288)

A common objection to an *established* (that is, governmentally favored) church is the fear of state persecution in the name of religion. Symington is conscious of this concern, but would urge against presuming that the state establishment of religion *necessarily* leads to persecution.

> It is quite a mistake to say, that the magistrate's giving his countenance to one set of religious opinions in preference to others, involves the essence of persecution.... [In adopting a creed] the legislature does not, in any sense, dictate to the subject what his religion shall be. It only determines what system of religious belief shall be taught with the aid and countenance of the state. (pp. 288–289)

The government might provide tax benefits to encourage college education, without thereby requiring that all citizens attend college. The government can establish certain testing standards and authorize certain textbooks for use in state schools, without thereby forcing all its citizens to embrace the beliefs promoted in those curricular choices. The government can adopt dietary standards to encourage good health without dictating what people eat. The government can recognize mainstream medical disciplines without hindering people's belief in alternative treatments. There are many ways in which government, for the sake of promoting the welfare of society, adopts various disciplinary standards. Symington believes a state can similarly adopt the creed which indicates that church which will receive the legal support and benefits of the state, without thereby compelling its citizens to believe accordingly.

3. *Government can protect the Sabbath*—The question of Sabbath-day laws was hotly debated in Symington's day. Symington devoted roughly ten pages to the subject (pp. 289–298). In short, he noted that government has no power to "compel" citizens to observe the Sabbath. It is the church's task to call people to assemble for worship and honor the Lord's Day. Nevertheless, the state can establish laws that protect citizens from being pressured by their jobs, distracted by public entertainment, or otherwise hindered from observing the Sabbath as commanded by their heavenly King. Symington writes,

> We know that the magistrate cannot enforce the spiritual observance of the Sabbath, and we do not ask him to do so. We know that secular authority can reach only to what is external. We know that it is the prerogative of God to touch, as it is His only to judge, the heart. But...might it not as well be pleaded that the magistrate should not make laws for the protection of human life, because he cannot restrain man from cherishing deadly hatred towards his brother man;... or laws against perjury, because he cannot impart to men a sacred regard to truth?... We contend that it is still competent for him...to secure to the nation a season of rest from public business and public amusements; and that, too, on distinctly religious grounds.... (p. 291)

Symington's point is that the state regulates the external dealings of society, the church addresses the conscience. There is no reason to suppose that the state's external regulation and the church's internal confrontation must operate from different standards of right. On the contrary, if both recognize the reign of Christ, then it should be expected that the Scriptures would provide the basis for each institutions' standard of right.

4. *Government can restrain gross idolatry*—Recalling that God punishes nations *as nations* for idolatry, Symington sees it as a legitimate task of government to restrain extreme and blatant idolatry or gross blasphemy. "A king that sitteth in the throne of judgment," King Solomon wrote, "scattereth away all evil with his eyes" (Prov. 20:8; cf. 20:26; 2 Chron. 24:2–5; Rom. 13:3–4; 1 Peter 2:14).

"This is confessedly a point of great delicacy," Symington admits, "and to define the full extent to which the magistrate is entitled or bound to go...must be acknowledged to be a matter of no ordinary difficulty" (p. 298). Symington is not pretending to have easy answers to what kinds of false worship or blasphemy warrant government intervention and what do not. Nevertheless, as is the case in many matters of government regulation, the general validity of national concern in this issue requires the government to wrestle (under Scripture) to discern where to act. Nonetheless, because idolatry and blasphemy are a threat to the nation as a civil society, its restraint is a valid matter for political concern.

5. *Government can financially aid the church*—Symington's last point is potentially the most controversial: "A nation may promote the interests of religion by contributing pecuniary support" (p. 302). He is careful to leave the precise nature of such financial support an open question. Perhaps a government might offer actual funding for certain religious activities, or perhaps the state's involvement would be limited to "giving encouragement to voluntary liberality"—that is, through measures such as tax deductions for contributions to the church (p. 302). His main point is that the state can legitimately provide financial support to the church, without necessarily violating its independence.

Symington notes the use of national taxes in the Old Testament to support the Lord's House (e.g., Neh. 10:32; 13:10–11). The prophets also described the New Testament age as a time when Gentile governments would offer gifts of gold and silver for the Lord (e.g., Ps. 72:10, 15; Isa. 60:3, 6, 9). Since states have much to gain *as states* by the establishment of churches throughout the land, Symington sees no reason why it should not be as appropriate for the state to contribute funds to church planting in poor and difficult communities as for the state to finance start-up schools or medical centers. Symington would undoubtedly be the first to urge Christians to give directly to the support of the church. Furthermore, he would resist any financial entanglements between church and state which would endanger the independence of either. Nevertheless, his point is simply that there is no necessary violation of church or state independence when the state looks for ways to economically facilitate the success of the church in its land.

> Shall countless sums be lavished on...prisons, and penitentiaries, and all the machinery of legal, judicial, and police establishments, for the detection and punishment of crime;

and shall not a single farthing be given from the public purse for the support of those religious institutions...[which] effect the suppression of crime of every name, and thus, not only... advance the comfort of the community, but...save the expenditure of the national funds? (p. 304)

It is within the state's rightful interests to find ways to economically benefit the church.

These five items are not comprehensive, but they illustrate the kind of state alliance with the church which Symington regards as proper. His conclusions are obviously controversial. He calls into question a number of deeply entrenched beliefs about church and state separation, widely embraced by Christians as well as politicians today. His aim in offering this list is to counter the assumption that state and church must be isolated from each other.

Christians, in Symington's view, often make the mistake of confusing biblical prohibitions against alliances with *the world* as though they restrict alliances with *the state*. James 4:4 says, for example, "Know ye not that the friendship of the world is enmity with God?" It is a misunderstanding of such texts, Symington warns, to presume that they imply a separation from government. When the Bible speaks of the evil of "the world," this refers to worldly immorality, not civil government. "The world of the ungodly...," Symington avers, "is the kingdom of Satan... [but] civil society...is the moral ordinance of God" (p. 306). Government, like the church, is *an ordinance of God.* Symington continues,

...All connexion of the church with the former [i.e., the world] cannot but injure her. [But] Civil society and the church of Christ, being both ordinances of God,... must be capable of dwelling together in friendly co-operation, and of exerting a mutual beneficial influence (p. 306).

The biblical injunctions for the church to abstain from entanglements with "the world" no less restrict her friendship with civil government than her cooperation with business leaders, charities, schools, or other institutions. In all of these, the church is only to insure she does not entangle herself in worldliness (i.e., ungodliness).

Some of those who advocate Symington's teaching overall have differed on certain points of state support for the church. In the 1884 American Edition of Symington's book, for example, the editors register their disagreement with points 2 and 5, above:

> At two points the American publishers...would dissent from the conclusions...[regarding] relations of church and state. These points are the adoption by the state of the creed of the church, and the bestowal upon the church, by the state, of direct pecuniary support.[1]

The reasons for this dissent include, on the one hand, that the church's creed includes many details of theology not relevant for government. In the view of the 1884 editors, the government can formally submit to Christ without ratifying a statement of faith as detailed as, for example, the Westminster Confession of Faith. On the other issue (financial support), the editors noted that Israel's tithes for the temple normally went directly to the Levites, not through the state. These proponents of Symington's teaching, therefore, differed with him on these two points.

Such debate would likely be welcomed by Symington. His main assertion is that the church and state are both ordinances of Christ, and that such matters of practical cooperation *ought* to be topics of discussion. But rather than discussing how to keep the church and state apart, as tends to be the trend today, Symington urges a positive expectation. How can the state and church improve their alliance under Christ? They have independent roles to fulfill, but they ought to fulfill them in amicable alliance. The practicalities of how that alliance should operate probably requires further development than the basic description produced by Symington.

Symington's teaching on church–state relations, as affected by the doctrine of Christ's mediatorial dominion, is summarized in his definition cited earlier:

> IT IS THE DUTY OF A NATION, AS SUCH, ENJOYING THE LIGHT OF REVELATION, IN VIRTUE OF ITS MORAL SUBJECTION TO THE MESSIAH, LEGALLY TO RECOGNISE, FAVOUR, AND SUPPORT, THE TRUE RELIGION. (pp. 264–265)

The Scriptures claim that Jesus Christ is the agent of all heaven's purposes on earth. All governments are to submit to His rule and support His church. No political body, once faced with this

---

1. "Introduction to the American Edition" [1884]

claim, can remain religiously "neutral." That government which has the light of Scripture is obligated to embrace Jesus' reign and support His religion, or to be counted among those kings who "take counsel together against the LORD and against his anointed, saying, 'Let us...cast away their cords from us'" (Ps. 2:2–3). Once a nation is confronted with the Scriptures, it becomes necessary for that government, as a government, to acknowledge Christ and to support true religion.

The resulting alliance might be roughly compared to the modern practice of "checks and balances." Many governments today are divided so that judicial, legislative, and executive powers operate independently from one another. In America, for example, executive authority is vested in the president, legislative authority is vested in Congress, and judicial authority is vested in the courts. Each of these branches of government has a strictly defined sphere and is independent from the others. Nevertheless, they are not separate. It is fully expected that these three branches of government will harmoniously serve the ends appointed in the Constitution. Through the separation of powers, American government *operates as a unity* despite each branch having independent spheres of activity.

This principle of "checks and balances" is not unlike the biblical church–state relationship defined by Symington. The ideal relationship for the church and the state retains their strict independence, while pursuing common ends under a single authority: the Word of Christ.

✦   ✦   ✦

The doctrine of Christ's mediatorial dominion is often overlooked in Christian pulpits, and neglected in Christian practice. Yet it is so prominent a teaching in all the Scriptures. Symington believes this is due to our tendency to gravitate away from teachings that place greater obligation on our shoulders. "It is, alas! too common," Symington remarked, "for men to shew a willingness to be interested in Christ as a *Priest,* while they obstinately refuse to submit to him as a *King*" (pp. 352–353). However, the doctrine of Christ's reign is not only a cause for duty, but also for comfort and praise. It is overlooked to the detriment of the believer.

In times of need, Symington states, the believer can take comfort in the knowledge "that the spiritual Joseph is ruler over all the land" and has everything under His command to care for His people (p. 350). In times of temptation and trial, the believer can look to Christ as not only that *Priest* who intercedes "that thy faith fail not" (Luke 22:32), but also as that King who "has every circumstance that can occur, every enemy that can arise, completely under His control" (p. 350). The ongoing intercession and dominion of Christ are twin subjects of profound importance to the Christian, both for edification, comfort, and for instruction.

The implications of Christ's reign for church–state relationships, and the consequent *obligation* upon states to establish *Christian* governments, is probably the most "attention-getting" aspect of Symington's work. The importance of that specific facet of Symington's work is indeed heightened at the current time because of widespread teaching (even within the church) that states should be secular. Nonetheless, the application of Christ's rule to the church and the individual, in all His roles, must not be overlooked. Whether or not the state pays homage to Christ, the church and the individual have services to perform for their King.

The church, *whose sole King and Head is Christ,* has every obligation to persist in her biblically defined calling no matter the circumstances of time and place. The Apostle Paul wrote in his charge to ministers,

> I charge thee therefore before God, and the Lord Jesus Christ, who shall judge the quick and the dead at his appearing and his kingdom; preach the word; *be instant in season, out of season;* reprove, rebuke, exhort with all longsuffering and doctrine (2 Tim. 4:1–2).

In "good season" or "bad season" the text could be more literally translated. Whatever the cultural or political "season," the church's charge from her King continues. The doctrine of Christ's reign gives the church the right, and the obligation, to pay all obedience to her biblical duties in all times and territories. Jesus Christ alone is King and Head of the church.

The reign of Christ further teaches the individual of his need to obey Christ in all His roles. Christ is not only our Savior, *He is also our King.* He is, in fact, the King over all other human authorities as well (at school, work, in civil society, and so forth). No human command (or social trend) can contravene our obligation to the King of kings.

Symington urges his readers,

> Nor let us be satisfied with anything short of an entire and implicit surrender of our hearts to King Jesus. It is possible for the subject of an earthly monarch to make a fair show of loyalty,... and yet, all the while, to be...a rebel at heart. In like manner, if we are not complying with the requirements of the gospel; if we are not walking worthy of the vocation wherewith we are called; if we are not living holy and obedient lives, in all godliness and honesty; we are unequivocally saying with our actions..., *We will not have this King to reign over us!* (p. 352; quoting Luke 19:14)

How inconsistent it is when Christians claim Christ as their atoning Priest, but ignore His rule over them as their gracious King. Symington would urge all those who would receive the benefits of Christ's priesthood to take care that they also show full respect for His crown:

> [Some] would gladly be *saved* from a coming wrath, but they are utterly indisposed to *obey*. Let them know that these things are inseparable; that the one cannot be had without the other; and that such as will not accept of Christ in all His characters, shall never obtain an interest in Him in *any*. (p. 353)

Those are words of strong exhortation, penned by Symington in the concluding pages of his book. They are aimed to bring to bear on his reader's conscience the full import of both doctrines, examined in both his works. Jesus is a Priest and a King (as well as Prophet) for His people. All who name the name of Christ have every reason to rejoice in these truths. All who name the name of Christ also have every obligation to live, day by day—personally, as family members, as professionals, as public citizens, and in every sphere—giving constant heed to this Prophet, in constant prayer to this Priest, and in loving obedience to this King.

In his typical fashion, Symington closes his book, *Messiah the Prince,* with a prayer on behalf of his readers:

> O Thou benign Prince!... put forth Thine efficacious grace

in our hearts. Make us a willing people in the day of Thy power. May we raise [on that final day], instead of the shriek of misery, the hymn of triumph, *Alleluia! salvation, and glory, and honour, and power, unto the Lord our God. Alleluia! [f]or the Lord God omnipotent reigneth!* We hail Thee, Sovereign of our hearts; we abjure for ever all other lords who have had dominion over us, and declare from the heart, WE HAVE NO KING BUT JESUS! (pp. 353–4; quoting Ps. 110:3; Rev. 19:1, 6; cf. John 19:5.)

✦   ✦   ✦

For unto us a child is born, unto us a son is given; and the government shall be upon his shoulder.... Of the increase of his government and peace there shall be no end, upon the throne of David, and upon his kingdom, to order it, and to establish it with judgment and with justice from henceforth even for ever. The zeal of the LORD *of hosts will perform this (Isa. 9:6–7).*

Excursus: Church and State in Old Testament Israel

One of the strengths of Symington's teaching is his concern to draw from both Old and New Testaments. The New Testament identifies Jesus as the prophesied Messiah—the Son of David who fulfills all the expectations ascribed to the Davidic throne in the Old Testament. It is Symington's recognition of this essential unity of the Old Testament royal hope, and the New Testament royal realization, that provides an important framework for this doctrine.

Although Symington draws upon various features of the Davidic throne, and numerous particulars of the church and state under the Old Testament monarchy, his book does not include a single, comprehensive overview of the Old Testament model of government. The Old Testament texts leave many particulars of ancient Israel's social structures unspecified, so that reconstructing a complete picture of Old Testament government is not necessarily possible. Nevertheless, the following "sketch" of its general contours helps to support Symington's overall arguments.

The first thing that can be observed is that, in Old Testament Israel, civil government and church government were generally independent of one another. The civil government was made up of elders and magistrates from each of the eleven tribes responsible for territories in Israel. It was the duty of these elders from the eleven tribes to maintain justice in their territories (e.g., Num. 11:16–17; 13:4–16; Deut. 21:1–9). Matters of worship were the concern of priests and Levites from the twelfth tribe: Levi (e.g., Num. 1:48–50). The tribe of Levi did not possess its own territory to govern in Israel, but rather administered church affairs throughout Israel, dwelling in cities *among* the other tribes' lands. The prohibition against other tribes presuming to interfere with the Levitical jurisdiction was especially severe, so that civil government and church government were carefully distinguished in Old Testament Israel.

Independence of Church and State in Ancient Israel

CHURCH GOVT
(Regulation of Worship
by <u>Levites</u>)

CIVIL GOVT
(Regulation of Society
by <u>Tribal Elders</u>)

Church and state were independent in Israel, but they were not unrelated. In fact, church and state in Israel enjoyed close cooperation. Civil magistrates in Israel were *legally enjoined* to consult the priests when difficult dilemmas of court justice arose. As experts in the biblical standards of righteousness, church officers in Israel were officially recognized by the civil government (e.g., Deut. 17:8–13). Conversely, church officers in Israel recognized the prerogatives of the civil government. Levites could work alongside civil officials and their teaching in the scattered communities served both the aims of religion *and of civil justice* (e.g., 2 Chron. 17:7–9). Although the actual governments of church and state were independent in Israel, much active cooperation was possible between them.

One of the reasons this was possible was because both the church and the state in Israel operated under the same Scriptures. Furthermore, both church and state enjoyed a common Head. Even prior to David, the patriarchs, Moses, and subsequent judges exercised leadership over both church and state matters. (This was possible because these leaders were prophets, and provided final decisions for both church and state matters through inspired revelation from heaven.) It was particularly when God appointed David as His anointed king, however, that Israel's distinct church and state governments were subjected to a single, permanent dynasty (e.g., 2 Sam. 7:13). The Davidic dynasty was set up "according to the order of Melchizedek" (Ps. 110:4). Melchizedek was the ancient *priest-king* of Jerusalem (Gen. 14:18); and the Davidic king likewise fulfilled both priestly *and* kingly functions at the head of the church *and* the state in Israel.

Union of Church and State under the King in Ancient Israel

It was David (and his sons) who organized the temple service rota (e.g., 2 Chron. 31:2), the choirs (e.g., 1 Chron. 15:16; 2 Chron. 35:15), and temple economics (e.g., 2 Chron. 24:1–14), who insured the continuing provision of sacrifices (e.g., 2 Chron. 30:24; 35:7), who called for reforms when worship was compromised (2 Chron. 29–31; 34–35:19), and who personally led in various national festivals (e.g., 2 Chron. 6:12; 30:18–19; 35:1). The Davidic king stood at the head of the Old Testament church. It was also the duty of David (and his sons) to guarantee justice for the people. The court of the king served as a court of appeal when lower courts failed to provide justice for the poor and vulnerable (e.g., 2 Sam. 14:4–7; 1 Kings 3:16–28). The king was responsible to insure that injustice was punished throughout the land (e.g., 2 Kings 21:11–16; Jer. 22:15–16). He was also charged to insure that the people were educated in matters of justice (e.g., 2 Chron. 17:7–9; 34:30). The Davidic king was responsible to God for the justice of society and was therefore at the head of the state, as well. The patriarchs, Moses, and the other pre-David judges had filled a similar role in leadership over the forming church and state of ancient Israel, but it was the appointment of the Davidic king that established a *permanent* office for the governance of both under God. Although established in Israel, it was expected that the Davidic king would gradually extend this rule over the many nations of the world (e.g., 2 Sam. 7:8–9; Ps. 72).

The tragic story which the Old Testament tells, however, is that David's sons failed to fulfill these duties. Solomon compromised Israel's worship (1 Kings 11:1–13) and was an oppressive governor (1 Kings 12:4). Subsequent kings likewise introduced both idolatry into the temple and injustice into society. God brought judgment upon Israel and Judah because of the failure of the kings to maintain the purity of the church and the justice of the state. Eventually, with the Babylonian exile, the remnant of Israel was scattered and the Davidic throne toppled.

Even though there was no longer any king on the throne of David, the prophets continued to announce that another Son of David was coming who would restore the throne (e.g., Amos 9:11). This coming King would perfectly fulfill the duties which David and his earlier sons had failed to fulfill (e.g., Isa. 9:6–7). Not only would this coming Messiah fulfill the Davidic duties *over the land and people of Palestine,* but He would successfully extend true worship and true justice *throughout the whole earth* (e.g., Isa. 49:6–7). It is this promised King which the New Testament identifies as being Jesus Christ. Jesus is the one who steps into the duties of the Davidic throne and assumes personal responsibility for both purifying the worship of the church around the whole world, and for establishing true justice now among the many nations of the earth.

Although His throne is from heaven (not visible on earth), and although His reign is now extended throughout the whole world (not restricted to the borders of Canaan), Jesus occupies the same throne as His forefather David. His is a rule over both religious *and* social spheres of mankind.

Church and State under Jesus, the Son of David

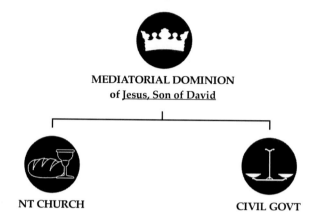

MEDIATORIAL DOMINION
of <u>Jesus, Son of David</u>

NT CHURCH   CIVIL GOVT

Even though Jesus' reign is much greater than that of David's earlier sons, His reign continues according to the same basic expectations. It is the consistent expectation of Scripture (both Old and New Testaments), that church and state governments *should be independent from one another,* but that they *should enjoy unity under a common King.* Once it was David in Israel; today it is Jesus over the whole earth. The New Testament Apostles do not speak of Jesus as establishing a *new* throne. Rather, the New Testament Apostles speak of Jesus as taking up all the duties and expectations of the *Davidic throne.* This Son of David, however, will not fail to accomplish His charge (1 Cor. 15:25), and He now exercises "all power" from heaven over the whole earth (Matt. 28:18).

One of the implications of this continuity between the Davidic throne and Christ's mediatorial reign is the usefulness of the Old Testament model for church–state relations, today. The pattern established in Israel was always a pattern intended for ancient Gentile nations to learn from (cf. Deut. 4:5–8). It is all the more relevant for nations around the world, today, now that Christ has been seen to have conquered death and ascended to His heavenly throne (Dan. 7:13–14; Matt. 28:16–20; Heb. 1:3). In availing of the Old Testament model, however, it is critical to recognize that the involvement of the anointed King in church *and* state matters is *not* the grounds for supposing civil government can thus interfere in both. The Old Testament kings foreshadow an office which Christ uniquely fills (as

He also uniquely fills the office of high priest). There is much which can be learned from the Old Testament cooperation of civil judges and elders on the one hand, and church officers on the other, when the Christological role of the king's office is borne in mind.